INTERNATIONAL AID

INTERNATIONAL AID

The Flow of Public Resources
from Rich to Poor Countries

I. M. D. Little / J. M. Clifford

With a new introduction by Osvaldo Feinstein

Routledge
Taylor & Francis Group

LONDON AND NEW YORK

First published 2006 by Transaction Publishers

Published 2017 by Routledge
2 Park Square, Milton Park, Abingdon, Oxon OX14 4RN
711 Third Avenue, New York, NY 10017, USA

Routledge is an imprint of the Taylor & Francis Group, an informa business

Library of Congress Catalog Number: 2005053556

Library of Congress Cataloging-in-Publication Data

Little, Ian Malcolm David.
    International aid : the flow of public resources from rich to poor countries / I.M.D. Little and J. M. Clifford ; with a new introduction by Osvaldo Feinstein.—AldineTransaction ed.
        p. cm
    Originally published: London : Allen and Unwin, 1965.
    Includes bibliographical references and index.
    ISBN 0-202-30794-8 (alk paper)
        1. Economic assistance.   2. Economic assistance, British.   I. Clifford, J. M. (Juliet Mary)   III. Title.

HC60.L53   2005
338.91—dc22   2005053556

ISBN 13: 978-0-202-30794-7 (pbk)

CONTENTS

PART II AID AND DEVELOPMENT

PART III DONORS' PROBLEMS

CONTENTS

CONTENTS

LIST OF TABLES

INTRODUCTION TO THE ALDINETRANSACTION EDITION

It may seem that forty years after its publication, a book on international aid can only have historical relevance. However, though International Aid, by Ian M. D. Little and J.M. Clifford (published for the first time in 1965) is indeed an important landmark in the history of international economic relations, the book is also important for current discussions on foreign aid.[1] Its senior author, Ian M. Little,[2] at the time of publication of International Aid was already a distinguished economist: in 1950 he published a critique of welfare economics that became a classic, with great influence in economics and economic policy.[3]

In 1958 he joined the India Project of the MIT Center for International Studies and thereafter became a development economist.[4] In the late 1960s, after International Aid, Little published with Jim Mirrlees (who in 1996 was awarded the Nobel Prize in economics[5]) the most important manual on project evaluation, and continued publishing celebrated articles and books, dealing with a wide range of development topics. Among the most recent ones, it is worthwhile to mention Economic Development, a magisterial comprehensive and critical survey of development economics, written for an audience of nonacademics and noneconomists interested in less developed countries, published in 1982 by Basic Books, and Ethics, Economics, and Politics, published by Oxford University Press in 2002 (a book that Little began to plan at the time of his eightieth birthday!); the concern with ethics and the interfaces of ethics with economics and politics, was already present in Little's initial publications and also in International Aid.

The preparation of International Aid took two years. Given that by 1963, when Little was asked to write the book by the Overseas Development Institute, his knowledge of developing countries (and of aid), was limited to India, he carried out a trip to Africa, which led to a short book on aid to Africa. Furthermore, the book draws on a vast bibliography, consisting not only of books and articles but also on reports from a variety of sources (several of the items included in the book's list of "works cited" were published just the year preceding the publication of the book).

In his Recollections, Little (1999, p.79) stated that most of what was written in the book "is still disappointingly relevant." This is even more the case in 2005, given the importance in the twenty-first-century discussions about aid of issues such as grants vis-à-vis loans, the "tying" of aid, aid coordination, the need to distinguish between development aid and aid for military expenditures, and the relationships of aid with security, themes treated in detail in International Aid. Furthermore, this book also adopted a valuable broad perspective, complementing economic analysis with a discussion of political issues as well as a consideration of moral and political philosophy.

Therefore, though the data and some geographical references in the book that are inevitably outdated, International Aid is a "classic" which provides an opportunity to be guided by a world-class economist in thinking about foreign aid and development issues.

Osvaldo Feinstein

NOTES

1. See references to Little and Clifford's book in Pronk (2001) and Kanbur (2003).
2. Juliet M.Clifford was Little's research assistant with no other known publication.
3. The book was reprinted in 2002 with a new preface by Little.
4. See Little (1999), a book which includes not only a compilation of some of Little's papers but also an autobiography spread across the book.
5. Recently Paul Samuelson (2005) wrote that a Nobel Prize to Abram Bergson along with Ian Little could have added lustre to Nobel awards in economics.

REFERENCES

Little, Ian M.D. 1999. Collections and Recollections. Oxford: Clarendon Press.
Kanbur, Ravi.2003. "The Economics of International Aid"
http://www.arts.cornell.edu/poverty/kanbur/HandbookAid.pdf.
Pronk, Jan. 2001. "Aid as a Catalyst," Development and Change, Vol. 32, pp. 611-629
Samuelson, Paul. 2005. "Abram Bergson, Economist: April 21, 1914 - April 23, 2003" Economic Journal, Vol. 115, pp. F130-F133

ACKNOWLEDGMENTS

Mr Little is a Fellow of Nuffield College, Oxford. He began the present work at the suggestion of the ODI, which undertook to provide him with research assistance. With the help of a grant from the Nuffield Foundation the ODI employed Mrs Clifford, the co-author, in this capacity. The travel expenses were paid jointly from the Nuffield Foundation grant and by Nuffield College. The authors are indebted to members of the staff of ODI for suggestions, and have drawn on several ODI publications. They are also indebted to several members of Nuffield College for comments.

The authors have had conversations with a great many UK officials at home and overseas. They have also had interviews with many other public and private donor agencies, the AID, OECD, UNEPTA, IBRD, CDC, Ford Foundation, as well as with officials and Ministers of many African Governments, and the Indian Government; and also some French and German officials. Those who have contributed to the authors' views in this way must number hundreds, and we regret that no more than a blanket acknowledgment can be made.

The following—not being government officials or members of ODI or Nuffield College—have read parts of the book and commented: R. E. Asher, D. Avramovic, E. Eshag, Sir Robert Hall, J. P. Hayes, A. S. Mackintosh, P. N. Rosenstein-Rodan, J. Saxe, R. Vernon, E. P. Wright. To these we are very grateful. Finally, of course, no individual or organization bears any responsibility for any of our views or mistakes.

We are also very grateful to Miss Jenny Bond for her cheerful and excellent typing of successive drafts, and for proof-reading.

I. M. D. Little, *Nuffield College, Oxford.*
J. M. Clifford, *Overseas Development Institute, London.*

INTRODUCTION AND DEFINITIONS

This book is about public non-military aid to poor or 'developing' countries. Public aid includes direct government-to-government aid, and also aid given through international organizations. We are not concerned with foreign private investment in poor countries, except in so far as its magnitude is a consideration affecting public aid. We also neglect private charities. These omissions are not because private investment and charitable activities are unimportant: but because public aid is a big enough subject on its own. Also, the flow of public finance to poor countries is much larger than that of private finance. This was not true when most public aid was for post-war reconstruction and relief, and flowed from the USA to war-damaged countries which now rank as rich. But now almost all inter-governmental finance goes from rich to poor.

Aid is an ambiguous word. Strictly defined, we believe it should refer only to the value of the subsidy implicit in the total flow of resources. Thus, grants of convertible currency are certainly aid to their full face value. But loans contain only an element of aid, sometimes an insignificant element. It is clearly misleading to lump these (and some other kind of 'aid') together, when assessing either the cost to donors and lenders or the benefit to recipients. Money-lenders may benefit their clients, but we do not think of them as giving aid.

But it has nevertheless become general practice to use the word 'aid' to refer to the nominal value of the direct and indirect flow of financial and other resources from governments of rich countries to those of poor countries. Thus one may read that aid from member countries of the Development Assistance Committee (DAC) of the Organization for Economic Co-operation and Development (OECD)[1] amounted to $6 billion[2] in 1963. This figure includes grants; net lending at rates of interest ranging up to 7 per cent and more, with maturities from five years upwards; sales of commodities for 'soft' currencies; and so on. One may even be told that DAC aid was more than $8 billion, this including private investment.

[1] Where initials of organizations are relatively unfamiliar we give the full name at the first mention. A glossary is also provided.
[2] Billion means 1,000 million throughout.

The main reason for this misleading terminology seems to be that 'aid' is a short word. It is cumbersome to replace it by, e.g., 'the flow of long-term financial resources to less-developed countries and multilateral agencies' (the DAC's own expression). After torturing ourselves without finding an acceptable alternative we decided to use 'aid' both as shorthand for the above expression, as well as in the strict sense defined earlier. Where the context requires a clear distinction to be drawn, we use 'aid proper' or 'aid content', or some such phrase, to refer to the real cost of the financial and other flows. Where we use the word more loosely, we sometimes use inverted commas to emphasize the fact.

There are other terminological difficulties. Current UN practice is to refer to recipients as 'developing countries' or 'less-developed countries'. We prefer the more descriptive term 'poor countries': but, for variety, we also use UN terminology, as well as the now outmoded 'underdeveloped countries'. Donor countries are, similarly, best described as 'rich'. But we use 'industrialized' and 'developed' as well. Even 'donor' is not quite accurate: strictly, 'donor' often means 'lender'.

The book went to the publishers in February 1965, but at a few points later information has been incorporated at the proof stage in May 1965. Policy shifts are sometimes quite rapid in the field of aid. We naturally hope the reader may be able to note that some changes have occurred in line with the authors' suggestions.

Any royalties from this book will accrue to OXFAM.

PART ONE

WORLD AID AND GENERAL PRINCIPLES

CHAPTER I

THE HISTORY OF AID

1. THE EMERGENCE OF AID AS A WORLD-WIDE PHENOMENON

Aid in the form of transactions between rich and poor, but independent, governments was very restricted in scope before 1960. France and Britain had been helping their colonies with development since the 1920s. The USA had run a number of programmes with increasing emphasis on development, but nevertheless concentrated heavily on military strategy and supporting friendly governments. The Soviet Union had begun to lend on a small scale to non-Communist developing countries, with avowedly political objectives. Other countries were just beginning to be involved in aid for development. Table 2 (p. 48) shows how little bilateral aid there was in 1957–9, from OECD members other than the USA and the colonial powers. The most important part of aid history is almost indistinguishable from an account of current aid programmes, since most important changes in aid policy since 1960 have not yet been completed. In preference to describing the emergence of aid chronologically, we shall first describe the big changes of 1959 and 1960, and then turn to the development of aid in the USA, USSR, Germany, and the main colonial countries, separately.

1959 and 1960 saw the admission to UN membership of a large number of former French, Belgian, British, and Italian colonies, most of them in Africa; independence of a few other countries, again mostly in Africa, was scheduled to take place during the next few years. Even now, it is hard to realize what a difference this made to international politics, especially in the UN. Before 1959, colonies looked to the metropolitan countries for most of their financial needs. Other countries—in Latin America and Asia—tended to look to the USA for bilateral assistance; or occasionally, for very small amounts of help under Commonwealth schemes as in India, Pakistan, and Ceylon, to the United Kingdom and other Commonwealth countries. Pressure was exerted in the UN for more multilateral assistance—resulting, for instance, in the formation of the

International Finance Corporation (IFC) in 1957 (but the volume of assistance from the USA was considerably greater than from all UN agencies combined). Change began with the Indian Second Five-Year Plan, and her urgent need for balance of payments support in 1958 which drew in USA and UK finance, and also funds from new sources like Germany and Japan, on an unprecedented scale. African independence, particularly of former British territories, later transformed the aid situation.

The main reason for change was the increase in both the need and demand for aid. Prices of most important commodities fell sharply from about 1952, and by 1958 poor countries' external reserves (especially in the form of sterling balances) had nearly all been spent. Independence itself brought new expenditure on overseas representation, on new buildings for government and parliament, and on compensation for large numbers of expatriates—mostly British but a few French—who could not remain in their posts under the old terms. Replacing the expatriates, either with newly-trained local people, or with more expatriates on contract terms, was an added burden. The problem was made more acute by the ex-British colonies' new financial relationships with Britain. Grant aid ceased at independence, with a few exceptions which, since about 1962, have almost become the rule. Loans from the British Government for independent countries are mostly tied to the purchase of British goods, although exceptions to this rule have also been on the increase. For all these reasons, developing countries taken together clearly needed new sources of aid.

Demands for aid outstripped even the increased need. The movement for independence had inevitably carried with it demands for a better material standard of living—one of the criticisms of colonialism was that it prevented economic progress—and virtually all of the new governments were pledged to grandiose plans for development. Demand increased most dramatically of all in India, because the cautious First Five-Year Plan of 1950 was followed by the large Second Five-Year Plan under which India's reserves of foreign currency were virtually exhausted by 1958, and which effectively implied a large and increasing balance of payments deficit.

The new countries were not slow to take their demands to the UN, and to make it clear that aid from any source, including the Soviet bloc, would be welcome. Pressure through the UN, reinforced by fear lest the Russians gain influence too easily, helped to persuade the rich countries to become more generous.

In the UN, the addition of new voices to the clamour for a Special United Nations Fund for Economic Development (SUNFED), together with India's deteriorating financial position and the financial weakness of the new countries, produced two useful new institutions: each was, in a sense, a partial substitute for the non-existent SUNFED, though the demand for a UN multilateral capital development fund has not even now been stifled. The first was the International Development Association (IDA) established in 1959, which makes low-interest, long-term loans for infrastructure projects of the kind acceptable to the International Bank for Reconstruction and Development (IBRD) in countries which are deemed to be too heavily in debt to receive more loans on IBRD terms. The IDA is affiliated to the IBRD, and administered in conjunction with it. It differs from the proposed SUNFED in size—currently, it cannot pledge more than about $300 million in any one year—and in the fact that the IBRD, and not the UN General Assembly (via the Economic and Social Council (ECOSOC)), is responsible for administering its funds. The second innovation was the United Nations Special Fund (UNSF), whose administration is responsible to the UN General Assembly, but this receives less than $100 million a year, and may spend money only on 'pre-investment' schemes—surveys, technical education, research, and the like. These have been the only concessions so far made, multilaterally, to demands for a world capital development fund.

Bilaterally, there has been a much greater response to demands for more development finance. Countries like Germany, Japan, and Italy, really only entered bilateral development financing in 1960—and of these only Germany is now a significant donor of aid proper. Countries with colonial histories like Britain, France, Belgium, and the Netherlands, far from reducing the volume of their aid when their colonies reached independence, have all increased it. The USA, having been in the aid business for nearly twenty years, was beginning to place more emphasis on development and self-help (the Cuban revolution gave more impetus to this policy change) and had for some time been widening the forms of her aid, as well as the political conformity required of recipients of aid.

The reasons for all these changes are a matter for speculation. Soviet activity clearly had a strong effect on USA policy; in 1953 and again in 1956, Congress cut the Administration's request for development assistance aid to India, on the grounds that Nehru was too pro-Communist; yet in 1957 aid to Indonesia was increased because of an Indonesian loan agreement with the USSR, signed in September

1956.[1] The USA document *Policy Guidance for Foreign Assistance*[2] states quite clearly that one object of USA aid is to prevent certain countries from becoming unduly dependent on Soviet aid. In general, Soviet aid has probably strengthened the USA Administration's case in Congress for aiding neutral countries. Federal Germany has also been influenced by Soviet activity, since one of its foreign policy objectives is to gain sympathy among uncommitted countries for its position in Berlin, and to prevent such countries from recognizing the East German Government.

Commercial motives have been strong; Germany, Italy, and Japan, began in the 1950s to compete for new markets, and export credit (which is frequently confused with aid, and cannot always be distinguished from it) has been a major weapon. These countries had at this time only recently emerged from post-war reconstruction; Germany was by the late 1950s well able to take on overseas commitments, but Italy and Japan still had serious regional development problems of their own, and were less equipped to provide aid proper in addition to commercially motivated credit. Other forms of aid, particularly technical assistance of almost all kinds, are also believed to promote exports. Refinance credits, which in 1959 accounted for more than 10 per cent of total gross 'aid' from OECD members, are equally justifiable on commercial grounds, since an extension of credit is often the only way of making eventual repayment possible.

Whatever their reasons, rich countries have responded to some extent to the need for extra finance, and for technical advice and training, for developing countries. We shall explain later how, despite the slogans of the UN Development Decade, this response has been limited, and how the forms in which finance and aid are provided severely restrict their usefulness to recipients.

Once it became clear that bilateral development aid would be increased, and that a large number of countries would be establishing new bilateral programmes, consultation between donors became an obvious necessity. This has been approached from two directions. On the one hand, the IBRD (and later other bodies) has sponsored consortia of 'donors' to certain recipients of aid, the most important being India and Pakistan. On the other, the OECD sponsors work on development through the DAC. The DAC's most important function so far has been the mutual examination, known as 'confrontation', of each member's aid policies in its *Annual Aid Review* and, as a by-

---

[1] cf. Charles Wolf, Jr., *Foreign Aid: Theory and Practice in Southern Asia*, Princeton University Press, 1960.

[2] Published in 1963 by the Agency for International Development (AID).

product of this, publication of the most comprehensive of available statistics of 'aid'. The DAC Secretariat also carries out research on the effects of past aid policies, and on the possibilities of closer coordination in more limited fields, like technical assistance, tying, and the terms of aid. In the process of confrontation, data collection, and reporting on members' policies, it is able to exert some pressure on members who fail to pull their weight, and has helped to bring about changes in policy by member governments; for instance, the reduction of German and British interest rates on some loans.

The events which led up to the changes of 1960 followed fairly independent courses in the various countries that provided aid before that date. Colonial powers were concerned only with their colonies, for which they had come to accept increasing responsibility as their concepts of the role of government changed. The USA became involved in aid to developing countries because of her world-wide political and economic strength and interests, and because the Cold War threatened those interests; and the Soviet bloc's aid seems to have been, initially, a counter-attack.

Other countries' 'aid' before 1960, as set out in the statistics collected in 1960,[1] was more or less a statistical accident, except for the small amounts subscribed and contributed to UN agencies and programmes. Bilateral grants from Austria, Norway, Sweden, Denmark, Switzerland, and Germany, totalled only $24 million for the four years 1956-9. Japan provided a further $182 million, but $177 million of this was debt cancellation rather than new grants.[2] Canada's grants totalled $164 million, but much of this was in the form of gifts of surplus commodities. Thus total bilateral grants, apart from surplus commodities, from these eight countries were of the order of only $60 million, over a four-year period. They also provided nearly $500 million in reparations, and $482 million in bilateral loans at unsubsidized rates of interest (mostly either as refinance credits or as loans tied to purchases from the lending country), but none of this is aid proper.

Although aid in the form of direct transfers of funds from one independent government to another with the intention of helping the people of a country is new, the use of finance in diplomacy has a long history, and some transactions that find their way into aid

---

[1] OEEC, *The Flow of Financial Resources to Countries in Course of Economic Development 1956-9*, Paris, 1961.

[2] A $177 million Indonesian debt to Japan was cancelled as part of a new reparations agreement signed in 1958. See John White, *Japanese Aid*, Overseas Development Institute (ODI), 1964.

statistics today are little different from their earlier counterparts.

The first diplomats to offer (rather than exact) subsidies as a tool of foreign policy seem to have been the Renaissance princes of Italy. Subsidies were extensively used throughout the seventeenth and eighteenth centuries to manipulate the balance of power. Compared with modern aid, subsidies were a relatively simple weapon, used to hire troops, or in lieu of sending troops, or to buy support or neutrality. George Liska (our source of information on this period of history) has written that this kind of aid depends on the assumption that 'there is a definable unit of fighting power or defence power that can be had cheaper outside a nation's military establishment'.[1] This is as true of military and related 'economic' aid today as it was then. The essential difference between the subsidy system and the modern system of aid is that 'the relation between the intention of the grant and the performance of the recipient has come to be less determinate',[2] in terms of both political and military objectives. It was still possible under the subsidy system to claim repayment of an already disbursed subsidy, if the recipient failed to perform.[3] It would be unthinkable to demand repayment of a modern grant to a developing country, however overtly political its purposes may have been, on the grounds that the recipient had failed to fulfil its side of the bargain.

In the nineteenth century, the use of direct government subsidies as a tool in the system of alliances was abandoned, probably because the decline of autocratic government made payments between rulers a decreasingly effective means of buying support. Instead, influence over the flow of private finance came to be used as a political weapon. This influence took varying forms, and was directed towards ends similar to those of subsidies, that is to forming and strengthening alliances, and to extending imperial rule. The supreme example of the unsuccessful use of private capital for diplomatic ends was France's involvement in Czarist Russia through the Franco-Russian Alliance. French loans were successful in helping to establish the alliance, but the sums of money invested in Russia rapidly became so enormous that even from a financial point of view the alliance came to be more important to France than to Russia, and Russia then acquired considerable influence over French policy in the Balkans. As things turned out, in return for a militarily unprepared ally in the First World War, France lost all her investments in Russia, and indirectly

[1] G. Liska, The New Statecraft, University of Chicago Press, 1960, p. 38.
[2] ibid., p. 61.
[3] ibid., p. 41.

was partly responsible, because her loans had effectively propped up the Czarist régime and strengthened its resistance to demands for social reform, for the form and violence of the Soviet revolution.[1]

The use of subsidies and loans in diplomacy involved many of the problems which now face those who make decisions about foreign aid. There is the difficulty that, once a donor has invested more than some crucial amount in a particular recipient country, its prestige (if not its financial interest) becomes so closely identified with that country's performance that the recipient acquires more influence over the donor than the donor over the recipient. Something of the kind has probably occurred in South Vietnam and Formosa—the fact that military strategy is involved does not alter the argument, since if USA prestige were not involved in these countries, their loss would not be of any great strategic importance. Other complications arose (and still arise) because aid to one country tends on the one hand to rule out and on the other to necessitate aid to certain other groups or classes of country; in particular aid to neutral countries damages the impact of aid to rather luke-warm allies.

We have given this sketchy account of some of the antecedents of modern aid in order to avoid giving the impression that modern government-to-government aid is unprecedented. In our accounts of the growth of aid from individual donor countries we shall concentrate entirely on the growth of government-to-government aid since 1900 or so, and ignore aid's less direct ancestry, except where private investment (as in the case of British aid to the colonies) was an essential part of the system until very recently.

The following sections describe the genesis of the government aid programmes of the principal donor countries. As we said at the beginning of this chapter, the main developments have taken place since 1960. But the USA and the colonial powers had been providing substantial aid to overseas governments for many years before that, and Soviet aid began in the mid-1950s. Thus these countries, together with Germany, the most important of the recently emergent donors, merit separate attention. We have not aimed to give a comprehensive account of the history, the administration, or the policies, of all these countries: but rather have tried to pick out those elements which appear to be particularly interesting, and which contrast with each other. The growth of aid from the four principal OECD donors, and from the OECD as a whole, is shown in Table 1 (p. 24).

[1] cf. Herbert Feis, *Foreign Aid and Foreign Policy*, St Martin's Press, New York, 1964, and *Europe the World's Banker*, Yale University Press, 1930.

TABLE 1

The net flow of official financial resources, 1956–63, from major OECD *donors*
$m

	1956	1957	1958	1959	1960	1961	1962	1963
Total OECD	3,270	3,859	4,381	4,349	4,942	6,134	6,014	6,048
France	648	819	884	832	848	943	975	863
Germany	161	298	278	325	343	615	450	424
UK	205	234	276	377	407	457	421	414
USA	2,006	2,091	2,410	2,322	2,801	3,488	3,573	3,721

Source: OECD, *The Flow of Financial Resources to Less-Developed Countries, 1956–63*, Paris, 1964, Table IV.4.

2. USA AID

The history of USA aid is the most important, since the volume of USA aid has far outstripped the total aid provided by other countries. Even in 1962, the USA provided more than half of world aid, and as recently as 1959 the proportion was as high as two-thirds.

Before the Second World War, and even in the nineteenth century, the USA Government had occasionally helped a friendly government (most often in Latin America) which found itself in difficulty or danger, but the scale of help was minute. During the war, she began lending on a larger scale to Latin American governments for the development of strategic industries, and for wartime import substitution. By the time the war had ended, the USA had become involved in heavy expenditure on relief and rehabilitation in a large number of countries in Europe and Asia; and soon afterwards in associated military aid to Greece and Turkey. As the Cold War developed, and Marshall Aid was introduced to strengthen Western Europe economically and politically, the volume of American assistance to other countries rose to a height that has never since been equalled. Since roughly the beginning of the Marshall Plan, the idea of aid for development of poor countries, as a logical extension of economic aid for the reconstruction of war-damaged economies, and military aid for meeting immediate danger to friendly countries, has taken root; and as some of the crises have been met, policy-makers have tried to take a more far-sighted view of the world.

For a number of reasons, USA aid for development in poor countries was very small initially, and has not reached the scale of Marshall Aid for the reconstruction of Europe. The main reasons for the low level of development aid around 1949 were, first, that the USA was already heavily committed to reconstruction in Europe, and to military aid in Greece, China and elsewhere; secondly, that the processes of development in 'backward countries' (as they were then sometimes called) were misunderstood, and many people under-estimated the difference between developing backward countries and reconstructing industrialized countries damaged by war; thirdly, that many developing countries were still colonial dependencies of European countries; fourthly, that the neutrality of others (especially India) in the Cold War inhibited the USA administration from assisting them on a large scale; and lastly that, in many developing countries, the most urgent need was for technical help with planning, administering services and projects, and training, rather than for finance, so that the amount of money spent depended upon the supply of technical advisers rather than on how much money could be afforded.

Since 1949, when President Truman's small 'bold new programme' of technical assistance to underdeveloped areas was launched,[1] the volume of USA assistance for development has gradually increased, and inhibitions about giving aid to neutral governments have been relaxed as competition with the Soviet Union and China, for influence in the uncommitted areas, has developed. Landmarks in the process have been the introduction of 'Food for Peace' in 1953 (most of which was intended for development projects and programmes rather than famine relief), the introduction of development loans in 1958, and the reorganization of most non-military aid under the Agency for International Development (AID) in 1961. This growth in development aid has been fairly steady, since (at least until the Clay Committee[2] reported in 1963) most serious criticism of USA aid administration was concerned with the high cost and waste involved in 'defence support' given to allies. A Presidential Committee[3] recommended in 1960 that, while recipients of USA aid should make more efforts on their own behalf, the USA on its side should increase the volume of development aid. The new AID made a valiant attack on the problems of development aid; Development Grants and Development Loans were doubled; economists studied the possibility of establishing criteria for the various types of development aid; and USA support was pledged for the Alliance for Progress, which commits Latin American governments to self-help measures as a condition for receiving aid.

Unfortunately, the American public has recently become very impatient with the aid programme at a time when it is still too early for

[1] The famous 'Point Four' of his inaugural address.
[2] *Report of the President's Committee to Strengthen the Security of the Free World*, March 1963.
[3] *Composite Report of the President's Committee to Study the Military Assistance Program*, 1959.

new long-term policies to bear fruit. Foreign assistance has been a large item in USA public expenditure for twenty years now, and development has been among the objects of aid for fifteen years. Yet the USA appears to have earned neither new allies nor gratitude, and these were the rewards which the electorate had been led to expect from USA aid. There is little understanding in Congress, or among the electorate, of America's real long-term interests in overseas development, and aid appears to the public as an expensive and ineffective means of pursuing military strategy. (Congress has always resisted proposals for spending money on explaining the aid programme to the public.) Consequently, the Clay Committee recommended in 1963 that total aid be reduced, in particular that African development be regarded as a European responsibility, and Latin American governments be required to carry out far more drastic reforms in social and economic policies before receiving aid from the USA. Congress followed this by reducing the AID budget request for economic assistance for fiscal 1964 from $3·1 billion to $2·0 billion. Most (70 per cent) of both the original request and the eventual appropriation were for development assistance. For fiscal 1965, $2·5 billion was requested and $2·2 billion appropriated, and the request for fiscal 1966 is only $2·2 billion. These figures exclude Food for Peace (given under PL 480), Eximbank Loans, and the Peace Corps, none of which is financed under the Foreign Assistance Acts.

Reaction in the USA against aid is unfortunate, but not difficult to understand. Aid for long-term development and remote political advantage is not a new idea to American economists. But it is new to the public and only half-understood. In the past, aid either had fairly quick results (like Marshall Aid, or post-war rehabilitation) or was presented as a strategic or political necessity, to buy allies or to stave off unpleasant occurrences for the USA (aid to shore up régimes in South Korea, South Vietnam, Formosa, Jordan, etc.; aid to countries providing bases like Spain, Morocco, and Tunisia; or aid to allies like Pakistan, Iran, and Thailand). When aid is given to neutral countries like India or Indonesia, and fails to produce either immediate goodwill towards the USA or rapid economic development (by analogy with Marshall Aid, or as might be expected from an optimistic reading of Professor W. W. Rostow's *Stages of Economic Growth*), the electorate fails to see the purpose of aid, and is easily led to oppose it. Moreover, there are frequent incidents involving expropriation or lesser hindrances to USA business, or State interference in industry beyond the level acceptable to USA businessmen, or plain corruption and misuse of funds. These can be used to build up a case against aid, as has been done with great success in Congress during the last two or three years. A further objection to aid, which carries considerable weight in Congress, is that it is a large item of Federal Government expenditure.

The USA is therefore having difficulty in substituting a long-term programme of aid for development for the more piecemeal approach, based on shorter-term military and strategic necessity, that was previously followed. American economists and political specialists have given far more serious thought to a world development strategy, than comparable experts from other countries. But their ideas have had much less impact on Congress, and on Congressional appropriations, than the ideas which lay behind the Marshall Plan. USA economic aid in 1949 was $8·1 billion, of which over three-quarters went to Europe; in 1962, total USA economic aid was only $5·1 billion, spread much more thinly over countries in Asia, Latin America, Africa, and southern Europe. Unfortunately, it seems at present rather unlikely that Congress will be willing to increase the amount of finance appropriated for foreign aid, until at least there is much greater public understanding of America's long-run interest in development, and of the immense difficulty of stimulating development in poor countries.

3. COMMUNIST AID

The Soviet economic interest in developing countries outside the Soviet bloc began in 1954, when the first trade agreements were signed, with Argentina and Afghanistan. Aid followed naturally from trade, since Soviet aid has been directly tied to specified Soviet exports. It nearly always takes the form of loans (most commonly at 2½ per cent, and repayable within twelve years), and is sometimes repaid by shipments of commodities specified at the time of the original agreement. The distinction between trade and aid agreements was sometimes blurred, in order to make trade agreements look like aid, as indeed they may have been in some cases. There has been a very long lag between commitment and disbursement. The peak for Sino-Soviet commitments was 1960, when $1,165 million was committed. In that year disbursements were only $186 million. By 1963 disbursements had risen to an estimated $425 million, and commitments had fallen to $319 million.[1]

It is not clear whether the Russian or Chinese governments think that accelerated economic development in poor countries will con-

[1] See OECD, *The Flow of Financial Resources to Less-Developed Countries, 1956–63*, Paris 1964, p. 56.

tribute to the long-run political aims of Soviet or Chinese foreign policy; in other words, that their faster economic growth will encourage the spread of Communism. If so, their beliefs run counter to those of Western governments, especially America! But, whatever their long-run theories, most Eastern aid has had more immediate political aims, closely allied to short-run foreign policy. One Soviet author has written '[The Soviet Union] strives to contribute all within its power to helping the peoples of [underdeveloped] countries to overcome poverty, economic backwardness, exploitation and coercion on the part of imperialist powers and foreign monopoly capital. The Soviet people consider such aid important and useful from the humanitarian point of view . . . as well as from the standpoint of the struggle for peace and peaceful coexistence of all people throughout the world.'[1] That competition with capitalist aid was an important factor in the Soviet decision to provide aid at all is suggested indirectly in a quotation by the same author from a speech by Khrushchev, who said, 'One cannot but regard the assistance which the capitalist countries are preparing to give to these states which have recently won their independence as a kind of assistance rendered by the Soviet Union to these states. Indeed, were there no Soviet Union, would the monopoly groups and imperialist states have offered aid to the underdeveloped countries? Of course not.' The speech seems to have been referring to the loosening of the 'strings' attached to part of USA aid from about 1956 onwards, but as USA aid to developing countries began in 1948, well before Soviet aid, the argument applies *a fortiori* to Soviet aid itself. Even Cold War clouds have silver linings.

The distribution of Soviet aid lends itself quite readily to interpretation along political lines. Much of it has gone to countries which have quarrelled with the West, or have suffered revolutions of a neutralist or 'leftist' character, and so have appeared to offer opportunities for a change either from a Western alignment to neutralism, or from neutralism to a pro-Soviet alignment. Instances are aid to Egypt for the Aswan dam; to Algeria; to Guinea and Mali when they broke with France; to Cuba after the Castro revolution. Of course, Western aid to Yugoslavia is not dissimilar. Other Soviet aid appears to echo the USA policy of trying to see that neutralist countries such as Indonesia do not have to become wholly dependent on Soviet aid. Aid to India and Yugoslavia may come into this category. Aid to Afghanistan and Iran clearly falls within the strategic category, as these states border on the USSR. This too echoes USA policy. It is in

[1] U. Rimalov, *Economic Co-operation between the USSR and Underdeveloped Countries*, Foreign Languages Publishing House, Moscow (no date).

fact easy enough to guess at the political motives of most Soviet aid. Given that there is relatively little of it, it is not surprising that its short-run political interest is so obvious. It presents a similar picture to that which USA aid might display if it were much smaller, and less ubiquitous, and not therefore forced to consider longer-run development aims.

In the last few years, open rivalry between the USSR and China, for leadership of the Communist movement, has naturally spread into the field of foreign policy and foreign aid. China, one of the poorest countries in the world, can afford much less than the Soviet Union, but makes the most of her scarce resources by concentrating on a few countries—at present East and Central Africa is particularly favoured—and by offering gifts in kind, and free credits, rather than loans. Since most Chinese aid commitments are very recent, one wonders how soon, and to what extent, they will result in much disbursement of real resources; if the pattern of early Soviet aid is followed, relatively little will be disbursed.

Aid from Eastern European countries has not followed the Soviet pattern exactly. Only during the past five years or so has aid from these countries become a significant proportion of total Eastern aid. In the period 1954–62, they provided 21·5 per cent of total Eastern commitments. The largest individual country contribution was Czechoslovakia's, with 9·2 per cent of total bloc commitments during that period—more in fact than China's 8·3 per cent (the big increase in Chinese commitments came after 1962). We do not propose to discuss the policies of each East European government, because they are clearly not independent of Soviet policy, and they are concerned with such a small proportion of world aid.

There are signs that Russian policy with regard to the strings attached to aid is changing. Early Russian aid, whether by design or necessity, was accompanied by much emphasis on the absence of strings, and of prying questions about the economic justification behind the projects which Russia agreed to support, and about who would operate the factories which they set up. Unlike the Americans, the Russians showed no concern for planning. Experience or new thinking about objectives seems to have persuaded them that this policy was shortsighted, since it has created too many monuments to aid of the kind known in Germany as 'development ruins'. Soviet aid was not properly integrated into the recipient's economy, and was generally under-administered.[1] This feature has not been unique to Soviet aid. More recently, according to the Press reports, the USSR

[1] cf. I. M. D. Little, *Aid to Africa*, Pergamon Press, 1964, p. 21.

has begun to ask very searching questions before finally committing aid to projects in Kenya and India. Their place as provider of aid, with no questions asked, has been taken over by China.

4. BRITISH AID

The growth of aid from colonial powers has followed a very different pattern from that in the major world powers. Politics on a world scale has not been the driving force behind aid, although pressures and disturbances overseas have certainly affected its distribution, and have sometimes accelerated general changes in policy.

Colonial powers have been providing aid for development for a long time, compared with other aid donors—but only for a short time, compared with the length of colonial ties. In Britain's case, development aid began in 1929, on a tiny scale, and did not become important until 1945. Recipients of this aid had by then been colonies for between thirty years and several centuries. France and Portugal, whose colonial policies were based on the theory of assimilation, tended to be more generous than Britain with government-to-government subsidies and loans, and with trade preferences and price support, for their colonies. Despite these important differences, there are many common characteristics.

In the nineteenth century, colonies were regarded by European business interests, and to an increasing extent by governments, as a source of wealth—hence episodes like the 'Scramble for Africa'. At the same time, *laissez faire* economic policies allotted governments a very limited role in economic affairs, so that transfers of finance from metropolitan to colonial governments would, on these grounds also, have been unthinkable, except as a temporary expedient in an emergency. In Britain, this attitude was strengthened by the theory that, as colonies were being prepared for ultimate independence, their financial arrangements should at all times be quite separate from the British Government's own finances. In contrast, French colonies have always paid taxes to the Government of Metropolitan France, which has therefore been directly responsible for those services which lay within the provenance of the central government. In the British case, however, it was found necessary even as early as 1878 to provide some colonies with grants-in-aid to cover ordinary budgetary expenses.

'Development' of colonies in the nineteenth century mainly meant private investment in mines and plantations. Public spending on roads, railways, and the few other services that governments were expected to provide, was financed from local taxation and from funds borrowed on the London market from private investors. Colonial Stock Acts, which gave these loans trustee status, enabled colonial governments to borrow at better terms on the London market than other overseas governments, but this was merely a logical consequence of their colonial status, and of the power of the British Government to ensure that their debts were paid. There was no deliberate British Government policy for colonial development. In the era of *laissez faire*, it was not considered to be any part of the duty of either metropolitan or colonial governments to concern themselves directly with developing resources by means of government spending.

From about the turn of the century, the UK Government began to take a slightly more active interest in colonial economies, and a variety of committees studied education, the use of natural resources, and similar topics in selected colonies. After the First World War, efforts were made to find and expand markets for colonial products in Britain, and colonial preference was increased by raising tariff rates on some imports from outside the colonies. In 1929, for the first time, provision was made for assisting colonial governments to develop their economies by means of grants and loans for what is now called 'infrastructure'; for improving transport, research, power and water supplies, land surveys, and so on. Education was excluded, and a strong subsidiary aim of the new Colonial Development Act of 1929 was to promote employment in Britain by stimulating the colonial economies and their demand for British exports. Funds therefore had to be spent on British products as far as possible. In retrospect, the scope of the Act and the sums involved seem tiny (not more than £1 million a year—and less than £7 million was actually spent in the eleven years that the Act remained in force). In 1935, total UK expenditure on the colonies was only just over £1 million compared with over £10 million spent by France in grants alone.

Throughout the 1930s the theory that colonies should be responsible for their own finances remained more or less intact, and Britain's own difficulties arising out of the depression limited her response to the even graver difficulties of many of her colonies. Grants-in-aid under the old system amounted to more (£12 million in 1930–9) than expenditures under the 1929 Act (£6·6 million), and over the longer period 1919–39 more than £100 million was borrowed on the London market by colonial governments. The terms of the 1929 Act carefully restricted the UK's possible commitment. Only capital projects were to be financed, and even these only if the colony's revenues could support the extra recurrent expenditure arising from a project. The exclusion of education had the result that the development of human resources was seriously neglected, and that the dependence of many colonies on expatriates at all levels of government remained as great as ever.

In 1940 UK policy was carried a stage further. Under the Colonial Development and Welfare (CD and W) Act of that year, £5 million per annum was made available for development and welfare in the colonies. Education was specifically included in the purposes of the Act, and recurrent costs were allowed to be met for a limited time after a capital project was completed.

In 1945, a new CD and W Act made £120 million available for a ten-year period, to be spent on projects organized into a development 'programme' in each colony. The last major innovation in British aid (which was still almost exclusively to colonies) came in 1948, when the Overseas Resources Development Act was passed. This set up a government corporation—the Colonial Development Corporation (CDC)—with power to borrow from the UK Treasury for investment in industry, agriculture, and any other profit-making field, in the colonies. The idea was that, by borrowing from the Treasury at slightly above the government borrowing rate for loans of any given maturity, the CDC would be able to take greater risks, and accept a lower rate of return, than private business, and would therefore exploit physical resources and provide employment and experience, in ways that would otherwise not be developed.

Throughout the 1950s, colonies remained the principal recipients of British aid, but by the end of the decade many former colonies had become, or were about to become, independent. Aid to independent countries was becoming the vital policy issue. The Government's policy on the eve of independence—before the true magnitude of India's need had become apparent, and when the floodtide of African independence had hardly begun—was summed up in a White Paper in 1957.[1,2]

Aid to the colonies was provided in the forms outlined above, namely grants-in-aid of administration, grants-in-aid for special purposes like flood relief and reconstruction, CD and W assistance (predominantly in the form of grants) for development, and CDC investment. Loans could be raised by colonial governments from

[1] United Kingdom's Role in Commonwealth Development, Cmnd. 237, July 1957.
[2] Ghana became independent in 1957, but was so much better provided with sources of revenue and educated citizens than other African countries that the latter were not expected to follow Ghana to independence for many years.

private investors in London, and direct loans from the British Government were rare. The system was on the whole a good one; most of its weaknesses arose out of administrative rigidities rather than general policy, and had more serious consequences for the very small or very poor colonies than for the large ones.[1] There were even then, however, signs that political change would create a need for new forms of aid. As early as 1953, the demand for colonial government stocks on the London market had begun to decline, principally it seems because the future of many colonial governments was becoming uncertain; yet not until 1959 was legislation introduced enabling the British Government to replace this source of finance with loans made directly from the Exchequer to colonial governments.

Up to 1958, the only independent Commonwealth countries that might have been considered eligible for aid were India, Pakistan, Ceylon, Ghana, and Malaya. These were all either relatively prosperous or possessed adequate reserves of foreign exchange, and it was still thought at this time that colonies should not become independent until their finances were 'sound' enough for them to have no need of government-to-government loans or grants.[2] The IBRD was considered by the British Government to be both more suitable, and perfectly adequate, as a source of external finance for such countries, and Britain as one of the founder members was by 1958 disbursing to the IBRD about £18 million a year out of her sterling subscription.

In the late 1950s India's balance of payments crisis, and the realization that many African countries must shortly be granted independence despite the weakness of their economies, made a change in policy inevitable. The IBRD, IFC, and IMF, did not together possess the resources to support India on the necessary scale, and some replacement had to be found for CD and W and other colonial forms of finance once African countries reached independence. The solution chosen was to make funds available on a fairly large scale under existing Export Credits Guarantee Department (ECGD) legislation. At the time this seemed a big step to take, but it can now be seen as an unfortunate compromise. Use of the ECGD implied that the money was tied to British goods, and that interest was charged at commercial rates ($\frac{1}{4}$ per cent above the rate at which the Treasury

---

[1] For a more detailed discussion of these administrative weaknesses as they still affect the remaining colonies, see English edition, Chapter XVI, pp. 310–11.

[2] Commonwealth countries were eligible on the same terms as foreign countries for ECGD loans in very special circumstances. The first ECGD loan to a Commonwealth country was made to Pakistan in 1954, on account of balance of payments difficulties. No more such loans were made until 1958.

could borrow). These characteristics appeared at the time to be virtues rather than drawbacks; the tying condition helped UK exports and so limited the cost to Britain's balance of payments, and the high rate of interest was considered normal and appropriate to the position of independent countries. These Commonwealth Assistance Loans (CALs) were initially available for categories of goods, or occasionally for projects, requested by the recipient, provided they were clearly for 'development'—i.e. for capital goods which would be used by the borrowing government. Project aid was still regarded as more suitable for multilateral than for bilateral donors.

British policy since the introduction of CALs has gradually eroded, without actually repudiating, the principle that 'aid' to independent countries should be 'hard', tied to British procurement, and not tied to projects except at the recipient's special request. But no comparable new principle has been enunciated. The White Paper of 1963[1] stated that independent countries might now expect to be eligible for a special financial settlement at independence, continuing access to the London market, continuing investment from the CDC, and CALs made through the ECGD.[2] It stated further that in several instances the British Government 'has joined with other donor governments to provide development finance', and had, exceptionally, given budgetary aid to an independent Commonwealth country. But there was no assurance that aid for these purposes would be provided in the future, or that forms of aid other than those listed in the previous sentence would continue to be available.

British policy since 1958 has thus been governed by an increasingly inappropriate principle, modified only when outside pressures became too strong to resist. For instance, although it has been plain for some years that India and Pakistan would continue to be able to meet service payments on 'hard' loans only if their gross aid receipts continue to be larger than their service payments, the British Government began only recently to lend to these countries at subsidized rates of interest. Similarly it was not until Sierra Leone and Uganda had proved unable to find uses for ECGD loans on the customary terms and conditions that the Commonwealth Relations Office (CRO) vote began to be used for making loans to African governments on less rigid procurement conditions. The necessity for these changes in policy was pointed out by the Select Committee on Estimates in

[1] *Aid to Developing Countries*, Cmnd. 2147, September 1963.
[2] Interest payments on ECGD Loans may now be subsidized, as a matter of general policy.

1959–60, but resulted in no immediate action.[1] British aid would have promoted recipients' development more effectively, had steps been taken earlier to provide aid to certain independent countries at lower rates of interest and on less rigid procurement conditions than those applicable to CALS.

Now let us turn to British technical assistance, and the changes which colonial independence has brought about in this field. Under the colonial system, as it operated in the 1950s, technical assistance of a kind was provided in two ways. First, the British Government recruited personnel for the colonial services. Secondly, advisers, teachers, scholarships, etc., were paid for out of CD and W funds. Neither of these activities was classified or regarded at the time as technical assistance. Officials recruited by the British Government were in any case employed and paid by the colonial governments, the British Government contributing only in so far as certain colonies were receiving general budgetary assistance. The British Government expected that officials who were dismissed, or chose to leave their posts when a colony became independent, would be compensated for loss of career by the successor to the colonial government which had employed them.

Independent countries' technical assistance needs have been catered for largely by means of regional programmes, often in conjunction with other donors. The earliest of these, the Colombo Plan, was inaugurated in 1950, and by 1963 the Department of Technical Co-operation (DTC) had sub-heads in its vote covering all possible recipients. There seems to have been less fear that willingness to provide technical assistance would be regarded by independent countries as an affront to their dignity than has been the case with financial assistance; but corresponding to the principle that soft loans or grants would not normally be made to independent countries has been the principle that technical assistance should be provided only in response to specific requests. Like the financial assistance principle, this has proved inapplicable in practice, though despite the statement in Cmnd. 2147 of 1963, that 'Technical Assistance involves the identification of the needs of individual developing countries', the old principle has not been officially abandoned. Expenditure on this kind of technical assistance has been small; in 1962–3 the total cost of Regional Programmes was only £3·9 million, though it rose sharply to £8·4 million in 1963–4.[2]

[1] Fourth Report, pp. x–xi.
[2] The increase is partly due to the inclusion of colonies in these programmes for the first time. See *British Aid 4. Technical Assistance*, ODI, 1964, p. 116.

For newly independent countries technical assistance—in the broad sense, including recruitment of administrative personnel—has proved if anything a greater headache than financial assistance. Administrative and other colonial officers left their posts at or soon after independence in much larger numbers than had been anticipated. The reasons for this were partly that a happy relationship was difficult to establish between the new governments and people who had served under the old colonial régimes, and partly because the terms of compensation provided many of these officers with a greater financial incentive to leave than to stay. Governments of newly independent countries were therefore faced with a desperate shortage of experienced administrators, and with the heavy cost of compensating their former employees for loss of career. In answer to this situation, the British Government introduced the Overseas Service Aid Scheme (OSAS) in 1961. This has been the principal channel of technical assistance since that date, and provides for two forms of help to newly independent countries and colonies. First, the British Government 'tops up' the salaries of expatriate officers to the extent deemed necessary to make their recruitment or retention possible, and helps to recruit new officers on contract. Secondly, it pays half the cost of compensation for officers who chose, or were asked, to retire prematurely.[1] In 1964–5 the scheme cost some £14·7 million, of which £6·4 million was for compensation, and some 12,000 officers were serving under the scheme in late 1963. The number of officers has been declining since 1961, and will continue to decline because of overseas governments' policies of Africanization (or its equivalent), but comparable schemes for 'topping up' the salaries of secondary school teachers and university teachers have been started under the title of 'Commonwealth Educational Co-operation', and these are expanding fairly rapidly.[2]

The number of British people serving overseas who had both been recruited by the British Government under aid programmes, and received part of their salaries from that source, was some 13,500 in late 1963. A further 500 were serving under subsidized programmes not regarded as aid (principally the British Council), and there were some 2,800 officers who had been recruited by the British Govern-

[1] It is doubtful whether repayment of compensation for officers who have already left their posts should be regarded as technical assistance. See also English edition, Chapter XVI, p. 298.

[2] The Overseas Development and Service Bill, now before Parliament, enables the Minister of Overseas Development to 'top up' salaries, or contribute to compensation, for employees of governments, inter-governmental organizations, local authorities, schools, universities, health services, public utilities, etc.

ment but whose salaries were paid entirely by their overseas employers. In March 1963, there were 50,100 students and trainees on courses in Britain, of whom about 2,300 were directly financed under aid programmes. Fee-paying students at British universities and technical colleges (around 23,800 in 1963) were paying fees which covered only a small part of the cost of their courses, on account of the general subsidy to all such institutions. Other forms of technical assistance—research, surveys, etc.—cannot be quantified in comparable physical units. The total cost (excluding subsidies to education in the UK) of bilateral technical assistance in 1963 was £24·2 million. Of this, £16·0 million was spent on experts,[1] £3·0 million on students and trainees, £1 million on equipment, £1·1 million on surveys, £1·8 million on research, and £0·6 million on consultants and other expenditures.[2]

It will have become apparent from this discussion that a large number of Ministries and Government Departments have been involved in administering British aid. The Foreign Office (FO), Commonwealth Relations Office (CRO), and Colonial Office (CO), together with the Treasury, have been responsible for policy decisions. The DTC, before becoming part of the Overseas Development Ministry (ODM), was subject to general policy direction from these Ministries, but took complete responsibility for the administration of technical assistance, and has carried funds on its own vote. The ECGD has looked after the technical aspects of drawing up ECGD loan agreements. The British Council has provided a substantial amount of educational aid to independent countries. Other Ministries and Departments—e.g. the Ministry of Education—have become involved in technical assistance from time to time, but their expenses were normally repaid by the DTC. The FO, CRO, CO, and DTC (also the Central African Office during its short life) are the only Ministries on whose votes aid estimates have been carried.

Much of this administrative complexity has been removed now that a new Overseas Development Ministry has been formed. Discussion of the new Ministry will be found in the English edition, Chapter XVI, concerned with current and future British aid policy.

5. FRENCH AID

Though France has provided more aid to her colonies and ex-colonies than the UK, neither did much until after the Second World War.

---

[1] Including compensation under OSAS.
[2] See ODI *Technical Assistance*.

38   INTERNATIONAL AID

Each then introduced a substantial programme of grant aid for colonial development. In 1956, the last year before the beginning of African independence, the total of French grants and loans ($648 million) was over three times that of the UK, and French private investment in developing countries was also substantially greater. Both France and Britain provided most of their aid to colonies rather than to independent countries at that time. On the other hand, the ratio of French grants to total 'aid' was lower than that of the UK (70 per cent against 85 per cent).

The two countries approached aid to their colonies in very different ways. As already explained, the British Government, believing that the colonies were all being prepared for independence (however distant that might be), attempted to maintain a rigid distinction between aid for capital expenditure and aid for recurrent costs, and provided the latter only under very stringent conditions. The French, aiming at the eventual integration of her colonies into metropolitan France, worried far less about such distinctions, and provided considerable amounts of aid in the form of what was in effect budget support. They also made much freer use than the British of price support for commodities exported by the colonies to France.

Differences between the two countries' policies were accentuated, rather than reduced, when their colonies became independent. The British Government has tried hard to uphold the principle that independent governments should only rarely, in exceptional circumstances, receive aid in the form of grants, or soft loans. The French Government has taken quite a different line. Budgetary aid, and technical assistance in all its forms, from administrative employees to teachers, and grant aid for development projects and programmes, have continued just as before independence. The African and Malagasy States[1] received almost exactly the same proportion of French bilateral aid in 1963 as in 1960, with no significant change in the terms. Aid to Algeria was maintained at its 1960 level until 1963, but has declined sharply since that year, both in total and as a proportion of bilateral aid; aid to Morocco has increased since 1960.

There have, however, been strings attached to this generous aid. Guinea, on rejecting membership of the proposed French Community in 1958, was cut off completely from French sources of aid. French officials leaving jobs in the Government of Guinea took away

[1] The thirteen French states which were formed out of French colonies in West and Central Africa—Central African Republic, Chad, Congo (Brazzaville), Dahomey, French Somaliland, Gabon, Ivory Coast, Madagascar, Mali, Mauretania, Niger, Senegal, Togo, Upper Volta—and the Malagasy Republic.

with them virtually everything movable, including records and statistics. Similarly, new financial aid to Mali was withheld for two or three years after the events which brought about the break-up of the Mali-Senegal Federation. France clearly regards the aid which she provides on such lenient terms to the African and Malagasy States as a powerful source of influence over their foreign policies.

Like other donors, France also uses export credits and small amounts of technical assistance as diplomatic and commercial weapons outside her normal sphere of influence. Countries which belong to the Franc Area have very close trading ties with France, and generally also have agreements which grant French firms, and now also firms registered in any European Economic Community (EEC) member country, preferential rights of establishment over other foreign firms. Aid to Algeria appears to carry no such stringent conditions, because an important motive behind it is the French desire to continue sharing in the exploitation of Saharan oil deposits; but aid to Morocco and Tunisia appears to depend partly upon the recipient government's treatment of French farmers and businessmen.

One result of the trade and monetary agreements between France and Franc Area countries is that the real cost of French aid disbursed within the area is hard to estimate. In effect, as a result of these agreements, the whole of French aid to Franc Area countries is as good as tied to the purchase of French goods, and the monopoly of trade by French firms which follows from this and other policies inevitably affects the price of imports. Part of French aid may therefore be regarded as a direct subsidy to certain French firms, in just the same way as part of contractually tied aid has the effect of subsidizing firms in other donor countries.

This argument is borne out by one of the calculations in the Jeanneney Report.[1] It is estimated that in 1960–2 the trading surplus of France with the Franc Zone countries, together with the value of services connected with trade in goods, and the expenditure on technical assistance, amounted to 92 per cent of net aid expressed in financial terms. Had it not been for the trade and financial agreements, one would have expected recipients to have spent more of their aid from France—which is not formally tied to French exports—on financing trade deficits with other industrial countries, and not to have spent almost the whole of their aid receipts in financing a deficit with France.

[1] See *The Jeanneney Report: an abridged translation of La Politique de Coopération avec les pays en voie de developpement*, ODI, 1964, p. 28.

Recent French policy statements suggest that the French Government would like to reduce the proportion of aid devoted to Franc Area countries. New commitments have in fact been made in Latin America, but the change has not yet shown up in published statistics of disbursements. It is unlikely that French aid to the African and Malagasy States will actually be reduced, but it may well be stabilized at its existing level. Aid to the rest of the Franc Area (excluding Overseas Departments and Territories, whose aid will presumably increase in line with French national income) will depend upon the political relationships that develop. In negotiating associated status with the EEC, for the African and Malagasy States, France was able to secure a substantial source of finance, via the European Development Fund (EDF), for these countries from the other five members of the EEC, and this in itself will allow France, if she wishes, to keep the level of her aid to these countries fairly static. Recently, progress has been made towards reducing budgetary subsidies to the African and Malagasy States, the amount allocated falling from 200 million French francs in 1962 to 65 million in 1964.

In line with financial assistance, French technical assistance to countries in the Franc Area is on a very large scale, and has not been noticeably reduced since independence. In 1963, there were 51,000 French technical assistance personnel working overseas, as against less than 14,000 British.[1] A number of factors help to account for the difference in scale between French and British technical assistance. First comes France's willingness to spend money much more freely on technical assistance, just as she decided to provide financial assistance on a much larger scale than Britain. Thus France spends roughly $3,500 per person against Britain's $3,100 as well as employing far more people. Secondly, the recipients of French technical assistance have thus far been readier to accept Frenchmen in their administrations, on a fairly permanent basis, than any of the former British colonies. Even those East and Central African countries—Kenya, Malawi, Uganda, Tanzania, and Zambia—which in comparison with West Africa still employ relatively large numbers of British citizens in government posts, are replacing them as fast as they can possibly can, whereas in former French colonies there is apparently no comparable pressure for Africanization. A third factor is the difference between French and British educational arrange-

---

[1] A further 3,000 British citizens were working overseas in posts for which they had been recruited by the British Government, but without receiving any part of their salaries from it, and 500 were serving under subsidized programmes not officially classified as aid.

ments. Fifty-seven per cent of French technical assistance personnel serving overseas are teachers, compared with 16 per cent of British personnel. It is clear that the French educational system, whereby teachers are all employed by the Central Government, who can therefore second them as it pleases, accounts for part of the difference. The British Government has been hindered in its attempts to arrange for teachers to go overseas by the fact that teachers are employed by Local Education Authorities, with whom arrangements for secondment, and guarantees of reinstatement and promotion, have had to be negotiated; but arrangements with LEAs for reinstatement, etc., are now working smoothly enough to allow a rapid rise in recruitment.

The administrative arrangements for French aid are in some ways comparable to those in Britain—before the ODM was established in 1964. One Ministry (Co-operation) is responsible for financial and technical aid to the African and Malagasy States, a second for the Overseas Departments and Territories, a third for Algeria, and a fourth (the Treasury) for financial aid to the rest of the world. Technical assistance is provided by the Ministries of Foreign Affairs and Economic Affairs, and by the various functional Ministries, principally the Ministry of Education. The Ministry of Co-operation is represented in the recipient countries by 'Standing Aid and Co-operation Missions', which transmit requests to Paris and check that projects are carried out, quite independently of the Embassies in those countries. In addition, the Caisse Centrale de Co-operation Economique, paying agent for aid to the African and Malagasy States and to the Overseas Departments and Territories, possesses funds of its own which it has recently used in Morocco and Tunisia.

The motives which prompt France to be so unusually generous with aid are complex. There seems little doubt that, despite the advantages which some sectors of the French economy derive from French aid programmes, aid is a considerable burden to France as a whole. We have already suggested some possible motives; that aid to Algeria is linked with French interests in Saharan oil and in nuclear testing sites; that aid to Morocco, Tunisia, and the African and Malagasy States, is linked to the treatment these countries offer French business and French residents. But these are only partial explanations. Political motives are also important, since France undoubtedly influences if not dictates the foreign policy of at least the African and Malagasy States, by means of explicit agreement that France shall be consulted before any important international meeting, and before important votes are to be taken in the UN. Then there

42   INTERNATIONAL AID

is the feeling, important also for British policy, that national prestige is involved in the economic and political condition and progress of former colonies. Finally, there is the well-known French desire to extend French cultural influence. This they have done very success-fully in all their ex-colonies (not excluding Guinea), but subsidies from France are necessary if the link is to be maintained.

The main differences between French and British aid policies probably stem from different beliefs concerning the possibility and value of cultural assimilation (corresponding to different theories in the past concerning political assimilation, and probably also to a different evaluation of the possible uses of aid in foreign policy). There have been signs in France recently of popular discontent with the cost of the aid programme, mainly on the grounds that the funds are misused, and that equally good results could be achieved from the expenditure of much smaller sums.[1] Nevertheless, there is little or no public disagreement with the notion that France should spend money on the propagation of French culture. The complaints seem unlikely to lead to an actual reduction in French aid. Indeed, current plans fall in with M. Jeanneney's suggestion that aid be increased at the same rate—5 per cent per annum—as French national income, i.e. that the current ratio of aid to GNP—1·5 per cent—be maintained.[2]

6. GERMAN AID

European countries, apart from Britain and France, which still possess colonies, or which possessed colonies until very recently—Belgium, the Netherlands, Portugal, and Italy—still concentrate most of their aid in their own spheres of influence, in much the same way as Britain and France. Even Germany, which lost its last colonies in 1918, shows a lingering interest in countries like Tanganyika, which once came under its rule, although the distribution of German aid is only slightly, if at all, influenced by such sentimental attachments.

Germany embarked on a capital aid programme in 1960. Reasons were many and complex, 'but they added up to a declaration that Germany, as a legally re-established and respected state, was once again able to take its place in the world and to assume wide inter-national responsibilities'.[3] The partition of Germany, and the ever-present tension over Berlin, gives her an interest in Cold War politics second only to that of the USA, Russia, and China. Also, German

[1] cf. Raymond Cartier, *Paris Match*, Spring numbers 1964.
[2] op. cit., pp. 30–1.
[3] See John White, *German Aid*, ODI, 1965.

enthusiasm for promoting private enterprise in developing countries appears to have an ideological foundation similar to that found in the USA. In a world where aid is an essential political and commercial tool for any important power, and is in particular an important element in the Cold War, it was inevitable that Germany should become a donor on a substantial scale.

The new programme did not start completely from scratch. As early as 1953 a small technical assistance programme had been launched, mainly in the form of training in Germany. Guarantees for private export credits had been used by the Government to promote trade—culminating in 1958 in the need to consolidate Indian debt to the German firms who had supplied the steel plant at Rourkela. The German Government had contributed its share (albeit based on an out-dated post-war assessment of ability to subscribe) to the IBRD and other UN bodies, and had invested substantial public funds in IBRD bonds. Through the EDF Germany had also contributed to the development of EEC associated territories—principally former French colonies. But apart perhaps from the export credit guarantee programme, which was clearly not very satisfactory because of developing countries' inability to finance imports on short-term credit, these activities hardly constituted a programme.

German aid policy is distinguished by the clarity of its concepts. Its most fundamental premise seems to be that aid should promote indigenous private enterprise, and from this there stem rules such that grant aid is appropriate only for technical assistance, that financial aid should be on a project basis and used either for revenue-earning projects at commercial rates of interest, or for infrastructure investment at subsidized rates of interest (3–3½ per cent being usual). There is a certain conflict between the desire to promote private enterprise and directly productive investment, the unwillingness to lend direct to private enterprise, and a reluctance to put money into public sector projects of a type normally considered appropriate to the private sector. For the same reason, i.e. that aid is for development and not export promotion, most aid (as opposed to export credit) is not officially tied to German exports.

Administrative weakness has unfortunately made a mockery of this coherent, if over-simple, approach to aid. The Co-operation Ministry, set up in 1961 to co-ordinate aid which had formerly been channelled directly through other Ministries—the most important of these being the Foreign Ministry and the Economics Ministry—has always lacked influence in the Cabinet because of coalition politics; and inter-ministerial rivalries have prevented Ministries from co-operating

44   INTERNATIONAL AID

in applying the principles evolved by the Co-operation Ministry. In particular, no proper aid administration has been established overseas, so that although the Government now believes that it should help to stimulate requests, it has no means of doing so. Requests continue to be stimulated largely by representatives of German business interests. This has been the principal reason why so much untied German aid has been spent on the products of German firms, and has given the German aid programme its probably justified reputation for being by far the most strongly commercial of all the major aid programmes.

One of Germany's most interesting innovations has been the general advance commitment, whereby the Government undertook to provide aid over a period of years, up to an agreed ceiling, to a particular recipient. This is a policy which the DAC has repeatedly pressed other donors to emulate, given the difficulty of planning expenditure and using aid rapidly, when aid is committed at yearly intervals and never for more than a year in advance. Unfortunately, and partly because of Germany's lack of aid administrators who could stimulate requests for commitment to specific projects, the lag between general advance commitment and project commitment, let alone between general advance commitment and disbursement, became so long and so variable that the policy of making general advance commitments has been dropped, and with a few exceptions only project commitments are now undertaken.

German aid has become very widely dispersed throughout the world since 1960, mainly because of the absence of strong colonial ties. The Hallstein doctrine prevents West Germany from providing aid to any government that recognizes the East German régime, and has led to a withdrawal of aid from Ceylon; an awkward relationship with Tanzania because the former Zanzibar Government had allowed an East German Embassy to be established in Zanzibar; and a tense and embarrassing situation in Egypt, when the President's invitation to Herr Ulbricht to visit Cairo raised the difficult question of what really constitutes recognition of a régime. The doctrine seems to limit, rather than to determine in any precise way, the distribution of German aid.

German aid has not had the impact hoped for in 1960, on the one hand because too much was expected of it, and on the other because of the administrative muddle that has prevented improvements in the programme and has allowed commercial considerations to eclipse all others. The public have become disillusioned—as in the USA and to a lesser extent in France—and though commitments for 1963 were higher than in any earlier year, budget appropriations have been decreasing since 1960. This decline must, if it continues, eventually be reflected in declining commitments and disbursements.

7. UN AID

Among the objects of the UN, as stated in its Charter, is 'to achieve international co-operation in solving international problems of an economic, social, cultural or humanitarian character', and members are pledged to co-operate with the UN Organization in promoting 'higher standards of living, full employment, and conditions of economic and social progress and development'. This marked a great advance on the League of Nations, which scarcely concerned itself with economic questions. But UN machinery for carrying out its obligations to poor countries was slow to develop, and the UN has never channelled through its own organizations more than a small percentage of world aid. In 1963, only 7 per cent of total OECD disbursements went to multilateral agencies.

The first UN agency to be explicitly concerned with developing countries was the International Bank for Reconstruction and Development. As its title suggests, emphasis was initially placed on reconstruction—for the first decade of its existence—although lending for development in poor countries began in 1948. Since then its development activities have expanded rapidly, and it has acquired two affiliates. One reason for the early neglect of development was that most developing countries were still colonies, and were regarded as the responsibility of the colonial powers. This is well illustrated by the fact that not until 1949 was legislation passed in the UK allowing the IBRD to lend to the governments of British colonies under a UK Government guarantee.

Other UN Specialized Agencies—the Economic, Social and Cultural Organization (UNESCO), the Food and Agricultural Organization (FAO), etc.—whose main purposes are to promote international co-operation, research, exchange of ideas, etc., have always used some of their funds for technical assistance schemes to developing countries. The most famous of their schemes has probably been malaria eradication carried out by the World Health Organization (WHO). It soon became clear that these separate programmes were too small, and too unrelated to one another, to use resources efficiently for development. The Expanded Programme for Technical Assistance (UNEPTA) was consequently initiated in 1950. This programme is financed by voluntary contributions from member governments of the UN, or of the Specialized Agencies. It is administered by a Technical Assistance Board (UNTAB), responsible to ECOSOC, and hence to the UN General Assembly; and is largely executed by the Specialized Agencies acting as agents for UNTAB. The Specialized Agencies now provide far more technical assistance under the UNEPTA than they do through the 'regular programmes', which they finance from their own funds, so that a certain conflict has developed within them. Their official function, for which they were set up, is to promote international co-operation and research in their own specialized fields. This demands a set of priorities different from those needed for programmes designed for maximum economic development in particular countries and particular areas. Malaria eradication is a good example: it makes sense from the WHO's point of view to press ahead with eradicating malaria throughout the world, and so to prevent re-infection. But the countries now worst affected by malaria have other more pressing problems, for which they prefer to use their resources. This conflict of priorities has tended to restrict UNEPTA's usefulness, since employees of the FAO, WHO, and other Specialized Agencies, have suffered from divided loyalties. It has now been decided that UNEPTA and UNSF should amalgamate, and their combined expenditure will amount to some $120 million a year (the target is $150 million); it will be interesting to see whether their combined strength will allow the new agency to resist the pressures of the Specialized Agencies more successfully.

UNEPTA was the first UN programme aimed solely at developing poor countries, to which UN members were asked to contribute. Soviet bloc countries have been unenthusiastic, and have caused difficulties by contributing in blocked currencies (this not only raised a question of principle, but also made their use a complicated administrative exercise). Nevertheless, for them, and for many other countries, this was their first entry into the field of aid. UNEPTA has been a useful channel of aid for some non-colonial, especially Scandinavian, countries which could afford some aid, but had no experience of developing countries and were dubious about setting up administrative machinery for giving aid bilaterally. Over 10 per cent of total aid from Norway, Denmark, Sweden, Switzerland, and Canada, in the years 1956–9, took the form of contributions to UNEPTA and UN relief agencies; whereas France, Britain, and the USA, contributed only 2 per cent of their total aid in this form over the same period.

Throughout the 1950s developing countries have canvassed the idea of a UN capital development fund (SUNFED), which would make grants and soft loans on a large scale, and replace much of the aid that is at present provided bilaterally. Rich countries have opposed the idea on a variety of grounds—that they cannot afford subscriptions in addition to their bilateral commitments, and that such a scheme would be feasible only if world disarmament were achieved, thus releasing a large new source of funds—but the biggest reason is disagreement over the form of control. The IBRD and its affiliates are controlled by a voting system in which the number of votes cast by a delegation is related to the size of its (assessed) contribution, so that IBRD policies are controlled by the donors and not the recipients. Even with this safeguard, donors have not been willing to subscribe generously to the IDA, the Bank's 'soft loan' subsidiary. The SUNFED idea is popular with developing countries, because it would be controlled by ECOSOC and the General Assembly, in which they have a large majority of votes. If they had their way, contributions to the Fund from the rich countries would be disbursed according to decisions made by the recipients themselves. Donors have shown themselves unwilling to provide large sums of money to an organization of this kind.

However, the strong demands for SUNFED have had some results. In 1959 the IDA was set up as a subsidiary of the IBRD (thus meeting donors' objections to SUNFED) for the purpose of making soft loans for the kind of projects hitherto financed by the IBRD. Countries whose external financial situation was too weak to meet IBRD criteria, but could put up projects which on their own merits would be acceptable to the IBRD, would qualify for these loans. IDA members have been niggardly in providing finance for these operations, so that the IDA has been consistently short of funds, at times appearing to be in danger of extinction. But contributions have recently been assured for another three years, and the IBRD is planning to give it some of its own income. These two sources should provide an annual income of over $300 million. But the marked preference of donors for bilateral or regional forms of finance, rather than for even this carefully controlled form of multilateral aid, has disappointed many who would like to see the latter increase.

The other partial substitute for SUNFED is the UNSF. This was established in 1959 to finance (by means of grants) any form of activity that would improve the opportunities for investment in poor countries. Education has been the most favoured activity, followed by surveys and feasibility studies, and research. Contributions, which are voluntary, have run at about $50 million a year, rising in 1963 to some $70 million, but have not so far approached the target of $100

TABLE 2

Changes in the amount and composition of aid from OECD donors, by category of donor, 1957–9 and 1961–3

$m

	1957–9				1961–3			
	Colonial and ex-colonial[1]	USA	Other[2]	Total	Colonial and ex-colonial	USA	Other	Total
Multilateral	317	167	645	1,129	509	690	662	1,861
Bilateral (net)	3,359	6,656	1,446	11,461	4,164	10,092	2,079	16,335
Grants	2,570	3,339	380	6,289	3,180	4,168	362	7,710
Reparations	—	—	462	462	—	—	456	456
Loans (gross) for more than 1 year	917	1,467	825	3,209	1,226	3,165	1,797	6,188
Repayments	−128	−740	−221	−1,089	−242	−955	−545	−1,742
Other bilateral	—	2,590	—	2,590	—	3,714	7	3,721
Total (net)	3,677	6,823	2,089	12,589	4,672	10,782	2,742	18,196

[1] Belgium, France, Netherlands, Portugal, and UK.

[2] Austria, Canada, Denmark, Germany, Ireland, Italy, Japan, Luxembourg, Norway, Sweden, and Switzerland.

million. There has been pressure to extend UNSF's interest to actual capital investment projects. But a recent decision to merge the administration of UNEPTA and the UNSF suggests that its limitation to 'pre-investment' activity will not be allowed to widen into investment proper. In any case, unless it had more money to spend, it could do very little in any broader field.

8. FINAL REMARKS

Many of the ideas about aid that have become current since 1960 have still hardly been translated into practice. There is no doubt that the pattern of world aid has changed quite markedly in the last four years. The group of non-colonial donors, excluding the USA and the Eastern countries, has overtaken the former colonial powers in the volume of aid given. The dominance of the USA has been reduced. Most donor governments are even now ambivalent about the advantages to themselves which they hope aid will bring. Aid from one independent government to another is still largely determined by rather short-sighted Cold War politics; by colonial ties whose rationale has not been properly analysed; and by commercial interest.

Tables 2 and 3 show clearly how the composition of aid differs between the important categories of OECD donor. In particular, the USA and countries with colonial or post-colonial responsibilities provide a higher proportion of their aid in the form of grants, and a lower proportion multilaterally. The differences between the three categories of donor narrowed slightly between 1957–9 and 1961–3, but were still substantial in the latter period.

TABLE 3

Changes between 1957–9 and 1961–3 in the percentage composition of aid provided by different categories of OECD donor

per cent

	1957–9			1961–3		
	Colonial & ex-colonial	USA	Other	Colonial & ex-colonial	USA	Other
Multilateral	9	3	31	11	6	24
Bilateral (net)	91	97	69	89	94	76
Grants	70	49	18	66	39	13
Reparations	—	—	22	—	—	16
Loans (net)	21	11	29	21	20	46
Other bilateral	—	38	—	—	35	—
Total (net)	100	100	100	100	100	100

Table 4 shows how USA aid has grown considerably faster than aid from either of the other two categories of donor, and therefore constituted a higher proportion of total OECD aid in 1961–3 than in 1957–9. The main reason for this is that the even more rapid growth of German aid over the same period (see Table 1) was masked by the slow growth in aid from countries like Japan and Italy.

TABLE 4

The percentage growth in total (net) aid from each category of donor, 1957–9 to 1961–3

Colonial	27%
USA	58%
Other	31%
Total	45%

CHAPTER II

THE QUANTITY OF WORLD AID 1962-3

---

1. THE FLOW OF GOVERNMENT FINANCE

A great deal is now known about the flows of finance which make up aid, as it is defined by international bodies. About aid proper less is known, published figures providing no more than a rough guide. Total real aid may be defined as the real cost of all actions by governments and individuals in rich countries that are intended to raise incomes in poor countries. Military aid is therefore excluded. Aid statistics as now published need amending in many ways to yield estimates of real aid in this sense, even if we restrict ourselves, as we do, to aid provided by governments.

First, the amount of subsidy implicit in every government loan should be substituted in the statistics for the gross value of each loan disbursement. Secondly, the loss of value due to tying aid to products exported by the donor country should be subtracted from the total amount of aid (this loss of value can be regarded as a domestic subsidy paid by the donor government to its own export industries). Thirdly, aid may be part of a 'package' including trade and payments agreements, which can be valued only as a whole; the 'package' may be worth more or less than the nominal value of that part which would currently be included in aid statistics. Fourthly, commodity price agreements, such as the world-wide agreement for coffee, the French agreements with African producers for coffee, cotton, ground-nuts, etc., and the Commonwealth Sugar Agreement, are all designed to subsidize producers as a group at the expense of consumers as a group, and therefore constitute aid even though the amounts involved are difficult, if not impossible, to quantify. Fifthly, important transactions not normally ranked as aid may involve one country in costs on another's behalf. Thus, where a 'donor's' currency is overvalued, and capital outflow is restricted, investment overseas, undertaken for private profit, will entail some social cost; where universities are subsidized, fee-paying foreign students will benefit; where there is a shortage of skills, each skilled emigrant will represent a transfer of scarce resources. Transactions of this kind frequently involve resource transfers from poor to rich countries as well as vice versa (Indian doctors and African nurses in British hospitals). They cannot be regarded as aid, unless governments purposely stimulate them for the sake of poor countries, but policy decisions about aid and about other resource transfers between rich and poor countries must be consistent with one another. In particular, policy with respect to private investment in developing countries is intimately bound up with aid policy.

Most important of all policies affecting donor-recipient relationships is trade. Removal of tariffs or internal taxes on goods produced by developing countries, or the introduction of preferences in their favour, can have effects on their economies as far-reaching as the results of aid.

Aid from the recipients' point of view looks rather different. The distinction between aid (provided by governments) and other sources of finance is much less important to recipients than to donors. Grants, soft and hard loans, and import-tied credits from governments or the IBRD, shade through loans from commercial development banks to private export credits (which may or may not be government guaranteed). If a development programme is to be financed, the problem is simply to get the money on the best possible terms and conditions, from any or all of these sources, and there is no point in making a distinction between aid and private sources of finance. The same is true of technical assistance; a bewildering variety of experts is needed and offered, or available through private firms of consultants, on all kinds of terms (terms are sometimes not made clear until after preliminary agreement has been reached); and experts subsidized in the name of aid will not always be as suitable as, or even any cheaper than, hired consultants. Some totally unnecessary experts may even have to be accepted, and part of their expenses paid, as part of a capital aid project. In general, the cost of aid to a donor government is not very closely correlated with its value to the recipient, when aid is taken project by project; and aid may at times be less valuable than private finance.

Laying aside these qualifications for the time being, let us look at the state of 'aid' as conventionally defined. Both the UN and the DAC publish figures of grants and long-term loans (over 5 years' maturity) made by governments, and the total of these is widely taken to represent total aid. The DAC also publishes figures of private investment in order to arrive at an estimate of the 'Flow of Financial Resources to Developing Countries and Multilateral Agencies'.

Their figures are by far the most comprehensive and up-to-date statistics available, and cover all major world donors outside the Communist countries.

Total aid in the above sense was of the order of $6½ billion in 1963; estimated net private investment in developing countries added about another $2 billion, to make a total (net) flow of financial resources of nearly $8½ billion.[1] OECD countries, of whom the USA is incomparably the most important, supplied about $6 billion of the public funds, and all of the private investment; and Communist governments disbursed an estimated $0·4 billion. Disbursements by other industrial countries amounted to less than $100 million.[2] A number of countries which are themselves 'developing' (notably Israel and India) provided some bilateral assistance, and developing members of multilateral organizations contributed to them some $100 million (partly in local currencies), but none of this can be regarded as assistance from rich to poor countries.

Aid disbursements by rich countries are not identical with recipients' receipts because of the activities of intermediary multilateral institutions. In 1963 about 7 per cent of total aid from OECD donor countries, and 13 per cent of total grants (counting subscriptions as equivalent to grants), was disbursed to multilateral agencies, and not directly to developing countries.

Since 1957, there have been two basic types of multilateral programme, those sponsored by the UN or one of its Specialized Agencies, and those sponsored by less universal bodies. Sources and uses of funds vary with each agency. The UN Programmes—UNEPTA, UNSF, UNICEF, etc.—are financed from voluntary contributions made by members (both developed and under-developed) of the UNO or of one of the Specialized Agencies; the money is disbursed in the form of grants for technical assistance. The UN Specialized Agencies (the IBRD is the most important of these in the aid field) derive their incomes in the first instance from assessed subscriptions from members (including less-developed members). The IBRD and one of its affiliates, the IFC, also raise money by floating bonds and selling participation in their projects to private (or official) investors. The form of disbursements of the Specialized Agencies varies. The IBRD and its affiliates lend or invest their funds, in the case of the IDA at very low rates of interest and for long periods; the other Specialized Agencies—WHO, FAO, UNESCO, etc.—all run small programmes of grant aid for technical assistance, financed from their

---

[1] Net, in DAC terminology, means net of amortization, but not of interest.
[2] Australia, New Zealand, Finland, and South Africa.

annual membership subscriptions. These UN Specialized Agencies also act as paid agents for UN programmes (UNEPTA, etc.). UN programmes and agencies provide in these ways assistance on terms ranging from grants to hard loans and equity investment.

The other multilateral agencies—the European Development Fund (EDF), the Inter-American Development Bank (IDB), and the European Investment Bank (EIB)—differ from UN agencies in that membership and eligibility for assistance is determined by political affiliation, and in a sense also by geography. The EDF receives from full members of the EEC assessed subscriptions which are disbursed in the form of grants to Associate Members (which are all developing countries). The IDB, like the IBRD, levies subscriptions from all its members, sells bonds and participations to private investors, and disburses loans to developing members. Membership of the IDB is restricted to members of the Organization of American States. The EIB raises money from private investors in the EEC, and invests principally in backward regions of the EEC itself. It may also, however, invest in Associated Territories, with the help of an interest subsidy from the EDF.

The principal effect of all multilateral agencies is to channel finance from rich to poor countries. But, in the case of all agencies except the EDF and the EIB, this effect is somewhat masked by the fact that subscriptions and contributions come from all members, not only from rich members, and by lags between receipts and disbursements. Developing members, however, pay relatively little (a total of $142 million for the average of 1962 and 1963, most of this in their own currencies, against $541 million from industrial and Sino-Soviet members, virtually all of whose subscriptions were in hard currencies). The consolidated accounts of the multilateral agencies are presented in Tables 5 and 6. Table 5 shows the sources and uses of finance. Table 6 shows the flows from the developing countries, and to the underdeveloped countries.

There are a few countries, on the borderline between developing and developed countries, and even a few which are undeniably not developed, which both give and receive aid. The most important of these is Japan, which despite its poverty by European standards is a member of the OECD and the DAC, and is classified by the OECD as a donor, but which still receives aid (in the form of fairly hard loans) from the USA. Its own aid programme, however, consists largely of reparations, and relatively short-term credit at high rates of interest which is almost completely tied to Japanese goods and services. Thus, appropriately in view of its relative poverty, Japan's voluntary

TABLE 5

Receipts and disbursements of multilateral agencies. Average of 1962 and 1963

$m

(Disbursements marked —)

Type of Country	Grants and capital subscriptions (1)	Official bond purchases net (2)	Private bond purchases net (3)	Repayments to IBRD IFC and IDB (4)	Total flow to multilateral agencies Total columns (1)–(4) (5)	Gross disbursements of grants and loans by multilateral agencies (6)	Net resultant flow to multilateral agencies Column (6)+(5) (7)
Industrial OECD countries	516·2	6·1	172·2	149·8	844·2	−97·5	746·7
Other industrial countries[1]	17·6	1·4	−0·2	43·8	62·7	−50·9	11·8
Sino-Soviet countries	7·1	—			7·1	—	7·1
Less-developed countries	142·2[2]	15·9	0·2	144·3	302·5	−821·0	−518·5[2]
Total	683·0	24·1[3]	170·6[3]	337·9	1,215·7[3]	−969·4	246·3[3]

[1] Australia, Finland, New Zealand, and South Africa.
[2] Very roughly half of the grants and capital subscriptions paid by developing countries to multilateral agencies took the form of subscriptions in their own currencies to the IDA and the IDB. Thus the net flow of foreign exchange to poor countries was of the order of $600 million.
[3] Column totals do not add up because of unclassified changes in private holdings.
Source: OECD, op. cit., p. 41.

TABLE 6

Multilateral agencies' net receipts of grants and subscriptions from industrial countries, and gross disbursements to developing countries. Average of 1962 and 1963

$m

	Net grants and subscriptions from industrial countries	Gross disbursements to developing countries
IBRD	41·5	435·7[1]
IDA	146·0	64·7
IFC	—	14·9[2]
IDB	30·8	56·0[2]
UNTAB	209·2	188·5
EEC	112·7	61·3
Total	540·2	821·0

[1] Repayments were $141·6 million.
[2] Repayments to the IFC and the IDB were $2·7 million together.
Source: ibid., p. 40.

aid (apart from reparations) costs little.[1] Israel is another country, richer in income per head but much smaller than Japan which, while still receiving aid from the USA and Germany, has embarked on a significant bilateral aid programme; it consists almost entirely of technical assistance, and has been concentrated on African countries south of the Sahara. Israel's political motive—to gain allies or at least neutral sympathizers in her confrontation with Arab countries —is plain, but her comparative affluence and her ample supply of skilled people would, even in the absence of special political motivation, mark Israel as a potential donor. Other donor-recipients, such as India, Malaysia, and Formosa, restrict their aid almost entirely to technical assistance, often provided through the Colombo Plan and similar organizations. India also provides Nepal with substantial amounts of financial assistance, for strategic reasons.

2. THE COST OF AID, AND DONORS' SHARES

The figures we have used up to now in this chapter have referred to what in Chapter I we called 'aid', a crude concept which is far from homogenous. We shall now look at the composition of this 'aid' with special reference to its cost to the donor. It is possible to classify with any accuracy only the 'aid' provided by members of the OECD, but as this accounted for $6 billion (net) out of a world total of some $6½ billion this restriction is not too serious.

The principal determinants of the cost of a given amount of nom-

[1] See John White, op. cit.

inal aid are the terms on which it is provided, and the extent to which it is provided in kind or on condition that it be spent on goods produced in the donor country. The latter affects the cost of aid to the extent that it enables firms situated in the donor country to sell their goods overseas at prices which they would not be able to obtain except under aid-financed contracts.

Aid can be analysed according to its terms quite satisfactorily from published documents.[1] The $6·6 billion gross ($6·1 billion net) provided in 1963 by OECD members consisted of $3·1 billion in grants, $1·3 billion in 'grant-like contributions' (finance or commodities provided against immediate or deferred payment in recipients' currencies), and $2·2 billion in loans (gross of amortization). The loan portion was provided at an average interest rate of 3·4 per cent, and an average maturity of 24·6 years.[2] Tables 7 and 8 show how these various categories of aid were distributed between the major OECD donors, and how interest rates and maturities for the loan portion of their aid differed from donor to donor. The quantitative importance of the USA, and the exceptionally good terms on which it lends, emerge clearly. Table 9 shows who were the principal recipients of aid from these donors.

It is much more difficult to give a precise picture of the extent to which aid is tied, and it is in any case not possible to calculate the extent of the reduction in the cost of aid due to tying. The main purpose of tying is not to reduce cost, in terms of resources, but to relieve any strain on the donor's balance of payments which aid might impose; and its main effect on the recipient is, in combination with project-tying, to create difficulties connected with local financing and project selection.[3] Neither of these principal effects, nor even the secondary cost effect, which arises when tied aid is used to buy goods in a market other than the cheapest, can be quantified. A further difficulty is that contractual tying is only one method of ensuring that aid is spent on exports from the donor:[4] therefore, since statistics showing the amount of (nominal) aid that is tied refer only to contractual tying, they tend to understate the real extent of tying; on the other hand contractual tying is ineffective in certain circumstances,[5] and

---

[1] DAC, *Development Assistance Efforts and Policies*, and OECD, *Flow of Financial Resources*, both published annually.

[2] The figures for average interest and maturity refer to commitments and not to disbursements.

[3] See Chapter VII.

[4] See Chapter XII.

[5] See Chapter XII.

TABLE 7

The composition of aid disbursed by OECD member countries and by principal OECD donors

Average of 1962 and 1963

$m

Category	All OECD	USA	France	UK	Germany	Other OECD
A. Bilateral, net	5,523	3,445	848	375	373	482
Grants other than reparations	2,532	1,362	727	211	54	178
Reparations	149	—	—	—	70	79
Loans repayable in recipients' currencies, net	360	360	—	—	—	—
Sales for recipients' currencies	930	928	—	—	2	—
Gross lending[1]	2,054	1,035	159	201	303	356
Amortization received	-502	-240	-38	-36	-56	-132
B. Multilateral[2]	522	218	72	42	64	126
Grants and capital subscriptions	516	218	72	42	68	116
Purchase of bonds, net[1]	4	—	—	—	-4	8
C. Total, net	6,043	3,663	919	417	436	608

[1] For more than 1 year.
[2] Includes net official multilateral contributions of Iceland, Ireland, and Luxembourg, of $1 million.
Source: ibid, pp. 130-3.

TABLE 8

Terms of OECD bilateral commitments, 1963

$m

(a) Distribution by maturities

Country	More than 1 to 5 years inclusive	More than 5 to 10 years inclusive	More than 10 to 20 years inclusive	20 to 30 years exclusive	30 to 40 years exclusive	40 years and more	Not available	Grants and grant-like contributions
Total OECD	-3·0	393·9	1,006·2	546·3	39·2	988·0	0·6	3,775·6
USA	-84·0[1]	177·0	228·0	171·0	35·0	988·0	—	2,448·0
France[2]	4·7	25·0	126·7	17·1[3]	—	—	0·6	696·8
UK	2·6	29·2	20·9	183·9	4·2	—	—	219·3
Germany	15·5	4·0	394·0	110·0	—	—	—	163·2

(b) Interest rate structure

Country	Less than 1% and interest free	1 to less than 3%	3 to less than 4%	4 to less than 5%	5 to less than 6%	6 to less than 7%	7% and more	Not available	Total loans
Total OECD	1,049·8	187·6	503·6	41·3	859·6	269·1	30·1	30·1	2,971·2
USA	1,040·0	75·0	112·0	3·0	283·0	1·0	1·0	—	1,515·0
France[3]	1·4	45·6	55·7	2·8	53·7	14·3	—	0·6	174·1
UK	6·6	50·8	9·8	1·6	144·4	—	—	27·6	240·8
Germany	—	14·0	279·0	16·0	145·0	64·5	5·0	—	523·5

[1] Negative figure results from recording new commitments less larger offsetting consolidation credit entries.
[2] Disbursements.
[3] May also include loans with maturities of more than 30 years.
Source: ibid., pp. 151 and 153.

TABLE 9

Principal recipients of net bilateral aid from the four major OECD *donors*
Average of 1962 and 1963
$m

(a) *The* USA

Recipients	Grants	Net Lending	Total
India	392	246	638
Pakistan	255	100	356
S. Korea	225	12	237
Turkey	187	7	194
S. Vietnam	184	—	184
Egypt	155	20	175
Brazil	83	66	149
Yugoslavia	103	31	134
Others	1,066	31	1,379
Total	2,650	795	3,445

(b) *France*

Recipients			
Algeria (including Sahara)	280	28	308
African and Malagasy States	265	26	291
Overseas Departments	98	17	116
Morocco and Tunisia	29	30	59
Overseas Territories	26	3	30
Others	29	17	46
Total	727	121	848

(c) *The* UK

Recipients			
India	7	54	61
Kenya[1]	29	16	46
Tanganyika[1]	23	10	33
Uganda[1]	13	9	23
Pakistan	5	15	21
Others	134	59	193
Total	212	163	375

(d) *Germany*[2]

Recipients			
Israel			64
India			49
Liberia			33
Pakistan			31
Turkey			26
Chile			19
Others			151
Total			373

[1] Including grants and loans to the East African Common Services Organization, allocated according to the following percentages: Kenya 48 per cent, Tanganyika 30 per cent, and Uganda 22 per cent.

[2] The $64 million to Israel was all in grant form. Of the remaining $309 million, only $75 million was in the form of grants. A breakdown by country into grants and loans is not available.

Source: ibid., pp. 75, 76, 84, 108 and 114.

for this reason there is an opposing tendency for the statistics to overstate the extent of effective tying.

Because tying by means other than clauses in aid contracts is so important, and because the effects of contractual tying may be very different according to the degree of simultaneous project-tying, and the extent to which aid may be used to finance general imports equivalent to the local cost of a project, OECD does not publish statistics showing the extent of tying. Nevertheless, we have a reasonable knowledge, for the four main OECD donors, of the extent to which their aid is tied. French aid is nearly all tied in practice, because of Franc Area trading and financial agreements, and because of contractual tying conditions attached to aid to countries outside the Franc Area. Most German aid—with the exception of multilateral assistance, reparations, and re-finance credits (which together amounted to $110 million in 1963)—is spent on German exports, though only about half is contractually tied. Most USA aid is contractually tied, or takes the form of gifts of commodities. But the USA is more willing than Germany to extend lines of credit for consumer and minor capital goods, in order that recipients can meet the increased demand for imports which results from local spending on development projects. British aid to independent countries is mostly contractually tied, except for re-finance credits. Our guess is that close to 80 per cent of bilateral aid as reported to the OECD is spent in the country of origin, either as a result of contractual tying, or because other means are used to ensure that it is so spent. This does not take into account secondary effects—the varying degrees to which aid-financed imports may be substituted for other imports from the donor, so that they are not in fact 'additional' imports, and the related difference between tied aid for the import content of selected projects, and tied aid for general balance of payments support. For these and other reasons, estimates of the extent of donor procurement cannot be used as measures of the ultimate effect of aid on the donor's balance of payments.

Non-OECD members' 'aid', of which Communist countries provide the bulk, cannot be analysed in the same detail as OECD aid, since not even aggregate disbursements are known with any certainty. All we can say about the terms of non-OECD aid is that it is nearly all lent, that rates of interest may be anything from zero to 5 per cent—2½ per cent has been most commonly charged by the Soviet Union—and that maturities also vary, though they tend to be shorter on average than for OECD lending. Virtually all Communist aid is tied to donor procurement and to specified projects, because this is an inevitable consequence of the Communist policy of balancing trade bilaterally, as far as possible, with all trading partners.[1] Some Communist governments have recently, however, offered to lend the proceeds of their exports to a developing country to that country's government, to help cover the local cost of projects for which capital goods are being supplied.

The amount of detailed information which is available concerning DAC members' nominal aid makes it possible to hazard a rough estimate of the total cost of each member's aid. The first published estimate of this kind was made by John A. Pincus in 1963,[2] for the 1962 aid commitments of DAC member countries. He defined the cost of aid as 'the combined nominal (or market) value of all forms of aid less the discounted present value of loan repayments, discounted at a rate of interest reflecting the alternative employment of long-term public capital'. He made three different estimates for each country, the first using a discount rate equal to the domestic long-term borrowing rate in the donor country; the second using a discount rate of 5¾ per cent, the IBRD's lending rate, to represent the international lending rate; and the third using a discount rate of 10 per cent, to represent the rate of interest which private investors would require if they were to invest in the recipient country concerned. He also made two alternative estimates, using (roughly) USA support prices and world market prices, of the value of USA commodity aid commitments, but made no corresponding attempt to estimate the real cost of other forms of tied aid. According to his calculations, depending on which assumptions one takes, the cost of total DAC aid commitments lay between 61 per cent and 77 per cent of their nominal value. For the USA the corresponding figures were 62–83 per cent: for France, 88–91 per cent: for the UK, 29–51 per cent: and for Germany 45–61 per cent. Of the major donors, the UK thus gave the worst terms; but there has been some improvement since 1962. The average interest rates charged, and maturities, are given in Table 10 for all DAC members' commitments in 1963.

We have made our own estimates of the cost of aid disbursed by DAC members in 1963. Our methods are broadly similar to those used by Mr Pincus; loans have been discounted at three different rates of interest, USA commodity aid has been valued according to two

[1] There have been occasional exceptions; for instance Somalia received a grant of £1 million in hard currency from China in 1963, and similar grants have been promised to Egypt, Kenya, Tanzania, etc.
[2] 'The Cost of Foreign Aid', *The Review of Economics and Statistics*, November 1963.

TABLE 10

Average rates of interest and maturities of DAC lending, 1963

Country	Average rate of interest per cent	Average maturity years
Canada	6·50	13
Italy	6·00	9
Japan	5·85	9
Netherlands	4·92	23
Germany	4·50	17
UK	4·40	22
France	4·00	15
Portugal	3·58	25
Belgium	1·76	12
USA	1·75	36
Denmark (grants only)	—	—
Norway (grants only)	—	—

Note: These averages are based on data for commitments; see Table 8.

different assumptions, and we have not attempted to calculate the real cost of other forms of tied aid or of commodity aid from other sources. There are several differences of detail; the discount rates we have chosen are 6 per cent, 10 per cent, and 15 per cent, against Pincus's domestic borrowing rate, 5¾ per cent, and 10 per cent. In our calculations, 6 per cent stands for both the domestic borrowing rate and the international lending rate, 10 per cent stands (as with Pincus) for the rate that private investors would want to earn in developing countries, and 15 per cent takes account of the fact that it is already clear, and recognized by donor governments, that many of the loans currently being made will not be repaid on time, and may never be repaid in full. Part of the 15 per cent, in other words, represents a risk premium. A more detailed account of how we reached our final estimates of the cost of DAC aid—set out in Tables 15, 16, and 17—may be found in the Appendix to this chapter.[1]

One of the main functions of the DAC is to consider the distribution of the burden of aid between its members. But nominal aid, expressed as a percentage of the donors' GDP, is a poor measure of the burden, unless it is implicitly assumed that interest and capital will never be repaid. So long as donors act as if repayment is eventually to be made from the recipients' own resources, one can proceed only by assessing the burden on this basis. The probability of non-repayment can best be allowed for by using a high discount rate,

[1] It is impossible to make any good estimate of the cost of Communist countries' aid. Not only is information about the volume and terms of their nominal aid very scanty, but also the goods which they provide on aid credit, and the goods which they accept in return, are not always valued at world market prices.

TABLE 11

Grant equivalent of DAC 'aid' compared with GDP and GDP per head, 1963

Grant equivalent of aid as percentage of GDP (at factor cost)

Rate of discount		6%		10%		15%			
Average grace period	GDP at factor cost	1 year	5 years	1 year	5 years	1 year	5 years	Nominal aid as percentage of GDP	GDP per head $
Country									
Belgium	11,204	0·82	0·82	0·82	0·83	0·83	0·83	0·83	1,215
Canada	33,615	0·19	0·19	0·21	0·22	0·23	0·24	0·30	1,807
Denmark	6,471	0·14	0·14	0·14	0·14	0·14	0·14	0·15	1,390
France	61,083	1·22	1·23	1·27	1·29	1·31	1·34	1·46	1,300
Germany	73,866	0·27	0·27	0·35	0·37	0·41	0·44	0·62	1,349
Italy	34,542	0·01	0·01	0·01	0·02	0·02	0·02	0·02	688
Japan	47,803	0·19	0·19	0·22	0·23	0·26	0·28	0·28	504
Netherlands	11,831	0·24	0·24	0·26	0·27	0·28	0·28	0·33	1,003
Norway	4,789	0·21	0·21	0·21	0·21	0·21	0·21	0·21	1,316
Portugal	2,502	0·68	0·72	1·04	1·12	1·32	1·40	1·88	279
UK	68,824	0·39	0·40	0·45	0·47	0·50	0·52	0·64	1,288
USA Method I	502,187	0·66	0·67	0·70	0·71	0·73	0·74	0·81	2,691
USA Method II		0·40	0·40	0·44	0·45	0·46	0·48		

Note: For the two methods of costing USA aid see the Appendix to this chapter.

such as the 15 per cent we have used. No doubt, the DAC has made some impressionistic allowance for varying terms in its assessment of the burden of aid. But it is useful to be more systematic than that. In Table 11 we show six different estimates of the cost of aid for each DAC donor, other than the USA for which there are twelve estimates, together with their GDPs and nominal aid levels. In Table 12 we express the highest and lowest of such estimates as a percentage of GDP for each donor, list the donors in order of wealth (GDP per head), and then give their ranking as donors for both the low and high cost estimates. The difference in the estimates in fact makes little difference to the ranking. These estimates are derived from the Appendix to this chapter.

TABLE 12

Wealth and cost-of-aid ranking, DAC *members, 1963*

Country (ranked by GDP per head)	Cost of aid as % of GDP Low	High	Donor ranking Low cost	High cost
USA	0·40	0·74	4	4
Canada	0·19	0·24	9	9
Denmark	0·14	0·14	11	11
Germany	0·27	0·44	6	6
Norway	0·21	0·21	8	10
France	1·22	1·34	1	2
UK	0·39	0·52	5	5
Belgium	0·82	0·83	2	3
Netherlands	0·24	0·29	7	7
Italy	0·01	0·02	12	12
Japan	0·19	0·28	9	8
Portugal	0·68	1·40	3	1

Taking account only of wealth, Canada, Denmark, and Norway, stand out as the mean donors; and Portugal, France, and Belgium, as the generous. The USA, UK, and Germany, of the absolutely large donors, are neither particularly mean nor generous in relative terms: this is also true of the Netherlands among the small donors. Italy is mean compared with other poor donors, but not on an absolute scale, for her GDP per head is barely high enough for one to expect her to be a donor. Relative only to the non-colonial powers, the USA stands out as the most generous. Relative only to ex-colonial or colonial powers, and considering the extent of her erstwhile empire, the UK stands out as the meanest of this group. Portugal's startling performance is very doubtfully comparable. One does not know how much her aid benefits the indigenous peoples of her colonies.

3. THE MAIN RECIPIENTS OF AID

In Table 13 we have selected the twenty-four countries (and two

TABLE 13

Principal recipients of aid from OECD *member countries and multilateral organizations*
Average of 1962 and 1963

Country	Net lending $m.	Grants and grant-like contributions $m.	Population in 1962 millions	GNP per head in 1962 $	Loans per head $	Grants per head $
French Overseas Departments	17	98	1	—	17·0	98·0
Israel	31	93	2	940	15·5	46·5
Jordan	3	75	2	200	1·5	37·5
Algeria	23	321	11	281	2·1	29·2
S. Vietnam	3	196	15	94	0·2	13·1
Tunisia	16	44[1]	4	175	4·0	11·0
Liberia	48	9	1	133	48·0	9·0
S. Korea	19	230	27	83	0·7	8·5
French Franc Area south of the Sahara	108	320	40	81	2·7	8·0
Congo (Léopoldville)	−5	96	15	88	− 0·3	6·4
Turkey	35	190	30	209	1·2	6·3
Yugoslavia	65	112	19	—	3·4	5·9
Egypt	39	158	28	123	1·4	5·7
Formosa	8	67	12	154	0·7	5·6
Kenya	15	38	9	85	1·7	4·2
Morocco	33	41[1]	13	164	2·5	3·2
Pakistan	166	284	99	78	1·5	2·9
Chile	124	19	8	445	15·5	2·4
Venezuela	54	16	8	726	6·6	2·2
Colombia	66	25	15	274	4·4	1·7
Thailand	19	32	29	100	0·7	1·1
Brazil	105	86	78	187	1·4	1·1
Indonesia	19	98	100	85	0·2	1·0
India	434	428	459	81	0·9	0·9
Mexico	57	11	38	319	1·5	0·3
Argentina	86	5	22	451	3·9	0·3
Total of Above	1,588	3,123	1,077	—	1·4	2·9
Total All Developing Countries	1,902	4,152	1,511	—	1·3	4·1

[1] Plus $31 million in French grants not broken down as between these two countries.
Source: ibid., pp. 44-5.

groups of countries or territories) that received most nominal (net) aid from OECD and multilateral sources in 1962. These twenty-four accounted for 62 per cent of total aid from those sources. For each of these countries we have tabulated GNP, official loans, and official grants, all on a *per capita* basis, and rearranged the countries in order of grants per head, to see whether there was any correlation between these quantities. One might expect to find a low GNP associated with either a large amount of total grants and loans, or with a high ratio of grants to total aid. As we had expected, no such correlation is apparent from the Table,[1] and differences between countries need to be explained in other terms, largely political and historical.[2]

Perhaps the most striking single feature is the position of India. She receives more grants and net loans than any other country in absolute terms. But when, as in Table 13, the countries are arranged according to grants per head, she falls almost to the bottom of the list. The most convincing explanation is a very simple one, that India is so large that to provide the same aid per head to her as to, say, Yugoslavia or Turkey, which lie in the middle of the Table, would swallow up half of the total of OECD aid. Indonesia, which is also very large, fares equally ill on a *per capita* basis: but, in Indonesia's case, size is certainly not the only reason. At the other end of the scale, Israel's high position is slightly misleading. Of the $93 million grants she received, $70 million consisted of war reparations from Germany, and though this money was no doubt used for development, it was obviously paid for reasons different from those which determine the flow of other types of aid. If this $70 million is subtracted from total grants received by Israel, she drops from second to fifth place in the table, still remarkably high in view of her very high income per head.

Given that a country is regarded by the western world as 'developing', and that it is not closely attached to Moscow or Peking, there seem, on the evidence of Table 13, to be three main alternative ways in which it can qualify for a large amount of grant-aid per head. First, it should be closely attached to France, preferably as an over-

[1] For the countries and areas for which GNP figures are given in the Table there is actually a positive correlation between aid and wealth, but this is dominated by Israel, 56 per cent of whose receipts consisted of reparations. Without Israel, it is negligible. There is also a negligible correlation between the proportion of grants, and wealth.

[2] There are countries, too small to appear in the Table, whose receipts of grant-aid per head are larger than those of many countries included. Cyprus, which with a population of 0·6 million received $20·1 per head in grants, is an example. Such countries have been excluded because the aid they receive is not a significant proportion of world aid, and because there is a strong tendency for very small territories, most of which are still colonies, to receive large amounts of grant-aid per head. The French Overseas Departments, which are included in the Table as a single unit, are not unique in this respect, though they probably receive rather more aid per head than most other countries' colonies. This having been said, we feel it would be a waste of space to list the very small territories, like St Helena, Nauru and Ocean Island, Reunion, etc., etc., when their total populations are so small, and their total receipts of aid are a negligible proportion of world aid.

seas department, but failing that as a member of the Franc Zone. Secondly, it should have a common border with one of the Communist countries, or be thought by the Americans to be in immediate danger from Communism, or tolerate American bases. Thirdly, like Algeria and Liberia, it should have some newly discovered resource of interest to foreign business.[1] Jordan, Israel, and Egypt, are the only countries whose receipts of substantial grant-aid per head cannot be explained in one of these ways. Jordan is easy to explain, because its survival and stability are considered by the USA and the UK to be essential for the maintenance of peace in the Middle East. Egypt is one of the classic examples of a country where East and West are competing, by means of aid, for popularity and influence. Israel's position is a special one which hardly needs explanation.[2]

It is not possible to analyse, recipient by recipient, the cost or the value of aid receipts beyond classifying them into the usual OECD categories, which in Table 13 we have telescoped into grants and loans. Nor are any details generally available on procurement conditions. A few countries, including India and Ceylon, publish their own statistics of external aid received,[3] but not always in a form that can easily be compared with OECD date for donors' outgoings.

The few remarks made in this section on the distribution of aid, and its prima facie paradoxes, are intended only as a curtain-raiser. What determines the distribution of aid shown in Table 13? We have given some initial hints, but no more. Whatever it is, is it justified? These questions occupy us in large parts of the rest of the book.

4. THE END-USES OF AID

A recent OECD publication includes a new breakdown of OECD bilateral disbursements by purpose, or end-use.[4] This is a classification which is of great significance to recipients. Many difficulties are said to have arisen in the course of classifying the data, and the final result is fairly tentative. The results are given in Table 14.

---

[1] Algeria is also a case of a country which gets aid to purchase the land of departing colonists. Kenya is another example.

[2] A statistical explanation of the distribution of world aid is referred to in Chapter III, p. 87.

[3] *External Assistance*, published annually by the Government Printer, New Delhi, India; and *External Economic Assistance, A Review from 1950–64*, published by the Ministry of Finance, Colombo, Ceylon.

[4] OECD, op. cit.

TABLE 14

Official bilateral commitments by OECD *members and commitments by multilateral agencies, by purpose*
1962 and 1963 Average

$m.

	Total OECD and multilateral agencies	Total multilateral agencies	USA	France	UK	Germany	Others
	3,438·0	1,069·7	1,136·0[1]	427·2[1]	176·9	342·0	278·5
I. Capital project financing:							
(1) Agriculture, Forestry and Fishing	392·3	146·2	114·0	66·6	26·4	27·0	12·1
(2) Transport and Communications	874·1	370·4	244·0	70·0	23·4	81·8	84·5
(3) Development of energy resources	791·1	303·2	273·0	68·3	22·8	75·5	48·3
(4) Indus Basin Fund	48·1	—	30·0	—	2·2	5·0	3·2
(5) Industry	781·1	184·2	259·0	33·4	54·9	136·0	113·6
(6) Social infrastructure	508·1	51·2	216·0	189·0	27·4	17·3	7·2
(7) Still unspecified, or multi-purpose	43·3	15·7	—	—	20·0	—	7·6
II. Contributions for clearly specified current expenditures	205·0	—	20·0	171·9	9·4	0·5	3·2
III. Non-project assistance	3,176·9	—	2,696·0	—	243·4	46·1	191·4
(1) Not directly linked with imports	394·6	—	138·0	—	154·4	2·1	100·1
(2) To finance current imports	2,782·3	—	2,561·0	—	89·1	44·0	88·2
IV. Technical co-operation	965·8	69·7	406·0	276·0	75·3	83·5	55·3
V. Consolidation and re-financing credits	90·1	—	10·1	10·2	14·0	18·3	37·6
VI. Other	351·8	62·0	78·0	—	—	89·9	121·9
VII. Total	8,227·5	1,201·4	4,344·0	885·2	519·0	580·3	690·0

[1] Sector breakdown largely based on OECD estimates.
Source: ibid., pp. 160–3.

The categories used are as follows:
(1) Capital project financing. This applies to all funds which have
    to be assigned to specific projects as a condition of disburse-
    ment. Funds available for more general purposes but used by
    recipients to finance capital projects are not included. No dis-
    tinction is made in this category between finance for direct
    imports only, and finance which may be used for local expen-
    diture.
(2) Contributions for 'clearly specified current expenditures' are
    similar to (1), except that they are used for the operating costs
    of existing institutions, rather than for the capital cost of
    establishing new ones.
(3) Non-project assistance is divided into two categories according
    to whether it must be used for direct imports, or whether it may
    be used for local or overseas expenditure at the discretion of
    the recipient. Where non-project assistance is restricted to
    imports of capital goods it tends, if the restrictions are narrow
    enough, to become indistinguishable from project assistance,
    and the OECD has left it to the reporting country to decide where
    the line should be drawn.
(4) Technical co-operation includes grants for students and
    trainees, subsidies to private institutions for training purposes,
    payments to experts who work in developing countries, and
    payments for equipment supplied as part of a training pro-
    gramme or expert survey.

The significance of the above categories of aid will become clearer
in Part II. The most important omission is the failure to distinguish
in category (1) between capital project aid that may be spent only on
imports required directly for the projects in question, and capital
project aid that may be used to finance local expenditures. The distinction between these two types of project aid is important to the
recipient. If aid is available for financing local expenditure, then,
given good project selection, the only effect of project-tying is to
ensure that the donor is satisfied that its aid is being well spent; but
if aid is tied to the import-content only of projects, its utilization can
create serious difficulties for the recipient.[1]

A few preliminary remarks on Table 14 are in order here.

Consider the totals in Column 1. First, non-project assistance is
nearly 40 per cent of the total. This does not mean that most countries
get a lot of non-project assistance, for it is heavily concentrated in a
few countries. Secondly, note that the direct linking of a high pro-

[1] The reasons for this are explained more fully in Chapter VII.

portion of non-project assistance to imports stems from the desire of donors to tie their aid to procurement of supplies from themselves. Thirdly, within the category of capital-project financing, the very small proportion devoted to agriculture, forestry, and fishing, is worth noting. It is a mere 11–12 per cent of the total, despite the fact that agriculture accounts directly for somewhere around half the output of the underdeveloped world. The proportion devoted to infrastructure is high, at least two-thirds of the total.

Turning to Columns 2–6, we note that the USA and the UK give relatively more non-project assistance than France and Germany. In the case of the USA, this is accounted for by commodity-aid, and supporting assistance to countries which support large military forces or operations. Removing these items would result in about as high a level of 'projectization' as for France and Germany. But the UK's high level of non-project assistance is not so easily explained, especially compared with France which also mainly aids ex-colonies. It is partly but no means entirely accounted for by general purpose tied loans to India. Thus the UK appears to insist much less on projectization than the other big donors, including the multilateral institutions which give only project-aid and technical assistance. The advantages and disadvantages of giving aid primarily in the form of projects are discussed in Chapter VIII. Another point to note is the very high proportion of technical assistance given by France— over 30 per cent of her total aid.[1] Despite her considerable technical assistance to East Africa under the OSAS, UK technical assistance, which includes some compensation and pensions for departed colonial civil servants, in total comprises only 14½ per cent of all her aid, about the same as Germany which has no colonial heritage.

5. SUMMING UP

The present distribution of world flows of aid is more easily explained along historical and political lines than according to any obvious economic or ethical criterion. In particular, donors seem to be inhibited from providing as much aid to India as its population, poverty, and relative efficiency would warrant, merely on account of its size, and the embarrassment which would result from concentrating a very large proportion of aid in a single country. (Conversely, the USA may be to some extent inhibited from providing aid on the scale its size and wealth would seem to warrant because, if it did so, its aid would be an even more embarrassingly large part of the world

[1] See also Chapter I, p. 40.

total, and of the total received by most recipients considered separately, than it is at present.) We shall return to the matter of distribution of aid among recipients in more detail in Chapter X, after discussing the principles by which aid should be distributed, and the factors which govern the amount of good which aid can do.

Members of the OECD provide between them 90 per cent or more of world aid. This means that discussion of, and decisions on, aid policy within the OECD have real significance for world aid, and that the OECD could become a powerful instrument for improving the distribution, terms, and conditions of world aid.[1] In view of the relative unimportance of Communist countries' aid—which is in keeping with their relative poverty—it is surprising that their aid has had as strong a political impact as it has, though it has been strengthened by careful selection of recipients.

Statistics of total 'aid' are frequently used in a misleading way, since figures of net or even gross flows of grants and loans on varying terms and conditions are used without qualification. It is a useful exercise to estimate the cost of aid in forms other than grants of convertible currencies in terms of its 'grant equivalent', and we have followed Mr Pincus in attempting this.[2] Nevertheless, no single definitive estimate can be made, not only because information is lacking as to the extent to which aid is tied, and the effect of this on the cost of aid, but also because the range within which plausible assumptions can be made about market rates of interest is wide. Despite the consequent range of results, such an exercise throws some new light on the total cost of world aid, and the extent to which current statistics, when used without qualification, overstate the cost of aid. It also gives a more reliable yardstick for comparing donors' efforts.

On the recipient's side also, there is a gap between the apparent amount of aid received, and the value of aid. This arises not only because of the difference between the gross or net value of total receipts, and the real cost of this aid, but also because conditions, such as procurement and/or project-tying, influence the recipient's use of its own resources; in the case of double (procurement plus project) tying this influence is frequently unfavourable. This difference between the nominal amount received and the real value of aid is not quantifiable, but we shall have more to say about it in Chapter VII.

[1] Aid matters are discussed in the DAC of the OECD. Austria, Sweden, and Switzerland, are members of the OECD but not of DAC, but as they provide only 0·5 per cent of total OECD aid, it makes virtually no difference whether one uses figures of OECD or of DAC aid.
[2] op. cit.

APPENDIX TO CHAPTER II

METHODS OF ESTIMATING THE COST OF AID

Taking the entries in the DAC's Table of 'The Flow of Long-Term Financial Resources to Less-Developed Countries and Multilateral Agencies, 1963' (pp. 108–9 of the 1964 *Development Assistance Efforts and Policies*) one by one, we arrived at our estimates as follows:

(1) 'Bilateral grants', including reparations, were valued as in the DAC Table, except in the case of the USA. Here, the value of commodities granted to developing countries under PL 480 Titles II and III was subtracted, and these commodity grants were treated separately as explained in (3).

(2) 'Loans repayable in recipients' currencies' were treated as grants.

(3) 'Transfer of resources through sales for recipients' currencies (net of resources realized by donor country by use of these currencies)', together with the grants of commodities subtracted from USA grants as described in (1), were valued in two different ways. Method I (see Tables 16 and 17) was to value both these items at the values reported to the DAC. Method II was to value both items at zero.[1] Method I treats sales for recipients' currencies as equivalent to grants.

(4) 'Government long-term lending, net.' To reach an estimate for the grant equivalent, each country's total gross lending for more than one year was treated as a single loan, whose maturity and interest rate was assumed to be the same as the average maturity and interest rate of that country's total loan commitments in 1962.[2] The grant equivalent of each loan was then taken to be the difference between the amount lent, and the discounted value of scheduled repayments of interest and principal. The discount rate was given three values, 6 per cent (to approximate the international—IBRD—lending rate), 10 per cent (to approximate a rate which private investors might earn), and 15 per cent (to make some allowance for the probability that many of these loans will not be repaid as scheduled). Alternative assumptions also had to be made to allow for the fact that 'maturity' is not a precise concept. The maturity of a loan means the period of time that elapses between disbursement and repayment of the final instalment of amortization, and the pattern of repayment can vary considerably for loans of the same maturity. Three initial assumptions about the pattern of repayment were made as follows:

(a) that capital repayments were made annually in equal instalments, together with interest on capital outstanding, and that there was a one-year grace period between disbursement and the first instalment of capital repayment;

---

[1] See Chapter VII, pp. 168–9.
[2] Calculated from information in OECD, *Flow of Financial Resources in 1962*.

(b) that repayment took the form of equated annual instalments of capital and interest, with no grace period assumed.

(c) as (a), except that the grace period before capital repayment began was increased to 5 years.

    We found that, in every case, the grant equivalent calculated on assumption (b) lay between the grant equivalents calculated on assumption (a) and assumption (c). Assumption (b) was therefore dropped.

    The two sets of assumptions (a) and (c) give us six different estimates of the grant equivalent of bilateral lending.

(5) 'Multilateral grants and capital subscription payments' were treated as grants. The capital subscriptions, to the IBRD, IDA, IDB, etc., are not strictly grants, but no date has been set for repayment and no interest or dividend is paid, and it is hard to imagine circumstances in which they might be repaid.

(6) 'Purchases and sales of bonds, etc.' from multilateral agencies. This is a very small item, and we have excluded it from the calculation of real aid, on the grounds that these purchases are made by official agencies on the same terms as private agencies (which buy the bulk of these bonds), and are therefore virtually commercial transactions involving no aid.

(7) 'Official bilateral loans for more than one year, up to five years' were included with longer-term loans (see 4). All other official and private transactions were ignored.

The results are shown in Tables 15, 16, and 17. Table 15 gives the six different estimates of the grant equivalent of loans. Table 16 gives the grants disbursed, there being alternative valuations for the USA. Table 17 combines the figures of Tables 15 and 16.

TABLE 15

Grant equivalent of loan disbursements by DAC members, 1963
$m.

Rate of discount assumed for capital repayments and interest on loans	6%		10%		15%		Loans (gross) as reported to the DAC
Average grace period assumed for loans	1 year	5 years	1 year	5 years	1 year	5 years	
Country							
Belgium	1	1	1	1	1	2	3
Canada	−1	−1	6	8	13	16	41
Denmark	—	—	—	—	—	—	−1
France	19	24	49	60	75	91	172
Germany	28	34	85	102	133	157	302
Italy	—	—	14	19	28	37	105
Japan	1	1	20	26	38	48	120
Netherlands	1	1	3	3	4	5	9
Norway	—	—	—	—	—	—	—
Portugal	8	9	17	19	24	27	42
UK	21	25	60	69	90	102	182
USA	459	505	661	722	792	858	1,106
Total DAC	537	598	916	1,030	1,198	1,342	2,082

TABLE 16
Grants disbursed by DAC members, 1963
$m.

Country	Bilateral grants excluding commodities	Multilateral grants and subscriptions	Alternative valuations of commodity grants and sales for recipients' currencies		Total	
			I	II	I	II
Belgium	76	16			91	
Canada	51	14			65	
Denmark	1	8			9	
France	697	28			725	
Germany	141	30			171	
Italy	25	8			33	
Japan	77	9			86	
Netherlands	10	19			29	
Norway	2	8			10	
Portugal	9	—			9	
UK	209	43			253	
USA	1,314[1]	217	1,335	0	2,866	1,531
Total DAC	1,612[1]	399	1,335	0	4,346	3,011

[1] Including $306 million loans repayable in recipients' currencies.

TABLE 17

Total cost of 1963 disbursements by DAC members
$m.

Rate of discount assumed for capital repayments and interest on loans	6%		10%		15%		Total aid (gross) reported to the DAC
Average grace period assumed for loans	1 year	5 years	1 year	5 years	1 year	5 years	
Country							
Belgium	92	92	92	93	93	93	93
Canada	64	64	72	73	78	81	101
Denmark	9	9	9	9	9	9	10
France	744	749	774	785	799	815	892
Germany	199	205	256	273	304	328	455
Italy	33	33	47	52	61	70	86
Japan	87	87	107	112	125	134	207
Netherlands	29	29	31	32	33	34	39
Norway	10	10	10	10	10	10	10
Portugal	17	18	26	28	33	35	47
UK	274	277	313	322	342	355	440
USA Method I	3,325	3,372	3,529	3,590	3,660	3,726	4,061
USA Method II	1,990	2,035	2,192	2,253	2,323	2,389	
DAC Total I	4,883	4,944	5,262	5,376	5,544	5,688	6,451
DAC Total II	3,548	3,609	3,927	4,041	4,209	4,353	

CHAPTER III

THE PRINCIPLES OF AID-GIVING

Chapter I already made it clear that governments do not give aid without expecting to achieve something which is in the interest of the donor country. Private charity is different, and it may be presumed that the motive is solely sympathy for the recipient. It may be true that there would be considerable public support for governmental programmes of aid for purely humanitarian motives. But most observers take the view that much less than the present level of aid would result if its sole support came from a simple desire to help poor people in other countries. Certainly, representatives of the people oppose aid when they can see no national interest in it, and the main support comes from exporting interests which may benefit.

It is easy to say that the importance of self-interest in determining aid levels is clear. It is much less easy to pin down exactly what the donor countries' interests are (apart, that is, from the interest of particular nationals whose business benefits). Indeed, there is great confusion. Public servants are sure that the donor benefits: they would be unhappy about spending the tax-payers' money otherwise. But when asked what are the UK's main interests and how it benefits (and we are sure the same would be true in most donor countries), officials give a wide variety of answers.

It may be asked, especially by those who want aid to be increased, whether this matters. Many purposes could be served by aid, and different people are sure to rank them differently in importance—the more reasons there are, or the more reasons people think there are, for giving aid, the more aid there is likely to be. We believe, on the contrary, that it is most important to think hard about what one is trying to achieve by aid. If there *are* different purposes to be achieved, then it is all too easy to achieve none of them effectively, because the different purposes may require aid in different forms, differently administered. Furthermore, if different donor countries could achieve some better consensus about the purposes of aid, there would be some hope of their programmes reinforcing each other. We might then be able to speak briefly and convincingly of the objectives of Western economic aid—something which is impossible at present. Let us, therefore, try to discover the self-interest in aid.

1. THE SELF-INTEREST IN AID

The possible interests of donors can be divided into (1) commercial and (2) political or strategic. For each class of interest, the question will arise as to how far it is served by aid directed as efficiently as possible to the economic development of recipients.[1] This must be asked, because perhaps the most important division of opinion—important because it affects the whole administration of aid—lies between those who think that economic development should be the sole purpose of aid, and those who believe that the donor's self-interest is not always best served by trying to maximize economic development. The former may think as they do, (a) because they believe that humanitarian motives should prevail, (b) because they believe that the whole of the benefit of aid to the donors arises via the enrichment of the recipient, or (c) because they believe that the pursuit of any other aim, while in theory admissible, is in practice unlikely to enhance the benefit of aid-giving.

(1) *The Commercial Interest in Aid-Giving*
Let us first discuss the commercial motives. Here it is necessary to distinguish (a) the collective interest of donors, (b) the interest of any single donor, and (c) the interest of particular individuals or groups within a donor country.

First, are donors' economies as a whole likely to benefit from aid-giving? Of course they would do so if 'aid' consisted entirely of loans at rates of interest which exceeded the productivity of capital in the donor countries, and if such loans in fact benefited the recipients. In other words, if capital were more productive in recipient countries, a transfer of capital could benefit both parties (if the loans were paid back). It is possible that this was the case with the capital that flowed from Europe, mostly from England, before 1914.[2] But such

---

[1] It is of course obvious that immediate military interests are not served by economic development—but throughout this book military aid is, so far as possible, ignored.

[2] Professor Cairncross's essay 'Did Foreign Investment Pay?' in *Home and Foreign Investment 1870–1913*, CUP 1953, comes to no very definite conclusion but the author seems to incline to the view that it probably did. Thus since the recipients surely benefited, it may have been true that some countries gained, and none lost.

private capital flows were, rightly, not thought of as aid.[1] In the eyes of the lender the benefit to the recipient was incidental to a purely commercially motivated transaction. Today, it is more difficult to find countries which, with likely long-run benefit to themselves, can afford to borrow much at commercial rates of interest. Indeed, if there is no apparent economic sacrifice on the part of the donor, there is no case for calling transfers of capital aid. One does not think of banks as aiding their customers, just because a customer may benefit from a bank loan. Equally, the customer benefits the bank by accepting the loan and paying interest on it.

To say that aid entails an apparent economic sacrifice by the donor could still be consistent with donors as a whole benefiting from aid. This would occur if there were certain long-run benefits which were normally omitted from the calculation of return on a loan. It is often claimed that such benefits would be conferred by having richer neighbours, because this would create opportunities for greater specialization and trade—a more extensive division of labour. Let us quote an example of this fairly widely believed argument:

> 'To maintain their present standards, the developed countries must continue to expand. But the volume of international trade among developed countries is much higher than that of the trade between developed and underdeveloped countries or among underdeveloped countries alone. The greater the number of developed economies, therefore, the higher the total value of international trade and the better the opportunities for expansion for any one country. In the long run, then, only the development of the economies (and the markets) of the now less developed areas will assure the continuing expansion and development of the now developed countries.'[2]

This argument is flimsy. The markets of already developed countries are already very large, and effectively could be made much larger still by the removal of barriers to trade. The extra possible gain from a further increase in the number of rich countries, on the grounds of trade and the division of labour, could be but slight. This is not to say that there would be no gain. Leaving the simple labour-intensive manufactures to poorer but developing countries—bicycles, radios, and above all textiles and clothing—would be of benefit to rich

---

[1] Although political strings were often attached, especially by France, to the 'privilege' of access to European capital markets.

[2] A. A. Fatouros and R. N. Kelson, *Canada's Overseas Aid*, The Canadian Institute of International Affairs, 1964, p. 28.

countries, permitting them to concentrate on things demanding the most capital and greatest skill. (Unfortunately, and for obvious short-term reasons, they do not behave as if this were so.) To go beyond this, and to argue that subsidizing the development of other countries is a more effective road to increasing one's own wealth than applying the same sum at home, does not seem plausible.

There is another argument, dating from Hobson and Lenin, to the effect that capitalist countries cannot absorb their own output of manufactures, and must therefore export capital and develop markets abroad to preserve full employment at home. The acceptance by the governments of capitalist countries that they too can influence the level of demand at home, and the capital-hunger still exhibited by highly developed countries when demand is maintained, should have shaken even the most doctrinaire out of this belief by now.

Counter-arguments are sometimes put forward to the effect that, in the long run, development of the underdeveloped world might harm the present developed countries. One such argument is that their development would raise the prices of raw materials, and so turn the terms of trade against the wealthy manufacturing countries. This is mere speculation.

To sum up, there is good reason for supposing that the subsidized transfer of capital or skill, which is properly called aid, is a genuine economic sacrifice. We believe there are very few economists who would go further than saying that this might conceivably be false. Yet it is quite often believed by others—we suspect mainly by those who are determined to be hard-headed and not to associate themselves with simple 'do-gooders', but who at the same time wish to deny that there is any political interest in aid.

We turn now to the possible economic advantages which individual countries may derive from aid. That, in a competitive world, the extension of credit may get one beneficial orders is obvious. Also, in a world in which most countries are, paradoxically, worried about their balances of payments, and in which therefore export receipts tend to be prized above their face value, it seems to all governments sensible to guarantee such private export credits. But, despite the government guarantee, normal export credits on commercial terms should not rank as aid. The government guarantee is there not to further the extension of credit to recipients, but to promote exports. But, if normal export credits may be obviously beneficial to any single donor in competitive export markets, it is clear that credits which contain a small element of aid, being at slightly subsidized rates of interest, or with rather longer than normal terms of repay-

ment, can also benefit the donor. Further, small *grants* of technical
assistance, which are clearly aid, may sometimes act like bread upon
the water. Thus, in a competitive world, there is no very exact dividing line between commercial credit and aid. We define 'aid proper' as
including only public grants and the subsidy element in public loans.
Even this may be consistent with some aid having a commercial
advantage on occasions for a particular donor country, especially
where use of the money is restricted to purchasing goods from excess
capacity industries.

The DAC does not provide a definition of 'aid', but the official
financial flows which it records tend to be considered as aid, even
although they include loans at rates of interest of over 6 per cent. If
loans of over 6 per cent were excluded as they should be, there would
be little left of the 'aid' of such countries as Italy and Japan. But as
we define 'aid', one can say that such commercial advantage as there
is in aid-giving is not great. For most donors it is not sufficient reason
to give aid. This is true even of those whose tying of aid (when there is
no compelling balance of payments reason for it), and whose choice
of recipient, suggests a strong commercial interest. It is rather the
case that such donors feel bound to give aid for other reasons, but
try to ensure that it costs them as little as possible by getting as much
commercial return from it as they can.

We turn now to a consideration of the commercial advantages,
which aid confers upon particular groups within donor countries. In
theory, and in the long run, no such advantages should exist. But, at
any one time, there are always industries with some surplus capacity
which would benefit from extra demand. More aid, especially if tied
to the products of that industry, will obviously benefit it (it is usually
less clear as to whether the donor country profits by thus assisting
excess capacity industries). In the USA the farming community is a
powerful backer of aid in the form of commodities. Given that the USA
is determined, as it appears to be, to produce excesses indefinitely,
giving them away costs it little or nothing.[1] Similarly, the UK has
made excess-capacity loans to help the North-East of England. Since
the latter are on commercial terms, the recipient is probably aiding
the UK as much as the reverse. Mutual assistance would be a more
accurate description than aid of this type of transaction.

Although it has been strongly denied that donor countries as a
whole derive any economic benefit from aid-giving, nevertheless it is
clear that there is a strong competitive commercial interest in it—
especially so when loans on commercial terms are wrongly counted as

[1] See Chapter VII.

aid. Furthermore, aid-giving may be used by governments to solve such domestic problems as those mentioned above.

To anticipate, it will be argued that aid for economic development should be a bargain by which the recipient has certain obligations: the donor should, in effect, be 'buying' economic development and, as the 'purchaser', have certain (non-political) rights. This position cannot be attained, or maintained, if donors clearly have strong interests other than the economic development of the recipient. And, as we have seen, the commercial benefits which donors seek do not arise from economic development, but rather from particular problems in their own countries, or from the fact that they are competing for export orders with other rich manufacturing countries.

Export promotion must not be muddled up with aid-giving, to the detriment both of the benefits which can be conferred by the latter, and of the image of aid which is projected to the recipient. A much clearer dividing line needs to be established, so that the donor can legitimately claim that his interest in aid-giving is the economic development of the recipient country. However, the case for this cannot be fully established until we have discussed the political and strategic interests of donors in aid-giving.

(2) *The Political and Strategic Interest in Aid-Giving*

Strategy and the Cold War. The purchase of fire-power from poorer countries, either directly or via the formation of alliances, has existed throughout history.[1] The military aid, as also the defence-support, given in the Far East and South East Asia by the USA is in the line of a long tradition.

It is surely impossible to deny that giving aid for strategic reasons is not only a legitimate interest for donor countries, but also that it makes good sense. Those who speak disparagingly of the fact that so much of USA aid is governed by Cold War considerations[2] can hardly be complaining that a country should not use all the means available to promote its own defence, but rather must be complaining that its defence strategy is unenlightened (has USA military aid to Europe been unenlightened?), or that economic aid should be better distinguished from strategic aid.

On the one hand, in trying to stop the encroachment of Communism in far off countries, the West, and the USA in particular, is

[1] See, e.g., George Liska, op. cit.

[2] In 1962, USA military aid and supporting assistance was about $1¼ billion, while economic assistance was about $2½ billion. But the direction of much of the latter was plainly also influenced by Cold War considerations.

probably doing little or nothing directly to promote its own defence
in the event of nuclear warfare: on the other hand, it would be a
poor advertisement of its own values if it showed itself unwilling to
try to contain or prevent Communism, and it may be the case that
one success for Communism makes another more likely. Communist successes which improve the USSR's missile platform or worsen
that of the USA are, of course, a direct strategic disadvantage.

That military aid should be distinguished from aid for development
is certainly important if possible—for aid suffers from a confusion of
objectives. Military aid is, in fact, separately designated. For instance, it does not enter into DAC figuring. So also is 'supporting
assistance', once called 'defence support', which is aid designed to
mitigate the burden of supporting a large military establishment,
rather than for economic development. The distinction is not really an
economic one. Even military hardware can promote development, if
it relieves the recipient from military expenditure it would have made
anyway. The same goes for 'supporting assistance'. The distinction
is really one of the nature of the donor's interest (although it may also
be made for administrative reasons, and to gain domestic support
for the programme). The giving of military aid, or supporting assistance, implies or should imply that the donor is interested in the
recipient keeping a more powerful military establishment than it
could otherwise afford. The *quid pro quo* is then clear. If the donor
does not have this interest, it should give aid for other purposes. Of
course, motives are not always as clear as this implies. The USA, the
UK, and others, are now giving military aid to India although it does
not seem certain that we are as interested as the Indians in their
having as large a military establishment as they now plan.

Political Aspects. Let us now ignore military assistance and defence
support, and inquire about the possible political objectives of aid,
other than those that accrue as a result of economic development.
Those who stress development would probably want to argue that,
military and related aid apart, all aid should be for development.
There must be no 'political strings'. This would imply that economic
aid should be no respecter of countries: it should go where it buys
most development (or maybe according to some other ethical or
economic criterion—the validity and applicability of such criteria are
examined below—see p. 92ff).

We believe that this position is impossible to defend. Whether or
not one country should give aid to another is a question which cannot but be related to the foreign policy of the donor. Should, for in-

stance, one give aid to one's enemies? It is possible to argue that one should. To go by development criteria alone might imply that a large part of Western aid should go to Communist China. Perhaps it should—but it is hardly a question which can be decided merely on economic grounds. Again, South Africa and Cuba might be good candidates for aid.[1] Or, again, giving aid to one country may infuriate another. The UK has managed to give aid to both Pakistan and India, but not to both Somalia and Kenya. Furthermore, there are such questions as whether British aid should be concentrated on the Commonwealth, and whether we should take risks with the Commonwealth by aiding Southern Rhodesia. If one thinks that the Commonwealth is a good thing—and the preservation of an international talking shop which cuts across many conflicting alignments and even hostilities may be no bad thing—then there is a strong non-economic argument for concentrating aid there.

Supposing then that one beats a retreat,[2] and admits that the distribution of one's bilateral aid must be governed partly by political and strategic considerations. It may then be argued that such aid as is given to a country—apart from military aid and defence support— should be given solely according to economic criteria. This is a much more viable proposition, but nevertheless difficult to support entirely. First, and most important, the development possibilities in a country depend very much on the political situation. A country, for instance, may be ruled by a reactionary government, which the donor knows would distribute any development in a very inegalitarian manner. If this government should fall, the donor would be discredited with the revolutionary régime. In such circumstances it might be better to wait, or only to give token aid. Donors cannot avoid assisting governments when they give aid, and, although it may be possible for them to hedge their bets a little, they may nevertheless find it hard to avoid association with any pre-revolutionary régimes which they assist. The USA has more than once made this mistake. Political judgment is required. What is wanted is the right political judgment—not none. Donors inevitably must take political bets, even if their interest is long-run economic development.

In short, political issues are highly relevant to economic development itself. But it is not even the case that a donor can never have a

[1] South Africa has a lower *per capita* income than some aid-receiving countries, such as Israel or Venezuela.

[2] This recalls the description of English empiricism attributed to Sir Isaiah Berlin—'Start from apparently self-evident premises, reach an unacceptable conclusion, and beat a hasty retreat'.

legitimate interest other than economic development. It may be good policy on occasion to prop up a régime with aid even if the régime is not very interested in sound economic development. In such a case, economic criteria may have to be muted. It may also be sometimes worthwhile to give token aid, as a demonstration of political interest and to preserve or widen contacts. Aid-giving may in fact increase opportunities for diplomatic persuasion and influence. Where one's aid is really diplomatic rather than developmental, it is likely to be bad policy to insist on what is false. Finally, one can never discount entirely the need to be diplomatic—the need to please, and sometimes to be more lenient with, say, prestige aspirations than the strictest attention to economic development might suggest. Despite the fact that economic development may be the donor's chief interest (and this we have still to argue), it is impossible to deny that the goodwill of the recipient government can also be important—and that these may be in conflict. But it may also, as we have seen, be the case that the goodwill of the recipient administration has negative value! The point is that these are essentially diplomatic considerations, which are unavoidable in the aid-relationship.

(3) *The Interest in Economic Development*
Why should the donor countries have an interest in development? We have denied that they have an economic interest. What then is the political or strategic benefit which they expect? It should be said at once that there seems to be no historical proof, or compelling presumption, that greater wealth leads to the kind of freedom and political institutions favoured by most Western developed nations, or to peaceful foreign policies. Even if one can accept that the present state of the world is evidence that wealth is related to non-aggressiveness or political stability, and freedom from Communism, one is calling in evidence countries which are so wealthy that they have no relevance whatever to the proposition that somewhat greater wealth for the presently aided countries is likely to make them more desirable and friendly neighbours for the Western donors. Thus, rather little weight can at best be attached to the theory that it is in the West's political or strategic interest that the rest of the world should be wealthier.

The theory should be stated more in terms of progress than of wealth, and in terms of support for governments which are either allies, or manifestly anti-Communist, or neutral. The emphasis on supporting such governments by encouraging economic development derives from the view that the desire and hope for economic and social advance have been so aroused among many of the under-developed countries, that economic progress is nowadays almost essential to the survival of any government which depends at all on democratic support. Only the tightest police state, like Portugal, seems likely to survive for long without it: even so, such a state, especially if grossly inegalitarian and traditional, is sitting on a potential revolution which international Communism is ever ready to promote and support.

If the above, as we believe, is the basic self-interest which donor powers have in development, it is to some extent in the diplomatic tradition of subsidies and political bribes. But there are or should be two essential differences.

First is the question of alliance. It has always made sense to strengthen the economies of one's allies and friends so long as this made some significant difference to the balance of power. People in the UK ought, perhaps, to remember that one of the biggest receivers of aid since the last war has been the UK (up to June 1963 the UK received about $4 billion in economic and military aid from the USA, far more than we have ourselves given. This is exceeded only by France with over $7 billion. We gave aid of only $1·4 billion). But, with some exceptions, the collection of allies among the under-developed countries seems to make little sense in a world of hydrogen bombs. It can hardly matter to us on which side Thailand or Togo, for instance, is to stand in the event of nuclear warfare. Nowadays, we want countries to defend themselves, not us, against external ag-gression. It appears therefore quite as important to support a genuinely neutral power as an ally.[1]

The second chief difference is the thirst for economic development, and the recognition that the best way to support those countries which are independent of the Communist powers is by developing their economies. Not only is the need for this recognized, but also the possibility scarcely existed until recently. It is only recently that the rich countries have become so rich that they are in a position to make a significant difference to the rate of growth of the whole of the underdeveloped world.

The USSR, and China, also give aid, not only to Communist countries, or to support those who make a break with the West

[1] In fact this is not fully recognized in the figures of either USA or world aid. A statistical analysis (Alan M. Strout, 'Factors affecting the allocation of Foreign Economic Aid', AID, 1964) has shown that it was worth $73 million of USA economic aid in 1960–2 to belong to NATO, SEATO, or CENTO. (Other donors redressed the situation slightly by giving these countries rather less aid.)

(e.g. Guinea or Cuba), but to neutral democratic countries like India, where aid was initiated even before the Sino-Soviet rift, and to countries which, like Egypt, imprison Communists. It is obvious enough that the USSR is not working on the theory that economic development reduces the risk of Communism. Or, if it does believe this (and in fact it probably believes the opposite), it must think that the effect is very slight, and is outweighed by the diplomatic advantages which it believes aid-giving can bring. The USA invented aid, as a device to win over, or at best keep neutral, the uncommitted countries. The USSR and China feared the diplomatic advantages and/or the general goodwill which this might bring to the West, and followed suit with what Americans have officially called the Sino-Soviet economic offensive. It is thus not really paradoxical that both East and West should both give aid to uncommitted countries. Nevertheless, there is, to some extent, a difference of principle. The West puts rather less emphasis than the USSR on the influence which aid can buy. This is exemplified by the famous story of the streets of Kabul. The Americans refused to pave them, seeing little economic development in this. The USSR paved them, putting more emphasis on doing what the recipient wanted. Those who argue the case for development must think the Americans right, despite the fact that any imposition of the donor's standards and values is apt to be labelled neo-colonialism.

The above statement of the self-interest of the Western donors[1] will be too frankly 'cold war' for some. For instance, some feel that it is in the long-run interest of the rich to give to the poor, having in mind, perhaps, the storming of Bastille. In their eyes, the division of the world is one of poverty versus wealth, or, very broadly, North versus South. One's flesh can perhaps be made to creep with the prospect of the ever increasing countless hordes of the underdeveloped overwhelming by sheer numbers the plutocratic North Americans, Europeans, and Russians.

This seems to us far-fetched. The interests of different countries, and groups of countries, in Asia, Africa, and South America, conflict probably even more than the interests of rich countries conflict with one another. It is highly unlikely that they would ever unite against the 'North'. The now famous seventy-five nations of the United Nations Conference on Trade and Development (UNCTAD) were united only on very broad generalizations, and when concrete policy changes came under discussion their unity quickly dissolved.

[1] Throughout this book the West is deemed to include, and the East to exclude, Japan. This is for the sake of brevity only.

Even if all the poor countries were to unite, industrial development and wealth are enormously more important than numbers. Of course, China has already exploded a bomb, and India, Egypt, and other poor countries, may also acquire nuclear weapons. But this has occurred, in the case of China, long before there was any possibility of her people reaching a standard of living which might make them less envious of the wealthy nations. And the same is, unfortunately, likely to be true of the other poor nations. On the other hand, it is very unlikely that they could develop the ability to deliver such weapons against the USA, or the USSR, with any hope of defeating their adversary, until they have become fairly advanced industrial countries. One can hope that, by that time, a reasonably large proportion of their peoples will not be in desperate poverty. If the rich countries have an interest here, and it is a remote one, it lies not so much in rapid development as such, but in development which will not produce a very powerful industrial sector in a country which remains, overall, very poor. It lies, in fact, in a reasonably egalitarian development. But this is mere speculation.

Nuclear weapons apart, it can be argued that both the West and the USSR have an interest in the political stability and non-aggressiveness of the underdeveloped countries, and hence in aid for development. Revolution, or local aggression, which may be partly caused by poverty, may spread and give rise to wider conflict which could lead to a Third World War. But this point has already been considered above: the only difference here is that it is posited that it is the developed world, and not just the Western powers, which is interested in stability. It may appear that the USSR, by exploiting revolutionary situations, has shown little interest in stability. But this is not clear. No one can expect that the poor countries will develop without, often, violent change. The West and the USSR are concerned to see that a form of economy, and political development, favourable to themselves emerges from revolutions, civil wars, or other manifestations of violence. The West involves itself in trying to influence such events, just as much as the USSR.

Nevertheless, the main danger arising from local wars and revolutions is precisely that the Cold War does still exist. This is not to deny that, if the Cold War really ceased to play a role, there would still be some self-interest for the rich countries in promoting political stability and above all preventing local wars (apart, of course, from the overwhelming humanitarian obligation to try to get disputes settled peacefully). After all, such events nearly always occasion some direct loss to the nationals of rich countries, either those who reside in, or have investments in, the troubled area: furthermore, some trade loss inevitably results. Nevertheless, it can hardly be denied that the self-interest of the donors would be enormously reduced. Aid would never have attained anything like its present level if it had not been for the Cold War.

We have now argued that the primary self-interest of the Western powers lies in promoting the kind of régime which will be both viable and as non-aggressive and favourable to Western ideas as possible, and that reasonably egalitarian economic development is a means to this. We have also argued that this self-interest arises mainly out of the Cold War, and its accompanying competition to 'capture' for one side or the other, or for neutrality, the political systems of the poorer countries. So far as the West goes this then should be a collective self-interest. But it is by no means true that all Western aid, even apart from any commercial interest, exhibits this self-interest. We have been, to some extent, discussing an ideal rather than the reality.

Cases in which the donors' interests seem to differ from the collective interest of the West in economic development fall into one of three categories. Either (1) the donors' political interests are identical with that of the West, but are not served primarily by economic development, or (2) the donors' interests are not identical with that of the West as a whole, or (3) they are neither in line with the collective interest of the West, nor primarily served by development. Now it will be part of our argument that the more Western aid can be oriented to development (or prevention of decline), and the more any special political objectives can be suppressed, the better will be the image of Western aid in the eyes of the recipients.

It is important for Western aid to be seen in a good light. If the sole benefit of aid to the donor were expected to flow via development this would not be the case. But it seems foolish to neglect the goodwill element. It is easy enough to be cynical, and say that the last thing one expects from aid is gratitude. This may be so: but anyway gratitude is not the point. What one wants is respect for the motives and purposes of the West.

Now to take case (1), if there is some aid which is intended to serve donors' interests directly, and not by means of promoting recipients' development, then it will be better for the image of development aid if such 'diplomatic' or 'strategic' aid-giving is not muddled up with aid for development. It is easy for the opponent of the West in an underdeveloped country to disparage aid for development by pointing out that the donor is, say, buying a base. Moreover, if the donor is, in fact, merely buying a base, he has no right to insist on the money being used for development. Of course, the recipient may want to be able to argue that it is not selling a base, in which case both may have to pretend the money is for development. But at least the nature of the bargain should be clear to the parties concerned. We believe that one reason why much Western aid (as also Eastern) has such a mediocre image in the eyes of recipients is not so much because they expect aid to be utterly disinterested—charity is not easy to accept— but because the nature of the bargain is not clear.

Now take case (2)—the donors' interests are not identical with the collective interests of the West in development, but they are thought to be served primarily by economic development. The clearest case in this category is French aid to the ex-French dependencies. The French are deeply interested in the preservation of a bloc of French-speaking countries, which are culturally oriented to France, and may be expected to side with her in international disputes. French interests are thought to be served by the development of these countries in much the same way as Western interests are served by the development of other underdeveloped countries. While many sections of opinion in all France's recipients would prefer not to have to rely on this special relation, France's generosity and the fact that other donors probably cannot operate so efficiently, makes it difficult to break. For this reason, while French aid can be regarded as having political strings, which are unnecessary, and therefore harmful to the collective interests of the West, nevertheless it is not clear that any rapid disruption of this special relation would be a good thing.

The fact that UK aid is concentrated on the Commonwealth might be regarded as a similar case. But it is not really so. The Commonwealth is a much more loosely-knit affair than the French Franc Area, and the UK plays a much less dominant role. Moreover, Commonwealth members are not tied to a single donor to nearly the same extent. (Of course, part of the reason for this is the UK's lack of generosity compared with France.) Even those smaller members who get most of their aid from the UK almost certainly feel themselves less dependent than the members of the French Franc Area.

The case of the Commonwealth suggests that, at least to some extent, special interests and aid relationships can exist without damage to a collective Western interest. In fact, it is probably not statistically worth anything to be a member of the Commonwealth so far as aid-receiving is concerned. So aid is not generally used or regarded as a lever or bait to maintain or increase the membership. (But, of course, membership is likely to result in a larger flow of aid from the UK itself, and this is probably one of the many fragile threads which maintains this highly improbable club.) Moreover, almost all UK aid to the Commonwealth is without any special political strings, and is aid either for development or for subsistence. Even in a case like Malta, where the aid is tied in with a defence agreement, it is clear that the recipient would have got a large part of the aid even if the UK had not been interested in maintaining the base.

Turn now to case (3), where the primary aim is not simply development, and is one which is not a collective aim of the West. Two cases which may be mentioned are those of Israel (if Israel counts as the West) trying to win friendship *vis-à-vis* the UAR, and West Germany trying to get non-recognition of East Germany. Of course, the aid given is designed for development, because this makes it look respectable. Now Israel is a very small country, and well-respected in many other developing countries for her economic achievements. Also, she is not regarded as a member of the Western bloc, and is not a member of NATO. Consequently her special interests do no harm. But none of this applies to Germany, and the political strings attached to her aid are certainly harmful to the general purposes of Western aid. The same is true of commercial strings (e.g. the non-consummation of aid to Uganda because Lufthansa was not granted landing rights in Nairobi). Still more important, in this respect, was Mr Dulles's dislike of neutrality. But, although alliance still plays its part in explaining USA aid figures, this is now mainly an echo of history, and the AID no longer appears to use aid as alliance-bait.

Now the Western world does not have a monolithic foreign policy. It is too much to expect that the political interests of donors in aid-giving will not diverge. But it is not perhaps too much to hope that donors should pay greater attention to the question of whether particular objectives, which they might be tempted to try to further by aid-giving, may not reduce the effectiveness of their own aid-giving, as well as that of others, so far as the major objectives of Western aid are concerned. We do not believe that it is the major political string—that you will not receive Western aid if you are allied to the USSR or China—which causes the resentment that political strings undoubtedly arouse among recipients.

2. THE ETHICS OF AID DISTRIBUTION

(1) *Redistribution or Development—Introducing the Main Issues*
While it has been argued that donors have an interest in economic

development (though, even apart from military aid, not to the complete exclusion of other political factors), it is also clear that they have a greater interest in the development of some countries than others. If we knew how to maximize economic development, this could be allowed for by giving a suitable political weighting to each country, and then maximizing the weighted development sum. There are those who advocate no political weighting, for at least a large part of aid, who would hand over aid funds to some multilateral body to distribute. But on what principles would such a body distribute aid? Should it try to maximize development? Not necessarily. Why should politically-disinterested aid be for development?

We have argued that the process of growing richer, rather than simply the possession of greater wealth, is at the heart of the donors' interest, now that the desire for progress has been so inculcated in poor countries. But if we are considering disinterested aid, it can be argued that the principle of redistributing wealth should govern aid-giving. Within countries, the States takes a hand in reducing inequality by aiding the poor from the proceeds of progressive taxation. It is not regarded as an argument against the receipt of social benefits that the beneficiary would spend it all on consumption, or that he is incapable of improving himself because he is demented or chronically ill. Giving aid for development seems almost the exact reverse. If aid all goes on consumption, donors are inclined to say it is 'money down the drain'; and if the recipient country is almost incapable of self-improvement it is said to have very low 'absorptive capacity', which is regarded by many as a reason for giving it very little aid.

So it could be argued that an international progressive tax should be levied on rich countries—say, starting with those with an income per head of $700—and the proceeds given to countries with, say, incomes per head of less than $600, in such a way that the poorer the recipient the more aid per head it would get. The recipient would have the right to its share of the proceeds, and no questions about development would be asked.

The weakness of such arguments is that they assume that if income is redistributed from rich to poor countries, redistribution of income from rich to poor people—which is the only morally desirable form of redistribution—will automatically be achieved. This assumption is far from justified, unless steps are taken to ensure that governments receiving aid use it in certain clearly specified ways. The right of a poor country's government to receive aid must depend on this condition. If the strings attached to the use of money within developing countries were, in part at least, development strings, we would have the half-way house, that development should partly determine the use of aid within countries, but not its distribution between countries. This would, we think, be considerably more appealing to the electorates of the donors, to whom many stories of the luxurious living of minorities in the underdeveloped countries would filter back.

The statistics of world aid distribution are in fact consistent with donors giving considerable weight to a country's capacity to use aid for development,[1] as well as some weight to questions of poverty and wealth. That the former should be the prime criterion is also official United States' policy.[2] Mr Smiles has been adopted as Uncle Sam's nephew.

Thus is it quite clear that the donors have some political interest in development. But is there any good moral or economic justification for favouring development, rather than just helping the poor? The first possible justification is that the amount of money which might realistically get transferred could make little difference to existing poverty. This is an old argument, but not necessarily the worse for that.

It is not only that, in a static world, redistribution alone could hardly make the difference to which either donors or recipients aspire, but that population growth is likely to render redistribution vacuous as a policy for reducing poverty. If economic growth is not speeded up, so that it significantly exceeds the population growth rate, which as a result would itself eventually be reduced, the transfers may well go 'down the drain', in the sense of making no lasting difference whatever to the poverty of the underdeveloped world. The Indian peasant is probably poorer than he was 100 years ago when

---

[1] Alan Strout (op. cit.), analysing DAC members' aid for 1960–2, shows that in the range $100–300 per head, a head is worth $2·40 in aid, while below $100 a head is worth only $1·48, and above $300 is worth $1·31. Thus while the ethical principle of the decreasing marginal utility of income may have operated above a certain point, the opposite principle operated at the lower end of the income range. The reason for this reversal is doubtless partly that donors have considered that poor countries have relatively little absorptive capacity for capital per head. At the same time it should be noted that many poor countries get more aid than the above figures prima facie suggest. This is because size and poverty are related (especially if India is excluded), and because there exists a 'small country effect' —i.e. small countries tend to get relatively high aid per head. In other words, countries tend to get some minimum aid quota regardless of how tiny they are. To the extent that this is not purely irrational, it may be to some extent justifiable on the grounds that states have certain irreducible political and administrative overheads.

[2] cf. *Principles of Foreign Economic Assistance*, AID, 1963, esp. pp. 29–32.

railway and irrigation investment in India began on a considerable scale. More than 100 years ago, Indonesia was probably in a state to 'take off': but, mainly as a result of population growth, the Indonesian peasant is as poor as ever. All that has happened is that there is much more rice, but correspondingly more people.[1]

The fact that there might be no lasting effect, is probably a knock-down argument with many electors in developed countries. It should not be, for one hopes that ultimately they will get used to the idea that international aid is here to stay for ever. But it is still a considerable argument, for people do not want to give money if it has no effect: still less if it merely increases the sum total of human misery, which is always a possibility if one of the main effects is to stimulate population growth.

Furthermore, one can argue that income redistribution within wealthy countries has done extremely little to alleviate poverty, or reduce inequality. The actual redistributional effects of tax systems are rather small.[2] It is mainly that the wealthy pay for common services. Similarly, in the international sphere, the wealthy now bear the main burden of defence, and thereby defend not only themselves. It is undoubtedly growth, and full employment, which has had the major effect: not redistribution. In so far as the social benefits arising from redistributive taxation have had any large effect, it has probably been where they have been paternalistically devoted to development—to compulsory free schooling, health insurance, and so on. The argument from the national welfare state can be more easily applied to proving that most aid should be for development than the reverse.

One of the accepted proofs of self-help is that recipients should have a high marginal savings rate.[3] This, admittedly, provokes the question, 'why, and with what possible justification, should we urge that the poverty-stricken should save more for future generations?' Why should we prefer the poor to save what we give, rather than consume it? Why should visiting economists go round advising how to raise the incidence of tax in poor countries?

There are several answers to this. The first is that the governments of many poor countries want the same as the donors. So far as they

[1] cf. Clifford Geertz, *Agricultural involution; the problem of ecological change in Indonesia,* University of California Press, 1963.

[2] cf. T. Barna, *Redistribution of Incomes through Public Finance, 1937,* Oxford University Press, 1945; A. M. Cartter, *Redistribution of Incomes in Post-war Britain,* Yale University Press, 1955; J. A. Brittain, 'Some Neglected Features of Britain's Income Levelling', *AER Papers and Proceedings,* May 1960.

[3] This concept is further discussed below.

dare, they attach a higher weight to the utility of future generations, as compared with the present, than does the electorate—where there is an electorate. The second is that there is scarcely any country which does not have some wealthy people, wealthier than many of those who pay taxes in the donor countries. Almost any country can save more, without affecting very poor people. Thirdly, a government, which is really interested in progress, is not likely to be happy to let the assistance it gets disappear into the pockets of the wealthy. Aid for development may well be more redistributional in effect, than a system under which the governments of all poor countries received free money to spend as of right.

The upshot is, we believe, that supporting development rather than merely redistribution makes good sense, and has some moral justification. But before we can take the argument further, and come to any firmer conclusion, it is important to be much clearer about what precisely we mean by 'supporting development' or 'maximizing development'. A formal definition of maximizing development is easy. By it we mean 'maximizing the present discounted value of all future increases in real consumption per head in the underdeveloped world'. We can begin to expose the problems implicit in this definition by showing more precisely how it differs, or may differ, from the redistribution principle.

First, the list of countries constituting the underdeveloped world must be agreed. Secondly, the phrase 'maximizing development' implies an equal weighting of consumption increases in different recipient countries, as opposed to the 'utility weighting' of the redistribution principle.[1] It will have to be discussed whether equal weighting is acceptable to anyone or has any rationale. The problem will generally be referred to as that of 'country preference'. Thirdly, there is the problem of consumption over time—or how to arrive at the present value of future increases in consumption. This is known as 'time preference'.

In the following section we discuss these problems, and also introduce the notion of self-sustained growth as a possible factor in the determination of aid giving. We come to the conclusion that maximizing development is rather an extreme policy, and probably almost as

[1] We leave aside the fact that there are considerable conceptual and statistical difficulties in comparing incomes in different countries. We take it in fact that, for policy purposes, it would be accepted that a dollar's worth of rupees represented the same real income as, say, a dollar's worth of East African shillings. It is recognized that this is not very easy to accept but we do not want to cloud the issue here.

unacceptable as the pure redistribution principle. Two general principles for aid-giving are introduced. It will not surprise any economist that the first is that of maximizing utility: the second is maximizing the donors' self-interest.

(2) *Country Preference, Time Preference, and Self-Sustained Growth.* Leaving aside the fact that some countries may not be aided for political reasons, we need to define the underdeveloped world. This is of some conceptual, and not merely of practical or political, importance, because it introduces the notion of 'self-sustained' growth. Thus, one possibility is to say that all countries are 'within the underdeveloped world', and need aid, if they cannot achieve a more or less steady growth in real income per head without it. This dividing line, as we have seen, may be different from a poverty line, although of course it is closely related.

The notion of 'self-sustained growth' (and the 'take-off' phase preceding it) is derived from the historical theories of Professor W. W. Rostow.[1] The concept has achieved much wider currency, indeed popularity, than the analysis of historical phases of growth has met with academic acceptance. Its popularity is probably due to the fact that both donors and recipients want to believe that eventually, and indeed in the not too far distant future, the underdeveloped countries will be able to 'stand on their own feet'—in fact be free of the need for aid. This, even in the poor countries, seems to be a much more popular notion than that aid should go on for ever as part of the process of redistributing the world's wealth.

We shall use the phrase 'self-sustained growth'. But its use does not involve us in acceptance of any historical theory. Indeed, we doubt whether there is any recognizable pattern of growth, definable in economic terms, which countries have followed, or must needs follow, if they progress from poverty to wealth. We do not commit ourselves to any Marxian, or any 'non-Communist', theory of history. Nevertheless, theory apart, history apart, one can make some fallible judgment as to whether a country is able to grow, without external assistance, at some politically satisfactory rate. We imply no more than this by using the phrase 'self-sustained growth'.

Thus, whatever the validity of Professor Rostow's analysis, there is nothing very controversial in the statement that there is little risk that the countries of Western Europe, of North America, and Australasia, will get poorer (provided, of course, that there is no

[1] W. W. Rostow, 'The Take-Off into Self-Sustained Growth', *Economic Journal*, March 1956, and *The Stages of Economic Growth*, CUP, 1960.

major war, or other political catastrophe). Indeed there is a strong presumption that they will get richer. They save enough themselves, and the resultant investment is, taking account of technical advances, productive enough to keep the growth of income ahead of the rate of growth of population.

The idea that there is, or anyway could be, some point in a country's history when the relationship of these variables is such that further growth without aid is very probable, not only produces an apparently logical definition of when a country is developed, but has also had some effect on aid-theorizing, and could (it is not clear that it has) produce a different criterion for allocating aid than that of maximizing development in the sense defined above.

Thus, one might regard the underdeveloped countries rather like horses in a race, some of them far from and some nearer the winning post, which marks the point of self-sustained growth. The donor powers could then give themselves objectives differing from that of maximizing development. They could, for instance, concentrate on getting as many horses past the post as possible in the next five, or ten, or twenty, years. All of these aims would, of course, produce different distributions of aid—and all of them different from that of maximizing development. Now if it could be shown that to produce some successes, and to discontinue aid to successful countries, would convince the US Congress that the aid-givers know what they are about, and that aid need not be for ever, and if such a policy of backing the winners is necessary to get more aid for development, we should not complain.[1] But, otherwise, we can see no ethical justification for it, as it would mean concentrating aid on the relatively wealthy (and speedy) even beyond the point that would maximize development (the total progress of all the horses).[2] It may also be

[1] 'Backing the winners' is sometimes used merely to refer to a policy of giving more aid to countries which use it better. This is, of course, quite consistent with maximizing development.
[2] It can be shown that, under certain rather extreme assumptions, giving more aid to a country at a certain point in its history will reduce the total quantity of aid it needs to receive before it can, without aid, sustain a given rate of growth. This suggests that a concentration of aid on one country at a time, or a limited number of countries, might conceivably reduce the total amount of aid required to be given before all countries have 'taken off'. But this is not very relevant, first because the assumptions are rather unrealistic, but more importantly because the minimization of the historical amount of aid required is not a proper objective. The 'burden' of aid must be related to the level of the income of donors when it is given. Alternatively, looking ahead, future aid must be discounted. The possibility that the *present value* of the future aid needed to bring the underdeveloped world to self-sustained growth would be reduced by a deliberate policy of con-

worth remarking that if the aim were to get all the horses past the post (anyway, all those with any chance of finishing) in the shortest possible time, with some given quantum of aid in each year, then some extra attention would, at some point in their history, have to be paid to the laggards. It is not surprising that, if this were the aim, the principle of utility would apply again, at least partly, because getting all the recipients to a state of self-sustained growth at the same time (which is implied by minimizing the period of aid for given quantities of aid) would probably mean that, at that point of time, they were of very roughly equal wealth.

However, sufficient theoretical attention has not yet been paid to the dynamics of manoeuvring a set of countries to the point of self-sustained growth, either in the shortest time, or with the least burden on donors, for very firm theoretical statements to be made. In any case, as we have said, it is very doubtful whether the point of self-sustained growth is sufficiently firmly established for any such analysis to have validity.

While there seems to be absolutely no ethical justification for aid distribution based on backing winners, one may still ask two questions, (a) whether there is some political justification, and (b) whether, as suggested earlier, there is a case for defining the underdeveloped world in terms of countries which are not capable of self-sustained growth.

There is no obvious political justification. Of course, there may be independent political reasons for giving a lot of aid to certain countries, which also happen to have large absorptive capacity and appear to be within striking distance of being able to sustain their own growth. More relevantly, it is just arguable that such countries are likely to be growing fairly fast anyway, and are therefore more likely to be favourable to the West. This is the argument that one is more likely to get credit for patting a passing express than helping a lame dog over a stile. It is a tenuous and not altogether attractive argument.

The question whether one can still use, or needs to use, the concept of self-sustained growth to define the underdeveloped world is more interesting. To do so implies, first, that all countries which cannot sustain growth by themselves need aid, and that no countries which can grow by themselves need aid. There is the obvious objec-

---

centrating aid on a few recipients at particular points in their history (to the extent that the current rate of total growth of income in the underdeveloped world was below its maximum), is even more remote.

tion that the first set may contain some very wealthy countries, and the second some very poor ones. Although there is some correspondence between wealth and assured growth it is by no means perfect. Therefore, before answering this question let us further discuss the question of country preference.

We saw that maximizing development implies giving equal weight to increases in consumption everywhere in the underdeveloped world. We must now anticipate the next section to the extent of saying that the essence of giving aid for development is that the donor attaches his own weights to consumption increases for different periods of time within a country. As consumption per head rises over time, according to the normal utility principle, one would attach lower weights to increases in consumption. In other words, the donor would normally discount the future.[1] Now a fairly extreme position for the donor to take, in favour of development rather than consumption now, would be not to discount the future at all—i.e. attach equal weights to consumption over time despite the expectation of rising income per head. This is obviously consistent with attaching equal weights to consumption in different countries with different levels of consumption per head. The combination, equal weights everywhere and at all times, will be our definition of maximizing development.[2]

If the aim is to maximize development, it is clear that one must have some definition of an underdeveloped country which makes no reference to standards of living. This is where the notion of self-sustained growth comes in. One maximizes development in that set of countries which are deemed to be incapable of growing (presumably at some satisfactory rate to be agreed) in income per head by themselves. This is a logical aim, but it still leaves one with the objection that a very poor country may seem to be growing satisfactorily, and hence be ineligible for aid, while richer ones are getting aid. A very wealthy but stagnant country might also become eligible.

Maximizing development is a special limiting case (equal weights) of maximizing utility. Maximizing utility implies that the donor attaches such weights as he pleases to increases in consumption, both over time and between countries, subject only to the rule that

---

[1] This is not what economic theorists always mean by discounting for reasons of time preference. Thus, a unit of real income in the future may weigh less than a unit in the present even if the real income level is unchanged. This is what may be termed pure time preference.

[2] Of course, one *could* go even further, and give greater weight to the future than the present, despite rising consumption. But this possibility seems so perverse that we ignore it.

the higher the level of consumption the lower the weight. One might normally expect the donor's preferences to be such that he would have a single scale connecting the level of consumption with the utility weighting. But this is not essential. For instance, we have seen that donors may be particularly interested in development, and may therefore not discount the future, at least until a certain present level of wealth is reached. This is consistent, however, with using a utility scale between countries at any one time. It would mean that the donor considered consumption growth within a country to be much more important than the level of consumption, but that levels of consumption as between countries (and individuals) mattered more.

If one aims to maximize utility there is no need of an independent definition of the underdeveloped, or aid-worthy, world. A country simply becomes 'developed' when, in donors' eyes, further increases in its consumption are valued no more than increases in consumption in donor countries. It should be noted also that there is nothing in the principle of maximizing utility which precludes a country with higher present consumption per head getting aid, while a country with lower consumption per head gets none. This is because the future must be considered. Thus the first country might be on the point of decline, without aid. This could make it aid-worthy despite its current level of consumption.

In the above discussion we have used what we have called utility weights to express donors' preferences. Since we are dealing with inter-personal comparisons, not merely between the living, but also between the living and many as yet unborn, it should surprise no one that there is nothing very objective about utility weights. Someone has to make the judgment about utility. Since the distribution of aid is the donors' choice—whether the donor be a government, a multilateral institution, or a charity—there is no escaping the fact that utility weighting not merely will, but must, be an expression of the donors' preference, both as between countries and as between present and future generations. The only 'objective' element in utility weighting, in other words the only restriction we have placed on the donors' preferences, is the rule that a given increase in consumption per head from a higher level cannot have a bigger weight than the same increase from a lower level, either within a country at different times, or between countries at the time of giving. Without this restriction, in the light of the history of the word, one would not be justified in calling the weighting a 'utility' weighting.

While utility weighting permits the donor to attach more or less weight to development, and to choose between quick maturing or slow maturing investments,[1] and within limits to choose between countries, utility maximization is not an aim which any individual donor government is likely to set itself. Thus donors will not generally help their enemies, however poor. To convert utility maximization (or its limit, development maximization) to the maximization of the donors' interest it is necessary to multiply the utility weights by another set of political weights (the enemy will generally have a political weight of zero). The various reasons for attaching political weights have already been discussed. When both sets of weights are used the donor is maximizing his self-interest.

It may be asked whether there is any point in keeping the two sets of weights separate. Does not the principle of utility vanish under the political weight? We think not. If, for instance, the UK gives a lot of aid to a poor and insignificant dependant, it would surely be misleading to say that this is solely because the UK attaches a high political weight. The reason would be partly that the country is poor (a high utility weight), and partly that it is dependent (a high political weight). This example draws attention to the fact that the political weight is, so to speak, rather a rag-bag, and includes every influence on aid-decisions other than relative poverty and growth potential.

Let us now recapitulate a little on the ethics of aid distribution. The general principle is that of maximizing utility. This formula permits any weighting by donors provided only that a low level of consumption gets at least as large a weight as a high level. Two other principles have been examined. First, there was the redistribution principle. In a pure form, this does not seek to maximize anything: nor is any stress laid on development. It is doubted whether many would subscribe to this. Secondly, there was maximizing development. This is a borderline case of maximizing utility, in which all consumption at whatever time in whatever aided country has equal weight. It carries with it the necessity of enumerating the countries to be aided. Political weighting apart, they are those which are not capable of self-sustained growth. It seems that something very close to maximizing development is subscribed to by some, especially by Americans concerned with aid principles.

But, before one can make up one's mind how much emphasis one should put on development (which, in general, implies a relatively inegalitarian weighting both through time and between countries) it is as well to have some idea of what is involved for the donor in trying to operate on the principle of maximizing utility (or development). To this subject we now turn.

[1] This is further discussed in the next section.

3. ON MAXIMIZING UTILITY (OR DEVELOPMENT)

In considering how aid should be used to maximize the present value of the increases in consumption per head we need to know,

(1) how much the transfer of capital from abroad will directly raise the national income in all future periods; this is termed 'the productivity of aid';

(2) how much each such increase in national income will itself generate further increases, via an increase in saving, and how much these further increases will themselves generate . . . and so on *ad infinitum*. This depends on what is known as 'the marginal savings rate'.

From this one can deduce the future course of consumption, knowledge of which is required to maximize either utility or development. But we further need to know the future course of consumption per head. For this we need to know,

(3) what will be the effects of aid itself, and the economic changes it produces, on the rate of growth of population. This we call the 'population effect'.

Finally,

(4) there is the possibility that the distribution of aid between countries will itself affect the values of the above variables. This we discuss under the heading of 'leverage effects'.

Of these four components of any estimate of the final effectiveness of aid we shall do little more than mention the first here, since its discussion belongs better to the following chapter. Moreover, it is obvious enough to all but the few who would subscribe to the redistributive principle that the productivity of aid must be allowed for. The other three components are discussed at length in the present chapter, because making allowance for them may be more controversial. In other words, the need to allow for them in maximizing utility or development might make some people want to retreat from accepting the utility principle.

(1) The Productivity of Aid

The first notion, how much aid from abroad raises the national income, is complex. Aid may be used to transfer skills (technical assistance), or capital. Even where it is capital goods, much wider considerations than the productivity of capital—its yield in the ordinary sense—may enter in. For various reasons, aid may have the effect of bringing into use productive resources already existing in the recipient country. It might then have a much greater effect than the

yield of capital would suggest. It may be, in some cases, most productive to use aid to transfer materials, or even consumption goods.
This will be discussed in Chapter VII. Here we need state only that
the productivity of aid—the effect it has in increasing the income of
the recipient—is extremely difficult to judge. The phrase 'absorptive
capacity' is much used in this context. A country with a low absorptive capacity can receive only a little aid before the marginal effect of
aid on its national income becomes very small.

(2) *The Marginal Savings Rate*

When an input of aid raises the national income, it will also raise
savings by an amount equal to the increase in national income
multiplied by the marginal savings rate (by definition). These extra
savings, turned into investment, will raise national income further,
and so on in decreasing increments. There is a multiplier effect.[1]
There are two questions to be asked about this effect. First, should
one take any account of it? This may well be asked because in evaluating investments one normally considers only the increase in income, and leaves out of account further increases in income which
will result if some of that extra income is saved. It is normal to ignore
these secondary effects, because income saved is not generally regarded as more valuable than income consumed. At the margin of
choice, the increased future income is discounted at a rate which
makes its present value equal to the amount of consumption foregone.
It would be double-counting to say, 'this investment yields 10 per
cent, but I shall save some of the extra income, and invest that in turn,
and therefore the real yield is more than 10 per cent.'

But the position of a donor government is different, because it may
want to discount the future at a different (lower) rate from the recipient government (and the latter may also discount the future at a
lower rate than individuals). This is, indeed, almost sure to be the
case. Governments, whether donor or recipient, who are keen on
development are normally trying to force up the savings rate, by
fiscal or other measures. Moreover, the donor government may have
the same time-preference for different recipients, while they themselves differ in this respect. Therefore the donor government, in
evaluating the value of aid as between different recipients, should
take account of their differing marginal savings rates. It establishes
its own present value of aid, given to a particular recipient, by

---

[1] The multiplier is $\dfrac{1}{1-vs}$ at infinity, where v is the output/capital ratio and s the
marginal savings rate.

computing all future increases of consumption per head consequent on the aid input, while discounting them at its own rate of discount. It thus computes an amount of 'aid benefit' which is comparable between recipients.[1]

So much for why the marginal savings rate of the recipient is relevant. The next question is whether it is important. Prima facie, not very. We saw (p. 104 f.) that the ultimate value of the multiplier effect is $\frac{1}{1-vs}$. Now a v of more than one-third is probably in most cases optimistically high, and equally a country which saves more than one-third of its increased income would, one might think, be doing extremely well. But these values would produce a multiplier effect of only 9/8.

On the other hand, if one tries to look forward to self-sustained growth, this concept seems to assume a greater importance. Unless population growth rates can be greatly reduced (see the next section), it is not very likely that a growth of income per head of 2–2½ per cent can be self-sustained with a domestic net savings rate of less than 15 per cent. If a country starts with a net rate even as high as 10 per cent (which is, for instance, probably greater than that achieved in India today), it takes a very long time to build up to the supposedly self-sustaining rate of 15 per cent, unless marginal savings rates are well in excess of 15 per cent.[2] The total aid required over the years reduces

[1] Where d is the rate of discount, and v the output/capital ratio (here assumed the same for aid as for internal capital), and s the marginal savings rate, the sum is

$$\frac{vd\,(1-s)}{1-d-svd}$$

This formula is valid for purposes of comparison only if one chooses to discount at a rate faster than the rate of growth. Otherwise the present value of consumption resulting from an increment of aid is infinite. The formula also assumes constant v and s, which is unlikely. But varying v and s (and perhaps d) over time merely complicates the calculation, without changing the principle.

[2] If Δt is the number of years required to achieve a savings rate of S_t which will sustain a rate of growth g, and S_0 is the initial savings rate, and s the marginal savings rate, then

$$\Delta t = \frac{S_t - S_0}{g(s - S_t)}$$

Let $S_0 = 10$ per cent, $S_t = 15$ per cent, then $\Delta t = \dfrac{1}{s - \dfrac{15}{100}}$. If s is 16 per cent, then it takes 100 years to build up to an average rate of 15 per cent: if s is 20 per cent, it takes 20 years: if 25 per cent, 10 years. But net aid would have to continue for longer than this, since part of the savings would be required to pay interest on the accumulated debt.

rather rapidly as the marginal savings rate rises above the average level assumed to be required.[1] But this, while interesting, does not affect the optimum distribution of aid between countries, to which the relevance of the marginal propensity to save was laid out in the previous paragraph. On the other hand, the marginal savings rate very much affects the weight of the interest and amortization payments which a country will incur before it reaches self-sustained growth. So, if donors insist on high interest rates, and are unwilling to continue net aid to finance development when a country's debt service obligations become very high in relation to its exports (a conventional measure of 'bankability'), then the actual distribution of aid will certainly be affected.[2]

The marginal savings rate has received considerable emphasis in American aid literature;[3] and also in that of the IBRD, for the reason given at the end of the last paragraph. It can be over-emphasized, for it is a less important variable than the direct effect of aid on national income. If income rises rapidly enough, the savings rate will follow in the end. It is also almost equally difficult to measure. The domestic savings rate is a very unreliable statistic in most underdeveloped countries, and the marginal domestic savings rate doubly so. Finally, the marginal savings rate is certainly less important than changes in the rate of population growth, if only because the former is partly determined by the latter, since it is easier for a country with a low population growth rate to save more. Thus if a country has a rate of population growth of 2½ per cent, and consumption per head should be allowed to rise at 2 per cent per annum in the interests of political stability, the savings rate cannot rise unless income grows at more than 4½ per cent.

---

[1] cf. R. I. McKinnon, 'Foreign Exchange Constraints in Economic Development and Efficient Aid Allocation', *Economic Journal*, June 1964. But the author neglects the fact that the sensitivity of discounted aid to the marginal propensity to consume is much lower than that of total aid. It is the former which is really relevant.

[2] The debt problem of underdeveloped countries, and its relation to interest rates and marginal savings rates is examined more thoroughly in Part II, Chapter IX.

[3] 'The best available measure of a country's achievement in improving domestic capital supply is the proportion of additions to national income which it saves. In serious development efforts, 20 per cent or more of increments to gross national product may be saved, even though initially the share of gross national product which is saved domestically may be only 6 to 8 per cent.' *Principles of Foreign Economic Assistance*, AID, p. 29.

(3) *The Population Effect*

It is part and parcel of the notion of self-sustained growth that population should not grow at a rate which threatens to equal or exceed that rate of growth of income which one believes the economy to be capable of sustaining in the long run. The now rich countries, including Japan, have struggled out of this Malthusian trap.

There has, of course, been progress in almost all of the underdeveloped countries also—there must have been, for they support more people. But in few has there been a lasting effect on income per head. In some, 'progress' has meant little more than that there was spare land, so that capacity to produce could grow almost effortlessly (there being little equipment) with the population. There was no requirement to adopt new techniques, or new and more productive ways of living. But in many other underdeveloped countries there has been considerable progress in techniques, and in some even the pessimist may think there are signs that the Malthusian cycle is being broken (as it appears to have been broken in Japan). In others, progress has meant only that a small rich class of big farmers or merchants, with even a sprinkling of industrialists, has been thrown up. The bulk of the people may or may not have adopted, or been able to adopt, more productive techniques. But where they have, any tendency for income per head to rise has been counteracted by population growth.

We know far too little of the dynamic interactions of population growth, and the growth of capacity to produce: and of how the changes in ideas and patterns of living caused by attempts to force economic growth, and indeed by short-run successes in achieving income growth per head, affect birth-rates and death-rates. One of the few things we do know is that the advance of medical techniques has made the problem of increasing income per head far harder for underdeveloped countries today than it was for Western Europe and North America in the nineteenth century. High death-rates were a sacrifice which the then present generation made, willy-nilly, for future generations. Today, the present generations in poor countries do not have to make this sacrifice, and are not likely to want to do so.

Death-rates have already fallen so far, with the introduction of preventive medicine, that population growth rates of over 2 per cent per annum are the rule; 3 per cent or more is quite common, and may very soon be the rule. There is a presumption, from the experience of the now wealthy countries, that birth-rates will eventually fall with the growth of income per head. But income in many underdeveloped countries will have to increase fast, say at 5 per cent or more (faster than it has ever grown in the UK), and increase at that rate for a very long time, before income levels are such that one might expect birth-rates to fall as a consequence of higher living standards. In the mean-time, income growth almost certainly has the reverse effect, that of increasing population growth rates. For instance, it might take India seventy years, at a $4\frac{1}{2}$–5 per cent growth rate (which she has not yet nearly attained), before an income level of even £100 per head is reached, and this is not a level at which, judging by others' ex-perience to date, one would expect the birth-rate to be much lower than it is at present. By then her population would be approaching 2,000 million if death-rates remained unchanged. Plainly, in a country which is already overcrowded with less than 500 million people, no such outcome is possible.

But what has all this to do with criteria for aid-giving? The facts of population growth certainly make the problem of increasing income per head far more difficult. But do they affect how one should distribute aid to maximize increases in consumption per head? Popu-lation growth is relevant to this problem only to the extent that aid-giving, and consequent increases in income, themselves affect birth-rates and death-rates. It is easy to set up a dynamic model in which these effects have a dramatic influence on the best distribution of aid.

Suppose, for instance, that there were two identical recipients, in both of which population growth and consumption growth were 2 per cent per annum, there being no change in consumption per head. If one gave half the available aid to each, consumption growth could be raised to 3 per cent. This, after a short lag, would cause an increase in the population growth rate to 3 per cent also. Aid would have done no lasting good.[1] But if all the aid were given to one country, the growth rate there could be increased to, say, $3\frac{3}{4}$ per cent. This would cause an increase in the population growth rate in that country to, say, $3\frac{1}{4}$ per cent. Gradually, income and consumption per head would increase. Ultimately this would result in a fall in birth-rates, and growth would accelerate. At this point, one could start switching aid to the neglected country, in which in the meantime both population and income had continued to march together. Finally then, both

---

[1] There would have been a small increase in income per head while the popula-tion growth rate was catching up. This might collect in the hands of a very small class of now permanently wealthier people: these, it can easily be supposed, would form a sequestered pocket of wealth with no further influence on the rest of the economy.

THE PRINCIPLES OF AID-GIVING

109

could be turned into developed countries (it would take centuries, with these illustrative figures!).

The above example is one in which maximizing consumption per head in the short run (in which it comes to the same thing as maximizing consumption) is very different from maximizing it in the long run. Splitting aid between the two recipients would result in an increased rate of growth of consumption of 1 per cent. For a year or so this would increase consumption per head by 1 per cent, but later by nothing. If all aid went to one recipient the increased rate of growth of total consumption would be lower at $\frac{7}{8}$ per cent (half of the extra $1\frac{3}{4}$ per cent which only one recipient would enjoy). Initially consumption per head would also grow at this same lower rate, but there would be the lasting effect of a growth of consumption per head of $\frac{3}{4}$ per cent, which would later accelerate.

Something quite similar to the above seems to have happened in some, perhaps many, underdeveloped countries. There was some progress, and consumption per head rose. But it did not rise fast enough to prevent the population catching up. This is by far the most serious argument for concentrating aid in big doses: more precisely, for giving more aid to some countries than would be warranted by maximizing the present value of utility-weighted consumption in the underdeveloped world. One might even argue that if, with aid, a country cannot achieve a growth rate of at least 4 per cent, then it is not worth aiding at all—there being too much risk that population growth will nullify the results. If the population growth rate is high, and the margin between it and the income growth rate is small, then there is too much risk that the population will increase so much, before income levels are reached at which one could expect a fall in birth-rates, that growth will become extremely difficult as a result of over-crowding on the land. In short, one fears that something like the Indian situation, but worse, is in the offing elsewhere.

But, of course, our example presupposes that aid and the growth of income itself raises the rate of growth of population. If high, and higher, population growth rates are going to occur anyway, then the best distribution of aid is unaffected. Now the population explosion of the last twenty years has very largely occurred independently of the growth of incomes, and independently of all but small doses of technical assistance. Malaria control, the primary effect of which is to reduce infant mortality, has probably been the largest single cause. Nevertheless, it is impossible not to believe that growth of incomes in poor countries has no effect in stimulating the population. Governments, whether they want to or not, will be bound to spend more money on health. Medicine apart, some improvement in health must occur as incomes rise, and must further reduce specific death-rates.[1] However, it could be argued that the effect of aid in stimulating population growth is, in the circumstances of today, probably so small that it can be ignored. Since we do not know whether this is true or not, and since it would appear to be morally repugnant to give little or no aid to some, in order to concentrate it on others even beyond the point of maximizing utility, it is an argument which many people would probably like to accept.

Of course, population growth may be affected, not just by the quantum of aid given, and the consequent growth of income, but also by 'strings' that donors may attach to aid, by technical assistance for birth control projects, and by the policies (whether affected by donor governments or not) of the recipient countries' own governments. This is also true of the productivity of aid, and the marginal savings rate. This consideration introduces our next section.

(4) *The Leverage Effects of Aid*

In the previous section, the effects of aid were discussed as if the reactions of the recipient country were data which had to be accepted. But part of the reason for some donors, notably the USA, putting emphasis on 'self-help' is to instil the belief that the recipient country will get more aid if it adopts policies which seem to the donor to be conducive to growth, indeed conducive to growth in a form which the donor believes will lead to a stable, non-Communist, political development also. This attempt to use aid to influence recipients in what is believed to be a wholly benign and socially desirable manner is being carried further by the USA in Latin America than by any donor elsewhere. 'The United States Government is embarked on a uniquely daring venture with its Alliance for Progress. It has become the advocate of land and other social reforms and is attempting to condition its aid on some progress in these matters. It is thus involving itself in the policy-making process of other countries to a hitherto unheard-of extent.'[2] It is hardly surprising that initial reactions to such an experiment have been very mixed, and some very hostile, It may be added that AID publications stress the importance of national development plans, and the United States' interest in improved economic policies, as well as the im-

[1] Of course, if the Malthusian cycle completed itself, death-rates would rise again when the initial rise of incomes had been wiped out.
[2] A. O. Hirschman, *Journeys towards Progress*, Twentieth Century Fund, 1963, p. 7.

portance of the private sector, and so on. The United States Government obviously hopes that recipients will take its hints, but until recently in Latin America there is little evidence that it has actually used aid as a lever.

How far can donors go in trying to influence the key factors which would appear to govern the effectiveness of aid, by making aid to some extent conditional on particular policies being followed? While the Alliance for Progress may go further than governments have elsewhere, complete non-intervention is the exception. First of all, most aid is given for specific projects, over which the donor generally exercises some surveillance. The donor may go no further than satisfying itself that competent engineers and contractors are employed; but often it also tries to ensure that it aids only projects which make economic sense, which appear to contribute enough to development, and possibly which fit into an overall development plan which it believes to be sensible. Certainly, aid has been an important stimulus to the production of development plans. This kind of 'intervention', which is limited in scope to the project itself, is usual to some degree, but naturally varies very much with the competence of the recipient. The reaction of the recipient varies from recognition of such surveillance as an essential and beneficial piece of technical assistance, to irritated accusations of neo-colonialism.

Economic development plans, and the proper degree of project surveillance, are discussed at greater length in Chapter VIII. Here we are more concerned with using aid as a lever to promote changes in development policy in a wider sense. The changes desired may be specific to the recipient, e.g. land reform. The donor might then make a clear bargain to the effect that more aid will be forthcoming if certain things are done. Obviously, such interference is extremely tricky to manage, and may easily boomerang to the discredit of the donor. If one is insistent enough on development, and does not mind risking making many enemies in the recipient country, such experiments may be admirable. On the other hand, the donor may not always know best. It has been suggested that it is facile to suppose that he should, given that the socio-economic systems of even small and apparently simple countries may be very complex, and that the consequences of reform are hard to predict.

But, the complexity of a small simple society's socio-economic system does not entail that foreigners do not know best. The nationals of such a society often lack the education to understand how it functions, and what will be the effect of reforms. Furthermore, it is often the case that the educated members of such societies are out of touch with the bulk of the people. Admittedly, in practice and at present, there are too many foreigners who do not know best: they do not stay long enough, and may get superficial impressions. They may nevertheless be better equipped than local people to acquire the relevant knowledge. Certainly, it is arrogant and facile of a foreigner to assume he knows best, and there is no doubt that much technical assistance, especially that provided by countries which have never had colonies, has suffered from such arrogance. At the same time it is often sensible to assume, first that no local has the required knowledge, secondly that wide knowledge of the socio-economic system must be acquired before aid can be given effectively, and lastly that the donors know better than the recipients what knowledge is relevant, and how it is best acquired. That foreigners often do not know best is an argument for having professional aid-givers who are allowed to stay in one country or area for long enough to know it very well, rather than an argument for 'aid without strings'. Moreover, the point is not to impose reforms which only foreigners think desirable, but to get extra leverage behind reforms which are widely believed to be desirable for development, especially by progressive elements in the recipient country.

Much less tricky than such particular 'reform-mongering' would be the attempt to influence variables which are quite generally favourable to increasing income per head, by stating and letting it be seen that countries will get relatively more aid than others if they are doing their best to improve such factors. We have seen that, quite generally, high marginal savings rates and low population growth rates, are favourable. We also came to the conclusion that there was, perhaps, not a great deal to be said for letting the values of these variables themselves influence the distribution of aid. But, if one takes into account the possibility of changing them, that is a different matter. Of course, one could not let aid depend mechanically on the value of the variables, because countries vary greatly in their capacity to achieve favourable values, and because one would tend, therefore, to give most to those who needed least. But one could try to make it clear by statement and action that the pursuit of policies to improve these factors disposed donors favourably to aid.

It should go without saying that donors should do all they can to assist self-help policies, particularly in birth control. Donors have been extremely reluctant to get involved, on the often justified grounds that this is a tricky field for donors and recipients alike. The excuse has, however, been overplayed, in view of the enormous importance of making progress in birth control.

Part of the purpose of emphasizing development planning was no doubt that plans would give donors a basis for judging the seriousness of recipients' efforts to help themselves. Certainly, recipients regard the existence of a plan as a factor in getting more aid, and in this they are right. But donors have not yet used recipients' plans as vehicles for promoting 'self-help' policies. There are several reasons for this. First, there has been little consensus among donors as to what standards of performance in what areas of policy are expected of recipients. Secondly, there have been only *ad hoc* and very general assessments of plans by donors' representatives, or by a multilateral organization such as the IBRD. Even where the IBRD has run a consortium of donor powers, there has been no sufficient consensus among donors for the consortium to operate in this way. Thirdly, most countries' plans, whether for lack of statistical knowledge or for other reasons, are insufficiently firm documents to enable desirable aid levels to be assessed on this basis.

Performance, rather than planning, is probably the only sensible basis for a general policy of trying to give relatively more aid to those who make serious efforts to tackle certain basic problems, like the taxation system or population growth, and less to those who waste a great deal of money on prestige projects. If recipients knew that the amount of aid received per head depended significantly on whether they had initiated a serious birth control policy, then the chances of ultimate success for aid-giving might be a little higher. The possibility of providing significant incentives to recipients, by means of a policy of giving more to the good boys to encourage the others, would seem to depend very much on a greater concentration by donors on the development objective, and on a greater agreement as to what facets of policy need singling out for 'leverage treatment'.

4. CONCLUSIONS ON WHY ONE GIVES AID, AND TO WHAT END

We think the most useful way to round off the discussion of motives and objectives of aid giving is by means of a personal creed. Such a creed should at least make it easier for the reader to produce his own.

(1) *What is Aid?*
One is tempted to start with the proposition that all aid must be disinterested, regarding this as a tautology rather than a recommendation. Buying something from a man may help him, but one does not speak of aiding him if it is something one wants. This very recently

developed but now universal misuse of language has helped to spread misunderstanding and cynicism about 'aid', which is not in the best interests of 'donors' or 'recipients'.

But the distinction between buying something one wants, and giving aid, is not clear-cut. Where the only interest of the transferrer of funds is in the subsistence or economic development of the transferee (for the somewhat tenuous, some would say far-fetched, reason that his subsistence or development will contribute to a world political situation favourable to the former), then only by straining language can we say that the transferrer is buying economic development, and we usually (legitimately) speak of the donor aiding the recipient. Nevertheless, it is at times useful deliberately to strain language, and speak of using aid to 'buy development', because the phrase indicates that both parties have some obligations—the recipient's obligation being to deliver development. In this special sense, aid is not disinterested. On the contrary, the donor *is* interested, and *is* buying development: but at the same time *is* a donor, and is entitled, e.g. in any reckoning of 'fair shares' among donors, to chalk up as aid a grant given solely for development.

Where the transferrer has a much more immediate and concrete interest, and could reasonably be said to be buying something definable, or making what seems to him to be a good investment, there is no reason to call the transfer aid. To do so, completely confounds any attempt to allocate 'fair shares' among donors, and worse, confuses recipients by lumping together transfers in relation to which they may have completely different obligations—e.g. to supply a base, be friends, or plan for development. Finally, aid proper would benefit if one drew a much sharper distinction between credits intended to promote exports and cheap long-run credits clearly designed as aid for development. If one could separate off all transactions which were really purchases, or really commercial, then one could claim that all aid was for subsistence or development. This would have many psychological and administrative advantages. But to go thus far is barely possible, and not altogether desirable.

It is barely possible because motives in actual transactions are not only mixed, but confused. Nevertheless, much unscrambling could be done. For instance, if loans were given either at full commercial rates and for no more than five years (not aid), or at definitely subsidized rates, say $2\frac{1}{2}$ per cent or less, and for twenty years or more, the distinction would be much clearer. Where political and economic motives are mixed, unscrambling may be harder, especially where the donor country itself does not really know why it is giving aid. Bases are easy. If we make some of our 'aid' to Aden or Cyprus conditional on defence arrangements, the purchase element is clear. This should not be called aid. Even so it may, in some cases, be desirable to be hypocritical and perpetuate the confusion for diplomatic reasons. Thus the recipient may prefer to be 'given aid', rather than be 'selling a base', which may be castigated as non-neutral or regarded as otherwise immoral. But although some purchases may have to be called aid officially, there should at least be no confusion between the parties as to the nature of the transaction. Where the 'donor' gives money for diplomatic reasons, and is not really interested in development, it is usually trying to buy something as vague as goodwill, or the probability of diplomatic support on some issue or other. Here the modern convention is to adopt the polite euphemism of 'development aid', not 'bribery'. Usually such diplomatic hand-outs will be relatively small, and they will be given to countries where a serious development effort is not in the 'donor's' interest. The relative lack of interest by the 'donor' in how the money is spent, should mark the distinction, even if the transaction has to be called 'aid'. There is the related administrative point that it is futile to retain a professional development aid mission in countries where money is really only given for prestige reasons, to buy goodwill, maintain contacts, etc. For example, the presence of AID missions in the French-speaking African countries south of the Sahara has been wasteful and senseless.

(2) *Aid Mostly for Development*
Trying to make all aid, as far as possible, genuine aid for development has so far been treated as a matter of aid-terms, of administration, and nomenclature. But we also believe that the diplomatic usage of aid should be kept to a minimum. Unlike some, we do not believe it can or should be cut out altogether, nor do we see anything wrong in it. Where a régime, for instance, is not really interested in development, and other conditions are unfavourable, it would be very wasteful, and probably impolitic, to try to give considerable amounts of development aid administered as such. Yet some token aid may, for many possible diplomatic reasons, be advisable. That such aid should be kept to a minimum derives simply from the view, which we share with most observers who are not professional diplomats, that it seldom does much good. One must beware ambassadorial views. Life is nicer for His Excellency if he can secure £1 million for the ruler's pet scheme.
 We believe that we—the West—should be interested in the develop-

ment of most underdeveloped countries which aspire to a neutral or Western-committed existence, and as much interested in the neutrals as the committed. Our interest derives from the probability that some considerable economic progress has become essential to the continued long-term existence of governments, or succeeding governments, which are likely to preserve neutrality or remain favourable to the West. The argument that economic advance may actually generate conditions favourable to the seizure of power by a ruthless minority, and that such a 'revolution' is more likely than not to be successfully exploited by Communism, may certainly prove valid in the sense that events will sometimes turn out like that. But if one is to accept it as an argument against our attempting to promote economic progress, then one must also believe that lack of economic progress is likely to stave off revolution indefinitely. In the present world, where, even in a long established autocracy like Ethiopia, the Emperor cannot (and does not wish to) prevent the infection of ideas of progress, this, we think, is an impossible argument to accept. We really have no choice except to back the view that reasonably rapid and well-disseminated economic progress, which is well balanced in the sense that it does not produce thwarted and disappointed minorities, is more likely to be favourable to us, than slow progress possibly limited to small sections of the population.

The anti-Communist objective which aid is given in the above account is nothing to be ashamed of. We, after all, believe that Communism is a major menace to the ideals in which we believe. Nor is the above account inconsistent with giving aid to Yugoslavia, for it is primarily Russian and Chinese-inspired Communism whose spread we wish to inhibit, and Yugoslavia is a nuisance to Moscow and Pekin.

One of the main difficulties arises when recipient governments are anything but progressive. This is one of the great preoccupations of the AID, which has to deal with many such. But, more generally, the fact that Western interests lie in the rapid development of as many countries as possible demands political, as well as economic, judgment of a high order when distributing aid. Our acceptance of the need to apply political judgment to aid-giving is quite consistent with our sympathy with some of the reasons which lead many people to want to keep foreign affairs' ministries out of the picture. Aid, and especially the threat of or the actual cessation of aid, has all too often been used by particular Western governments for purposes unrelated to the long-run interest of the West in economic development. How foolish, for instance, it would have been for the USA to withdraw aid from the UAR—as requested by Mr R. A. Butler in 1964[1]—because President Nasser's support for the Yemen Republic is in conflict with British interests in the Aden Protectorates. We believe that almost all the attempts to punish recipients by reducing or withdrawing aid, because certain aspects of their political policies were disliked, have failed. Most notably, of course, Mr Dulles's piqued withdrawal of USA interest in the Aswan Dam caused the nationalization of the Suez Canal (and was thus an essential link in the causation of the Suez War). Furthermore, such uses of aid or non-aid, even if immediately successful, do lasting damage to the possibility that the West's aid should come to be regarded as motivated only by the desire to see economic progress. We do not think we can be indifferent to the picture which Western aid as a whole presents to the underdeveloped world.

It is for the same reason that the tarnishing of Western aid by commercial competition in so-called aid-giving must be ended. This would be easier, if only we could get more agreement among Western donors as to what aid is, and what are its purposes. The competition to achieve a certain ratio of so-called aid to the donors' national income has, in this connection, probably done more harm than good.

To sum up, we believe that once economic aid for development has been properly defined, then donors should use that aid, to adopt our own terminology, to maximize the 'political value of development'. We doubt whether the resultant policy is likely to be, in practice, very different from a policy of maximizing utility. The main difference is simply that one would not give development aid to governments committed to Moscow or Pekin. The more realistic humanitarians should in any case be content, because much more aid is likely to be forthcoming if people can be convinced of their own interest. Finally, long-run 'politically-weighted' development is an objective which is surely in the interest of all Western countries (and Japan), to which they can all subscribe, and on the basis of which some better co-ordination of policies could be made.

[1] See *The Economist*, May 2, 1964.

PART TWO

AID AND DEVELOPMENT

CHAPTER IV

THE RECIPIENTS' WORLD

In Part I we discussed the origins and some of the characteristics of aid to poor countries. In this Part we shall analyse some theories about economic growth in these countries, and discuss how aid from outside can help to promote their growth. This chapter is concerned with the description, rather than analysis, of some important characteristics of aid recipients. Any quantitative discussion of donors and recipients requires one to enumerate the countries in each category. The UN and the DAC both provide lists of 'recipients' (some 'donors' are also in fact recipients of aid, and some 'recipients' donors). We adopt the DAC enumeration, which is as follows:

All Africa except the Republic of South Africa.
All America except the USA and Canada.
All Asia except the Sino-Soviet bloc and Japan.
All Oceania except Australia and New Zealand.
Greece, Spain, Turkey, Yugoslavia, Cyprus, Malta, and Gibraltar.

There are nearly 100 independent countries, and over fifty dependent territories in the above areas.

No single criterion separates the classes of donor and recipient. But a poverty line, drawn at $600 per head, conflicts little with the above enumeration. The most notable exceptions are Japan, Portugal, and South Africa, classed as donors with *per capita* incomes of less than $600; and Venezuela and Israel which are recipients with incomes per head much higher than $600. The Sino-Soviet bloc is excluded *en bloc* because next to nothing is known about capital flows within it, and because no members, except Poland, have received aid from Western countries.

When we describe the characteristics which some or all poor countries possess in common, we do not of course intend to imply that there is a sharp distinction between rich and poor countries at the borderline. It is obvious that Greece and Spain, for instance, have more in common with Italy than with India or Malawi. Nevertheless, we shall proceed to make such generalizations about recipient countries as seem useful and illuminating for descriptive purposes, without paying much attention to a few relatively unimportant borderline cases, or to the fact that some of these generalizations might apply to certain donor countries as well.

What then are the characteristics of the recipients' world? The first and most obvious is poverty, since poverty is the one factor which all recipients share virtually by definition. Sixty per cent of the population of recipient countries live in countries where *per capita* GNP is less than $100 a year. Thus all recipient countries are poor, and the majority are very poor. Not even the unreliability and incomparability of *per capita* GNP statistics can obscure this fact. Although it is certainly true that, in Britain or the USA, one could not keep alive on even the average Indian income, nevertheless it is generally agreed that estimates of *per capita* GNP, reduced to dollar equivalents, enable one to rank countries in order of real income with tolerable accuracy.

Apart from poverty, which in a sense sums up the whole of developing countries' characteristics, the most important and impressive common feature is the very high rate of population growth. Historically, as is still the case in a few countries, high birth-rates have been accompanied by high death-rates, especially among young children, so that the total population grew slowly if at all. But during the twentieth century, and especially since the incidence of malaria has been reduced, death-rates in many countries have fallen rapidly, while birth-rates have remained unchanged, or have, in a few cases, even risen a little. The reduction in the death-rate has been particularly large among young children, so the result has been not only that the total population of many countries is now rising at 3 per cent or more a year, but also that the age-distribution of population throughout most of the developing world has been seriously distorted. Forty-five per cent of the population of recipients live in countries where 40 per cent of the population is less than fifteen years old; and in several countries[1] more than 45 per cent of the population is under fifteen years old. These two factors in combination present grave problems. A high rate of population increase is likely to lead fairly quickly, in most countries, to pressure on land resources: even where there is unused land of reasonable quality, or where land could be farmed more intensively, feeding an increasing population will usually demand changes in techniques, of which irrigation is the most

[1] Kenya, Southern Rhodesia, Philippines, Sudan, and Taiwan, are the largest of these.

obvious example. Changes in techniques cannot easily be introduced to a population which is totally uneducated. But the high ratio of children to adults, typical of an area where population is expanding fast, demands an ever-increasing supply of investment in buildings, materials, and above all in teachers, if the existing level of education is to be maintained, let alone increased. Thus, if governments aim to improve the standards of education, as a means of improving the standard of living in the future, then the high ratio of children to adults will present a problem quite independent of the pressure on resources which is often, but not always, present.

The magnitude of the developing countries' population problem as outlined above can be made clearer by comparing poor with rich countries. In Britain complaints about the difficulty of satisfying the demand for public services of all kinds, especially housing and schools, are frequently heard. Yet the rate of population growth is only 0·8 per cent; and only 23 per cent of the population is below the age of fifteen. The USA, where a post-war rise in the birth-rate has caused some concern, has a rate of population increase of 1·6 per cent a year. In India, population is now increasing at over 2·5 per cent a year. In South and Central America, eleven independent countries[1] have rates of population growth of 3 per cent and more. In Africa also, some eleven countries are thought to have as rapid rates of growth.[2]

The impact of the population explosion on the growth of GNP per head emerges clearly from such statistics as are available. If we take the fifteen major developing countries for which statistics have been published by the UN for the years 1952–60 or thereabouts, we find that Thailand, which ranked fifth in order of growth of GNP, ranked only tenth in order of growth of GNP per head, on account of a 3 per cent rate of population growth. India, whose GNP grew at 3·8 per cent per annum, achieved a growth in GNP per head of only 1·7 per cent (population grew at 2·1 per cent), while consumption per head grew at little more than 1 per cent per annum. In eleven of the fifteen countries, population grew faster than GNP per head, and in two of them the rates of growth of population and GNP per head was the same. If these were at all typical, more than half of the growth in poor

---

[1] Costa Rica, Dominican Republic, Guatemala, Honduras, Mexico, Nicaragua, Panama, Trinidad, Brazil, Ecuador, and Venezuela.
[2] Burundi, Guinea, Kenya, Mali, Mauritania, Morocco, Niger, Nigeria, Somalia, Southern Rhodesia, and Uganda, are the countries referred to. But statistics of population are too inaccurate to assign any precise figures to particular countries.

countries' GNP in the 1950s was absorbed in supporting a larger population, leaving only a small margin for raising the incomes of the existing population.

It may be argued that the rates of growth of GNP and of population are not independent and that, if the rate of population growth were reduced, GNP would also grow more slowly. This is not plausible in the short run, if slower population growth is achieved by means of reducing the birth-rate, thus reducing the ratio of unproductive people to working population. In the longer run, it is also unlikely to be true, since in most developing countries the productivity of unskilled people is very low, and many unskilled people are unemployed or seriously underemployed. If the rate of increase of the potential working population were reduced, as a result of birth control, this would be unlikely to have a noticeable effect on the volume of production, since it would be the numbers of unemployed that would be reduced first, and since it would be easier to increase productivity, by means of better education and training and other services, in a country where population was not growing too fast.

The economies of most developing countries are characterized by a heavy dependence on agriculture for income, and an even heavier dependence on agriculture for employment.[1] A high proportion of agricultural output is for subsistence, i.e. it is consumed by the family of the producer without ever reaching the market. But pure subsistence agriculture, where no monetary exchanges occur, is by now probably very rare. Most systems of traditional land tenure—from tribal ownership to share-cropping—tend to discourage improvement and innovation, although so many other social and economic factors are involved that too much importance should not be attached to a single factor. Concentration of population in agriculture makes the task of improving education and other social and economic services more difficult, because an agricultural population tends to be scattered in villages or even individual huts or compounds, and because children can become productive workers in agriculture at an early age, so that allowing them to go to school is a sacrifice for the parents over and above their direct expenses (if any) on fees, books, etc. Yet without more, and better, education (in the widest sense, including agricultural extension) the prospects for a continuing improvement in net output per head are poor, even in those areas where good land is plentiful.

Because of the concentration on agriculture, and to a lesser extent

[1] Agriculture is here used loosely to include agriculture in the strict sense, animal husbandry, fishing, hunting, and forestry.

on mining—the only other form of production whose location is so closely tied to natural endowment—the exports of developing countries tend to consist almost entirely of primary products. This has several consequences. First, because countries within the same area tend to have similar natural resources, because primary products are more homogeneous than industrial products, because overland transport is slow and expensive, and for a variety of historical reasons, developing countries trade very little with one another. Secondly, each developing country's exports tend to consist of a fairly narrow range of primary products, one or two commodities often accounting for 50 per cent or more of total exports, so that any exogenous change in the market for a given primary commodity may have a serious impact on the export earnings of some developing countries. There is also a theory that the prices of primary commodities in general have a secular tendency to decline in relation to the prices of manufactures;[1] if this is so it implies that a primary-producing country must increase the volume of its exports faster than the volume of its imports, and this clearly places it at a disadvantage in relation to exporters of manufactures. This theory is not, however, by any means universally accepted.

While the above generalizations have validity, when one is comparing poor with rich countries, it is easy to give too stereotyped a picture of the recipients' world. A few of the important ways in which recipients differ from one another therefore need to be stressed.

Perhaps the most striking variation is in size. The typical poor country is small, with not more than ten million or so inhabitants, but the list of poor countries also includes the world's largest non-Communist country, India. With over 450 million people, India contains over 30 per cent of the population of the developing world, and the five next largest—Indonesia, Pakistan, Brazil, Mexico, and Nigeria—each with more than 50 million people,[2] contain a further 20 per cent. Thus though the typical country is small, the typical inhabitant of the developing world lives in a large country.

Closely allied to size is the extent of developing countries' dependence on exports. Concern with the problems of certain primary producers which has arisen because of fluctuations in the volume and prices of their exports, has tended to create the illusion that all

[1] See, for example, *Towards a New Trade Policy for Development*, Report by the Secretary-General of the UNCTAD (Dr Prebisch), UN, New York, 1964.
[2] Nigeria officially contains over 50 million inhabitants. But the latest census exaggerated, as a result of political rivalry between the regions. The real population is very probably less than 50 million.

poor countries are heavily dependent on exports. In a sense this may be true, since they are on the whole less able than industrial countries to produce substitutes for their traditional imports if for some reason their export earnings fall. But in terms of the proportion of GNP exported, it is not true. India exports less than 6 per cent of GNP; Brazil, Chile, and several others, export less than 10 per cent. Those developing countries which are very heavily dependent on exports are mostly quite small; Trinidad, with less than one million people, is an extreme case, exporting 74 per cent of GNP; Ghana, with seven million people and exporting 23 per cent of GNP, is perhaps more typical of the many other countries which export a substantial but not excessive proportion of GNP. The impression that it is in the nature of poor countries to be heavily dependent on exports has probably arisen because many of them are so small, and are for this reason quite heavily dependent on foreign trade.

The problems of countries whose exports consist principally of primary products have received a great deal of attention during the last few years, and a number of misunderstandings have arisen. First, there has been a tendency to equate primary exporters with poor countries, and vice versa, despite the fact that more than 40 per cent of the world's exports of primary commodities come from rich countries. The reverse proposition is broadly true, that all poor countries' export earnings come principally from primary products, though there are one or two minor exceptions to this rule, like Hong Kong and Israel.

More important, the simple classification of products into primary and secondary, which is useful for making certain generalizations about underlying economic tendencies, encourages one to make sweeping and misleading generalization about the problems which face exporters of primary products. In reality, the factors which influence markets for primary commodities, and so the countries which trade in them, vary enormously from one commodity to another. Very broadly, one can distinguish three groups of commodities, according to likely trends in future demand; foodstuffs, for which world demand is likely to increase more slowly than demand for other goods; agricultural raw materials, for which demand is derived from the demand for manufactured goods, and which are likely to continue to suffer from severe fluctuations in demand and increasing competition from synthetic substitutes; and minerals, demand for which will probably remain fairly buoyant though fluctuations are likely for the same reasons as for agricultural raw materials. Even within these categories, however, producers of different commodities will, judging by past experience, face very different problems. The prospect for exports of coffee from poor countries, for example, are better than for sugar, because no close substitute is likely to be produced outside the tropics. The class of minerals contains both tin, which has suffered from severe price fluctuations since the war, and demand for which has increased very little in the last fifty years; and petroleum, whose price has fluctuated very little even by comparison with manufactures, and world consumption of which has increased nearly forty times in the last fifty years.

A recent article has suggested that none of the traditional explanations of why poor countries suffer from greater fluctuations in export earnings than rich countries is of much use in explaining the difference. In addition, it suggests that the difference between rich and poor countries in this respect is not nearly as great as traditional theory might lead one to suppose.[1]

It is not therefore nearly as easy to generalize about the special characteristics of commodity markets as is commonly believed, and consequently the trade problems of poor countries as a group cannot be sharply distinguished from those of richer countries. Explanations of poverty that dwell too much on the disastrous effects of depending upon exports of primary goods are not therefore wholly satisfactory, though it remains true that when a high proportion of a country's output and employment is concentrated on a single export commodity, that country is exceptionally vulnerable to the effects of fortuitous shifts in demand for or supply of that commodity.

Very broadly, then, while there may be some descriptive validity in generalizations about poor countries, based on aggregate data, many of these break down in individual cases. Even generalizations based on separate statistical evidence for each country, on matters like the proportion of various age-groups attending school, or the numbers of doctors per head of population, may conceal wide differences in important matters of detail. For instance, India, which has a percentage of illiterates (about three-quarters of the adult population in 1961) not far short of that in many African countries, educates a far higher proportion to graduate level than any African country. In East Africa, on the other hand, the greatest weakness in the educational system is still at secondary school level, and the most pressing problem is how to staff government departments and other key institutions with qualified citizens in place of expatriates.

[1] Alisdair I. MacBean, 'Causes of Excessive Fluctuations in Export Proceeds of Underdeveloped Countries', *Bulletin of the Oxford University Institute of Economics and Statistics*, November 1964.

The important lesson for donors is that aid cannot be provided, and related policies effectively pursued, without a detailed understanding of the recipient's economy. For instance, stimulating the import of manufactures from poor countries would in the short run help Hong Kong and probably also India and Pakistan, but would scarcely affect Africa; supporting the price of coffee would help various countries scattered throughout the world, but would be useless to Ghana or Nigeria; providing more places for undergraduates to study in Britain would do little to help East African countries at present, and so on. Poor countries cannot be lumped together into a single category except in relation to the broadest possible political decisions, and economic theories about growth in poor countries—in so far as they differentiate at all between rich and poor countries—can be sketched only in the broadest outline.

CHAPTER V

SOME DEVELOPMENT THEORY

---

1. INTRODUCTORY

There are, broadly speaking, two types of development theory. The first is concerned with explaining the genesis of progress, or the lack of it: and the subsequent course of growth. The second is concerned with planning growth, hence with breaking the bottlenecks to a forced, more or less state-directed, process of growth. It is the second kind of theory which interests us directly: this is also the kind of theory in which many economists move with greater ease. It is forward-looking, and the models produced can be more abstract, and any figures more illustrative. It can and does rapidly degenerate into total irrelevancy.

The first kind of theory should throw light on how to plan for development, by spotlighting key factors and relations. But economic theories of the genesis and progress of development, or its failure, do not take us far.[1] There is the poverty-trap theory. The underdeveloped countries are too poor to save. This is unplausible, because all countries were poor once: and, anyway, there are always some relatively wealthy people who could save. Alternatively, there are no opportunities for productive investment, and so no one saves (or, if they do, they export the savings); or, more plausibly, no one has the entrepreneurial spirit required to undertake productive investment, and so the savings of the relatively wealthy are invested abroad, or go into land, the purchase of which supports the consumption of the sellers. The wheel may then be brought full circle when the land is split up again through excessive procreation.[2] This brings one to the Malthusian trap. There is some savings, and some investment: but not enough or not effective enough to prevent increases in population from catching up.

---

[1] See E. E. Hagen, *The Theory of Social Change*, The Dorsey Press, 1962, Chapter III, for a fuller criticism of economic explanations of growth.

[2] For an excellent account of this version of the dynamics of stagnation in an Indian village, see F. Bailey, *Caste and the Economic Frontier*, Manchester University Press, 1957.

Finally, and more recently, a balance-of-payments obstacle has been suggested. A country may have the ability to save more than it does, but more investment, using only indigenous resources, is not worthwhile: for reasons beyond its control, it can neither export more nor import less so as to leave a margin with which to buy those foreign capital goods or skills which would make investment more productive, and so make it worthwhile to save more. This is really an elaboration of the case already mentioned (not enough opportunities for productive investment: hence not enough saving). It is perhaps not very plausible as a main explanation of stagnation: but, like the other factors mentioned, it may be a contributory explanation of either stagnation or a very low growth rate. But it probably belongs more to the second kind of theory—which seeks not so much to explain, as to teach how to plan to accelerate growth. We shall discuss it at some length in Sections (3) and (4) below.

The above theorizing may seem to be somewhat banal. Nevertheless it points to the main concepts with which economists operate in planning development, and in analysing development bottlenecks—savings rates, the effectiveness of investment, the balance of payments, and possibly population growth (though this is usually treated by economists as a god-given datum).

We turn now to the second kind of economic theorizing about underdeveloped countries, which centres round the problem of how to accelerate growth. We shall discuss in turn the effectiveness of investment (in a very broad sense of the term); savings and the balance of payments; international trade and the need for foreign capital; and how all these are interrelated. Population growth has already been discussed in Chapter III.

It is worth remarking at this point that many economists have always realized that their aggregative concepts represent, as it were, the mechanisms through which more basic cultural or psychological forces operate: and also that the decision-making processes in a country—politics in general—are highly relevant. It is only recently, however, that some economists seem to have come to believe that, so far as development goes, it may be more important to study anthropology, social anthropology, sociology, politics and decision-making, demography, education, and even health. This does not mean leaving it to the professions concerned, for thinking in many of them is often not oriented towards development, and a number of distinguished economists have stepped outside their own disciplines.[1]

[1] e.g. Myrdal (sociology), Hirschman (decision-making), Hagen (psychology), Balogh (education).

We have much sympathy with this. But, for lack of knowledge and space, in what follows we mostly stick to our last.

2. THE EFFECTIVENESS OF INVESTMENT, AND ABSORPTIVE CAPACITY

In developed economies one usually speaks of the marginal productivity of capital, that is the rate of interest which makes the discounted value of the profits, accruing to the least worthwhile investment undertaken, equal to the cost of that investment.[1] Profits are theoretically the proper measure of additions to national income, and not the value of the output. This is because the other components of value—wages; salaries; and the cost of raw materials, fuel, and semi-finished goods—are the cost of inputs which, it is presumed, would have contributed to national income even if the investment in question had never been made.

In underdeveloped countries, it has become common to use the concept of the capital/output ratio (or its inverse) as a measure of the increase in national income consequent on an investment. If output means gross output, this presumes that inputs other than capital would have made no contribution to the national income. This in turn implies that one is dealing with a labour surplus economy, one in which the marginal productivity of labour is zero. This is, probably, close to the truth in some underdeveloped economies, e.g. India and Pakistan, but certainly not in most. Secondly, it means that current inputs other than labour are produced by labour alone, which is mostly absurd.

For individual projects, the value of the capital/output ratio approach lies in its emphasis that the increase in the national income may be much greater than the productivity of the investment, as conventionally calculated, suggests. This will arise when the investment permits hitherto unemployed indigenous resources to be used, or when there are significant benefits which do not actually accrue as receipts ('external' economies). Nevertheless the gross output/capital ratio is generally misleading in the opposite sense, because the real current costs of output, in terms of opportunities foregone, are seldom zero.[2]

---

[1] We here ignore the imperfections which make the 'present value' approach generally more suitable for project selection than the 'internal rate of return', which is described in the text.

[2] The marginal output/capital ratio is also much used, as we shall see, in an aggregative sense. As such, it is merely an observed relation between investment and income growth—but one which can or has varied widely from time to time and country to country.

The proper measure of the effectiveness of an individual investment is arrived at by discounting the future stream of profits (plus the money value of any net benefits which accrue to the community, but not to the investment itself) as struck after valuing all current inputs at the value which they would have added to the national income if the investment had not been made. Below, when we speak of the productivity or effectiveness of an investment, or of aid, it is assumed that prices have been used which properly reflect real costs and benefits, and that all 'external economies and diseconomies' have been allowed for.

Assessing the effectiveness of investment in this way is very difficult. It is, of course, done and thought worthwhile for many types of investment in developed countries—but not for all types, e.g. health and education. The difficulties are greater in underdeveloped countries. There are the greater risks attendant on operating processes with managers and workers who are not used to them. There is also much less knowledge of markets. There are greater possibilities of unforeseen external benefits or damage, resulting from, e.g. introducing industry or a foreign system of education into a traditional society. Investments are also, often, far less marginal to the economy, with the consequence that much complementary investment may need to be undertaken. It may be that the cost and benefit of a whole linked nexus of industrial activity, or of an integrated education system, has to be assessed. Then again, prices often do not reflect scarcities, or measure benefits, as well as they do in developed economies. Moreover, in the least developed countries, a particularly large part of investment tends to be in spheres where the quantification of benefit (though not usually of cost) is well-nigh impossible—education, health, and administration—and yet more in spheres where it is, to say the least, very difficult—e.g. road building and agriculture.

We saw, in Chapter III, that the concept of 'absorptive capacity' is often used as a criterion of the potential effectiveness of aid. In principle, it means assessing the productivity of investment. If, as we have suggested, this is often so difficult as to make the attempt practically worthless, how comes it that the concept can play any useful role?

In many of the least developed countries there is a grave shortage of people—in some they are virtually non-existent—who are capable of designing, building, or operating, projects which use substantial amounts of capital. This is the most usual reason for saying that absorptive capacity is very low. It appears that not much capital can be used before one approaches the point where schemes become so dubious that the return will probably be nil, or the money will simply fail to get spent.

This introduces the subject of technical assistance. Surely, if the immediate bottleneck to the efficient use of capital is the lack of indigenous skill, then would not comparatively small amounts of technical assistance permit large amounts of capital to be absorbed? Within limits this is true, especially of economic overheads—transport, power, water supply, etc.—and of social overheads—schools, universities, hospitals, etc. A high proportion of world aid has, in fact, flowed into such things,[1] not solely because of the need for them, but also because they are relatively easy for foreigners to undertake, and because they are usually in the field of public enterprise. Aid is given to governments, and many donors—e.g. the USA, Germany, and the IBRD—prefer not to support government enterprise in spheres where, in the Western world, private enterprise usually operates.

But the demand for power and transport depends very largely on the general development of the economy. Unless these things themselves have a marked capacity to stimulate their own demand—which is very doubtful—then productivity rapidly falls away. It is notable that power and transport tend to get relatively over-provided in the economies which have the least absorptive capacity, because donor governments find this an easy way of giving aid. In India, where lack of indigenous skills and entrepreneurship is much less of a constraint than in Africa, power and transport are recurrent bottlenecks, because there is so much else which seems worth doing: but in several African countries the overheads of power and transport have already been provided years in advance of demand.

Turn now to 'social' expenditure, and take education first. Education used to be, and often still is, treated by administrators as a consumption good. Investment in education was in buildings, which were thought of as analogous to consumption-good factories. The salaries of teachers were analogous to the current expenses of output, which was the education enjoyed by the pupils. Thus no conceptual recognition was accorded to the fact that educated people are more productive than uneducated—enormously more productive if the education is well adapted to the skills required in the economy. If education is planned to produce needed skills, then the final output of education is not learning for its own sake, but the increased output

[1] Probably around two-thirds of project aid: see *Financing for an Expansion of International Trade*, UNCTAD, E/CONF, 46/9 Geneva, 1964, Table 22.

consequent on a better and more appropriately educated population. Now the essence of capital expenditure is merely that some or all of the output occurs at a significantly later date than the input. Consequently, the changeover from a conception of education as supplying a demand for learning for its own sake, to a conception of it as creating the skills necessary for economic development, implies that all the educational expenditure required for development is investment, or capital expenditure. Equally, its conventional classification as 'social' rather than 'economic' is misleading, except where all education is of a kind which contributes nothing to the productive capacity of those educated.

If the capacity of a country to absorb capital to produce more final goods and services is severely limited by the knowledge and skill of the population, it follows that it has a prior and urgent need for investment in education (including, as we have seen, recurrent expenditure). We here use the word 'education' in the broadest sense, to include, for instance, agricultural extension; and the inculcation of trade and white-collar skills, and administrative know-how. But here too the possibilities of useful expenditure may be severely limited, because of a lack of teachers. For essentially technical reasons—the number of pupils which already existing teachers can efficiently handle, and the speed of learning—there are limits to the rate at which education can be expanded. In the meantime, it is useless to spend money on buildings and equipment when sufficient staff and pupils do not exist. It is another sign of lack of absorptive capacity, when investment in buildings proceeds ahead of the quantity and quality of their occupants. In these circumstances, of course, the supply of teachers, and extension workers of all kinds, from abroad, has top priority. But one should note at this point, that in some fields of education—most notably agriculture—there may also be limits set by the fact that neither foreigners nor natives always know what to teach, nor whether, for cultural or economic reasons which are difficult to alter, teaching will have much effect.

Much the same considerations apply to expenditure on health, except that it cannot be treated like education as an investment in increasing the future *per capita* output of the economy. It is all too likely, with its effects on population growth, to be counter-productive in this sense, despite the fact that a healthy man is a better worker. At the same time, it has to be remembered that the ultimate object of expenditure is consumption, and that health is a most important consumption good, in the provision of which moral considerations are often dominant. Recipient governments, which are keen on development, will probably not spend more on health than seems to be politically wise in the face of popular demand. Clearly donors cannot refuse to give either technical assistance, or capital aid, in this field. But, as with education, the rate of growth of health facilities and preventive medicine is limited primarily by the difficulties of securing a rapid expansion of trained people.

For such reasons as these the productivity of capital in providing social and economic overheads tends to be sharply reduced, and may even fall to zero, when a certain point is reached. We turn now to the most important of the final productive sectors, agriculture.

It is by now very widely agreed that increasing agricultural output has a high priority for development. But this has only recently been the case. A few years ago, industrialization was regarded as almost synonymous with development: and suggestions to the contrary were treated as old-fashioned and right-wing, even imperialistic. This is still true of some African thinking. It was thought that reducing the agricultural population was a high priority. Now it is realized that, starting from a usually very small industrial and commercial base, there is no possibility of creating enough non-agricultural employment to absorb the rapid rise of population. Secondly, food needs are rising fast, and even if enough food can be imported this will limit the country's ability to buy capital goods. Thirdly, in many underdeveloped countries agricultural output is over half the national income, and accounts for two-thirds or more of employment, while much of the output and employment in the service sectors is itself dependent on agriculture: this alone should make it obvious that rapid growth in general is impossible without a rapid growth in agricultural and other rural incomes.

Nevertheless, only about 12 per cent of world project aid has been for agriculture.[1] There are many reasons for this neglect, apart from the lack, until recently, of adequate realization of the need on the part of both donor and recipient governments. Much of the expenditure needed is current expenditure, and also has little import content. These are two bad reasons for neglect which will be discussed below.[2] They do not indicate lack of absorptive capacity. But it is also true that it is often difficult to spend much money effectively on agriculture and rural development. There are, as in other fields, far too few trained people to expand agricultural education and extension rapidly and successfully. Other schemes, such as credit extension, often require close and detailed administration which is very difficult

[1] ibid.
[2] Chapter II, p. 71 and Table XIV.

for donors to manage, and which also suffers from lack of trained people. Land-tenure systems are also often almost prohibitive obstacles both to improving the land itself, and to the formation of capital-intensive farms or plantations. In fact, most schemes for agricultural improvement have been failures. This is probably especially true of aid schemes in independent countries. The British, for instance, had some notable successes in the colonies—most notably of all, the Gezira Scheme in the Sudan.[1] With such difficulties in the way of more 'grassroots' agricultural development, difficulties which are especially great for foreign donors to overcome, it is not surprising that much of the 10 per cent of aid for agriculture has been for irrigation, which is itself more of an economic over- head than a directly productive investment. It is unfortunately notorious that much of the capital for irrigation has been wasted, and has had little effect on output (though we do not know whether this has been as true of foreign-aided irrigation projects). Either land-tenure has been unsuitable for irrigated farming, or the farmers have been unwilling to change, or have received insufficient help to enable them to make the radical changes in methods which are required. Sometimes too, canals have leaked, or there was inadequate drainage, with resultant loss of land through salinity.[2]

Finally, let us consider industry. Here the limits to expansion are of two quite different kinds: (1) lack of skills, and (2) the small size of the market. Lack of skill includes entrepreneurial ability and know- ledge, managerial ability at all levels, and of course technical and trade skills. This dearth is very variable as between countries. Some, like Brazil, Mexico, and India, have a considerable stock of indigenous managers, accountants, engineers, etc., whereas in most African and some Asian countries such people are almost non-existent. Technical assistance can help to overcome this handicap, especially in public industry. But a limit is often set to technical assistance by political demands for jobs for indigenous personnel, however inexperienced. Domestically owned but foreign-managed industry has not always been a harmonious combination. Foreign-owned and foreign- managed industrial investment is still the main form of industrializa- tion in many of the least developed countries. It can and does also play a significant part in countries where most industry is nevertheless domestically owned, e.g. India. The limits here are the willingness of

[1] For a history of the scheme see A. Gaitskell, *Gezira, A Story of Development in the Sudan*, Faber & Faber, 1959.
[2] See, e.g. Hirschman, op. cit., Chapter I; H. Ruthenberg, *Agricultural Development in Tanganyika*, Springer-Verlag, 1964, pp. 94–5.

foreigners to risk money in what are sometimes politically difficult countries in which to operate; the willingness of the recipient government to accept foreign enterprise, or private enterprise at all in certain fields (this is operative in India, and many other countries); and, as with all industry, by the size of the market.

Many of the underdeveloped countries are far too small ever to be able to support much industry on an economic scale, and also lack the great wealth of natural resources which can compensate for this, such as oil and ski-slopes. Manufacture for export is a possibility, but it is not easy to break into world-markets, even in the absence of protection in the wealthy countries. Regional development and common-markets, and federation, are obvious ways of trying to alleviate this condition. But the successful negotiation of such agreements is not easy, especially in the face of various vested interests, both economic and political, which may be opposed to them. But, again, this factor is highly variable as between countries. India is already a large enough market for most things to be producible on an economic scale, despite its poverty. It is more a problem of the number of countries in the underdeveloped world which have poor prospects of beneficial industrialization, than of the amount of population concentrated in these countries. More than 50 per cent of the population of the independent non-Communist underdeveloped world is in countries with over 40 million people. But 95 per cent of the independent countries have less than 40 million, and 82 per cent of them less than 20 million.[1]

So much for our cursory discussion of absorptive capacity. But sufficient has been said to show that it is an important concept which has some applicability. Very broadly speaking, small countries with a low level of indigenous skills and poor natural resources can absorb little capital per head for effective development before it becomes, so far as one can foresee, almost a complete waste. Technical assistance can mitigate this. For the sake of the poorest countries, there should certainly be much emphasis on technical assistance. Nevertheless, technical assistance is itself subject to difficulties of absorption.

On the other hand, countries with a high level of indigenous skills, with large markets, good natural resources, and willing enough to accept technical assistance (which they can more easily absorb, simply because imported skills are of relatively less importance), may be able to absorb large quantities of capital per head for development. We shall discuss the actual distribution of aid per head in Chapter X. But we may briefly anticipate ourselves here to say that, in fact, many

[1] See also Chapter IV.

small countries of low absorptive capacity get much more aid per head than those with more immediate promise. This is partly because many small poor countries get a lot of aid which is not for development, but just to keep them going at the existing level. The overheads of government, of law and order, etc., are excessively high per head in very small poor countries. It is also partly because a country is a country; which, however small, has a vote in the UN; and may be a member of the French Franc Area.

The problems which the governments of many poor countries have set themselves are enormous. Little is known about the springs of economic progress. We know that progress requires capital. But more capital is no guarantee of progress, let alone orderly and peaceful progress. Economic progress requires changes in institutions, laws, customs, and ways of thinking: it may require the elimination of tribal rivalry and caste divisions; or even the giving up of some newly won sovereignty. The governments of almost all developing countries are thus beset with political problems. They are, at once, faced with powerful demands for economic progress, and often with a deep reluctance to make the changes which progress requires. It is not surprising that large-scale industry, and prestige projects, which do least to interfere with basic attitudes and customs, and directly affect few people, are so popular. Nevertheless if they do not risk far-reaching and deep reforms, development may prove illusory; and such development as there is may fail to touch the mass of the people. But radical reformers may find themselves also in grave difficulties. There can be little doubt that the fully dictatorial system, where the ruler or rulers can rely on a loyal army, starts with a powerful advantage.

Many of the governments have to try to cope with these problems with grossly inadequate means at their disposal, both in skilled men and in material and financial resources. Without the men, the analysis of their problems, planning to overcome them, and implementing the plans, will be gravely deficient. Even the ordinary 'night-watchman' functions of government cannot everywhere be fulfilled. On the other hand, continued reliance on foreigners, except in the form of relatively ineffective supervisory experts and advisers, is politically very difficult. For many of them, the demand for progress, and the population explosion, have come before a sufficient educational and organizational basis was laid to cope with these problems. Even where this has not been so, the political, social, and cultural, problems to be faced, would often be more than enough for the best possible administration. In such circumstances, and where there is no thriving entrepreneurial-minded private sector, the ability to make good use of financial resources may be very circumscribed.

In such circumstances, the people, and governments, of the developed countries which hope to see the capital flow they encourage, and the aid they give, result in economic development must plainly be sympathetic and very patient. It is a mistake to expect too much, especially by way of efficient and politically ruthless development planning. At the same time, it is foolish not to be realistic. Donor countries will not do much good for development if they give to countries whose governments are either inadequately determined to promote change and development, or are quite incompetent to do so, unless they themselves have a sufficiently good knowledge of the economic requirements, and the socio-political background of the country, and sufficiently good political relations with it, to be able to ensure that aid is well used. On the other hand, if donor powers are really keen on economic development, they should give very freely to those reforming governments which are reasonably on top of their job.

3. SAVINGS, AND THE BALANCE OF PAYMENTS

A country which could use more capital, at a reasonable productive level, may still find that more rapid growth is inhibited by failure or inability to save more. Various writers have thus expressed the need for aid as the difference between absorptive capacity and some reasonable savings level, taking the poverty of the country into account.[1] For this purpose absorptive capacity has to be defined as the amount of capital a country can absorb per annum before its productivity falls to some agreed figure—zero or above. Agreement on such a figure is not easy; nor, as we have seen, may it be easy to assess absorptive capacity having agreed the figure. It is probably easiest in the case of very primitive economies where there may be almost a kink in the productivity curve; that is, productivity beyond a certain level of investment falls rapidly to zero.

Nor is it easy to say what a reasonable savings level is. To speak in terms of 'reasonable', implies that the government can control the overall level of savings, varying its own level of savings or dissavings,

[1] Max F. Millikan and Walt W. Rostow, *A Proposal: Key to an Effective Foreign Policy*, Harper and Brothers, 1957; B. Higgins, *UN and US Foreign Economic Policy*, Richard D. Irwin Inc. 1962; P. N. Rosenstein-Rodan, 'International Aid for Underdeveloped Countries', *Review of Economics and Statistics*, May 1961.

by adjusting either current expenditure[1] or taxation levels.[2] So far
as current expenditure is concerned, much is, of course, as essential to
development as is investment, e.g. justice, police, etc. One can only
expect such expenditure to be 'balanced', and not wasteful. Higher
taxation normally increases savings, provided it is not imposed merely
to finance higher public current expenditure; because, when private
incomes are reduced by taxation, private savings are not reduced by
as much. In other words, taxation can be used to reduce, or lower the
rate of increase of, private consumption. But clearly the level of taxation is a tricky political matter. In many underdeveloped countries
one finds that taxation of the relatively wealthy, especially in the
middle ranges, is low: but advocacy of higher tax rates may have to
be tempered by consideration for the political difficulties of the
government. Also, there are the real economic difficulties; that high
taxation tends to discourage the import of foreign skills and capital,
and may drive away a country's own skilled nationals and capital;
that taxation is hard to collect with an underdeveloped administration, and corruption has to be reckoned with; that controls over
capital flight or emigration are also difficult to enforce, and may be
regarded as undesirable.

While the size of the gap between absorptive and savings capacity
is hard to assess, and its estimation requires wide economic and
political judgment, there is no doubt that such a gap exists in at least
the great majority of underdeveloped countries. This is only to say
that some aid is useful.

We must consider next how the above concept of aid, as an adjunct
to savings, fits in with the common view that the purpose of aid is to
cover balance of payments deficits when a country has reduced its
own reserves of foreign currency to a minimum. Balance of payments
trouble has often been the immediate reason for an extension of aid
to a country—for example, India in 1957–8.

Now if a country can and does invest more than it saves, this
necessarily shows up as a foreign payments deficit. That is mere
arithmetic. Furthermore, the fact that transfers of capital from abroad
are intended to finance otherwise adverse balance of payments
positions, implies no more than that donors will not generally give to
countries for the purpose of increasing their reserves. But the pre-

[1] We have already noted that current expenditure usually includes some expenditure that is really investment. We are assuming that the division between
'investment' and 'current' expenditure has been, as well as possible, made on
economic grounds.
[2] There are other possible means of influence, but these are the most important.

sence of a foreign payments deficit is no proof that a country needs aid, for the accompanying excess of domestic investment over savings may not be a sign of high absorptive capacity and low savings potential at all: it can arise for a variety of quite different reasons. Equally, the absence of a foreign payments deficit is no indication that a country does not need aid. Its foreign account may balance merely because it does not try to force investment above the level of savings, and either stagnates or has a growth rate below that which could be achieved if the productivity of capital were the operative restraint.

Also, a poor country may have a monetary system which does not permit a balance of payments deficit to exist, or not for long. This was the case with British colonies where the currency-board system automatically produced a monetary deflation sufficiently severe to cure any deficit. A number of underdeveloped countries have not created central banks for themselves, so that the government has no power to borrow from the central bank, and an actual shortage of cash in the treasury can limit expenditure. In such countries, especially those where public investment is a major part of total investment, an inadequacy of savings relative to absorptive capacity shows up as an inability of the government to tax or borrow enough to finance the investments it would like to carry out. Although most of the new countries in Africa, where the currency-board system still lingers, are conservative in financial matters, nevertheless this system is not likely to last for long. As soon as a government takes full control over its own monetary system, it can quickly turn a shortage of savings into a balance of payments deficit. If it then deals with this deficit by import controls, it will find itself in the position of forcing up the domestic savings rate, by inflation, to the level determined by its own increased expenditure.

The above account suggests that a balance of payments deficit is nothing more nor less than the reflection of a deficiency of savings. This is necessarily true, *ex post*, as a matter of accountancy. But is there a causal connection such that an increase in savings will always result in a fall in the foreign exchange deficit? Furthermore, can we say that the need for aid is always to supplement savings, and that a balance of payments deficit (or inflation) is no more than a symptom?

The answers to these questions are in the negative. It is true that if the production of a country remains unchanged, then an increase in savings, with unchanged domestic investment, must improve the balance of payments by a like amount (this is the essence of what is called the 'absorption' approach to balance of payments problems). But, with a given exchange rate, one does not expect a reduction in domestic demand to be fully matched by the sum of any resultant reduction in imports and increase in exports. Some fall in domestic output is certain. However, there is nothing sacrosanct about exchange rates. So we must ask whether a country can, given the optimum exchange rate from the point of view of the balance, have a balance of payments deficit which is not merely symptomatic of a savings deficiency (in the sense that the level of domestic savings is less than a level of desirable investment, having regard to the productivity of investment and the need for growth). To answer this we must consider a country which, in the light of its wealth and its administration, could be reasonably expected to save enough for the investment programme deemed desirable. But it has a balance of payments deficit. Can this deficit be cured without compromising its investment programme or its current production? In short, does it need aid for imports, though not as an adjunct to savings?

First, suppose the country has a narrow range of exports, mostly materials, such that the world demand for its exports is inelastic for a fall in the exchange rate, and elastic for a rise. Alternatively the curve could be of unit elasticity. Then, whatever it does about reducing home demand, or changing the exchange rate, there is a maximum amount of foreign exchange which it can earn. So far so good. But we must also show that imports cannot be sufficiently reduced. Now, more savings, i.e. a reduction in domestic demand, will certainly reduce imports of consumption goods: but it will also reduce domestic output unless the exchange rate can be changed so as to ensure that this otherwise excess capacity is taken up by producing substitutes for the reduced imports, or by producing a greater volume of exports. If export demand is inelastic, this would also have the effect of reducing its foreign currency earnings. Nevertheless, provided export earnings remain sufficient to buy the imports of materials and components required for its own factories, it is theoretically possible, by a suitable combination of exchange rates and savings, and possibly controls over consumption good imports, to divert almost all consumption demand to indigenous output.

This might, of course, be a drastic business, which no one would really want to impose. Although, in theory, the investment programme could be financed, it might imply such a wrench for the erstwhile consumers of imports as to cause a revolution, which might not be favourable to the development of the country. But we need not rely on revolution to prove our point. For it may be that the maximum foreign exchange earnings of a country are insufficient to pay for both the imports required for the investment programme and for the materials and components needed to use its capacity (these latter are sometimes called 'maintenance' imports). Can, in such a case, anyone deny that aid is needed for balance of payments' reasons quite distinct from the need for aid as an adjunct to savings? Yes, the sceptic can advance one more argument.

It can be argued that, even in the unlikely circumstances described above, free-exchange rates combined with the right amount of domestic demand would nevertheless permit any desired level of domestic investment: and that the above example introduced an unnecessary and unrealistic rigidity in that it was assumed that some fixed part of domestic investment had to consist of imports. This argument is valid: it implies merely that the more expensive in terms of domestic resources is foreign exchange the lower will and should be the foreign exchange component in investment. But it ignores the possible change in the productivity of the investment programme consequent on a lowering of its import component.

Thus the counter-argument is that in a country which lacks the skill and the equipment needed to build machinery and large and complicated structures, an investment programme with a low foreign exchange component would have to consist largely of simple buildings and public works, executed mainly by men and women working with baskets and shovels, and that such investment would have too low a productivity for it to be worthwhile to make the savings required to finance it. Thus a foreign exchange shortage may reduce the productivity of investment, and reduce savings. Or, to put it in another way, imported capital may be more productive than domestic capital. Alternatively, even if some labour-intensive investment is worthwhile, a country may be capable of carrying out so much import-intensive investment as well, saving enough for both, that a foreign-exchange bottleneck still results. There is, in fact, a limit to the extent to which the import-component of investment can be reduced.

The above seems to be the essence of what is meant by saying that underdeveloped countries are faced with a structural problem.[1] It may all seem a little far-fetched. So let us illustrate with the actual

[1] The reference is to what is called the 'structural school' of Latin-American economists. The arguments about structuralism have arisen more in the context of explaining Latin American inflation, than in the context of the need for aid. For a brief account see D. Seers, 'A Theory of Inflation and Growth in Underdeveloped Economies Based on the Experience of Latin America', *Oxford Economic Papers*, June 1962. The argument that India has a structural balance of payments problem, was advanced by I. M. D. Little in 'The Strategy of Indian Development', *National Institute Economic Review*, May 1960, although the term was not used.

case of India. India's foreign-exchange earnings are so low as to be barely sufficient to pay for the materials and components needed to keep in full operation the already established capacity to produce, plus a very small element of consumption goods imports (excluding those which are 'aid', i.e. PL 480 imports from the USA). Thus she could buy virtually no foreign machinery, nor pay for foreign experts, if it were not for aid. At the same time her own capital goods industries are quite inadequate to make the equipment needed. Now, admittedly, one of the present authors has argued that India's investment programme should contain a much larger element of investment in land improvement (drainage, small-scale irrigation, local roads, levelling and contour-bunding, etc.) which can be effected very largely by hand (using indigenous materials themselves very largely obtained by hand), and would reduce the proportion of foreign plant and machinery in her investment programme.[1] It is possible that such investment would not be very productive, but this consideration is offset by the fact that its real costs would, in view of the excess supply of labour, be very low. But it was argued that such investment should be *additional* to the existing programme, and that India could, though not easily, find the additional savings required, If this is true, then given that India could not greatly increase her export earnings by devaluation, it follows that she needs aid for balance of payments reasons over and above that needed for savings reasons. This is not the place for an analysis of India's exports, but no observer suggests that devaluation could effect such a transformation[2] (this is not to say that devaluation would be a bad thing). While India is the most obvious example, there are probably other countries where the foreign exchange constraint bites before the savings constraint. These may include Argentina, Colombia, and Brazil.

A 'structural' balance of payments problem does not arise in developed economies which export mainly manufactures of a wide variety, for the condition of a low elasticity of export demand is then most unlikely to arise. Furthermore, most developed countries import a considerable proportion of consumer goods which are in relatively elastic demand. Moreover, they are generally capable of making a high proportion of investment goods at home. But it can arise in underdeveloped economies, where one is trying to accelerate

[1] Little, ibid.
[2] See G. D. A. MacDougall, 'India's Balance of Payments', *Bulletin of the Oxford University Institute of Economics and Statistics*, May 1961. Manmohan Singh, *India's Export Trends and the Prospects for Self-sustained Growth*, Oxford University Press, 1964, Chapter XIV.

growth by rapidly raising the level of investment when there is no, or only a very small, domestic investment-good industry. It is probably most likely to arise when a country has emerged from the most primitive stage in which absorptive capacity is low, and in which much of the most needed investment such as buildings, roads, and education, does not need to have a very high import content; but before industrialization is so advanced that investment goods' output and manufactured exports have become adequate.

Thus it is by no means generally true that the problem of under-developed countries is primarily one of foreign exchange. For instance, in most of the countries in Africa, exports would be enough to pay for materials and the essential import component of such investment as can be absorbed, provided savings were enough. The deficiency of savings is then the sole reason for giving aid. Indeed, several African governments, those which have not instituted central banks and taken powers to borrow from them, cannot find the money for the domestic currency component of investments the import component of which has been covered by aid.[1] This does not prove that savings are deficient, since it is possible that further monetary expansion than is at present constitutionally permitted would result in a non-inflationary expansion of output and income, which would itself produce the required increase in saving. But this is unlikely, and the basic deficiency in many such countries is savings rather than foreign exchange. There are also, of course, the countries which are lucky in having primary product exports for which the demand grows rapidly—the oil-producers being the most notable examples.

This question of whether the basic development bottleneck is, after taking absorptive capacity into account, savings or foreign exchange has been discussed at length because its implications are important. There are some who argue that trade is more important than aid: and even go so far as to say that if the developed countries did not protect against the underdeveloped then nothing more than a little technical assistance would be necessary. This is absurd. It is clear that most of the poor countries cannot reasonably be expected to save enough to finance all the investment which is feasible and would contribute significantly to growth. Even those few countries where the primary bottleneck is at present foreign exchange, in the sense that they could save more but cannot invest more without more foreign exchange, are already in receipt of aid and would certainly have a savings problem if this were not so.

[1] For a more extended discussion of what is known as the 'home cost' problem, see Little, *Aid to Africa*, Chapter V.

The structural problem should, with reasonably good planning (including regional planning and trade) on the part of recipients, and liberal trade policies on the part of donors, disappear much more rapidly than the problem of poverty, which is the basic reason for a deficiency of savings. Nevertheless, it has of recent years received more emphasis, largely because of the rather unfavourable changes in the terms of trade for most underdeveloped countries in the last decade. This emphasis, fathered by Dr Prebisch, then Secretary-General of the Economic Commission for Latin America (ECLA), culminated in the UNCTAD of 1964. We turn, therefore, to the trade problems of the poor countries.

CHAPTER VI

TRADE AND AID

---

1. LONG-RUN PROBLEMS

From 1928 to 1961, exports of primary products grew slowly relative to total world output, by 1·4 per cent per annum against 2·7 per cent per annum. This was due to a number of well-discussed factors. First, production of primary goods grew more slowly than total production, by 1·7 per cent per annum. The main causes of this have been the growth of synthetics and the fall in the raw material content of final output. Secondly, exports of primary products grew more slowly than their production, as a result of increased self-sufficiency in the rich countries, this in turn being the result of technological advances and protectionism. Since the poor countries in the aggregate export almost entirely primary products, this has meant a very slow growth of world demand for their exports, aggravated by the fact that the primary product exports of the rich countries themselves grew relatively fast.

In the more recent period 1950–61, primary production (excluding oil) has grown much more rapidly at 4·6 per cent per annum. This rapid growth is probably because the base year was still one when shortages of both food and materials were still in evidence. Nevertheless, the exports of the poor countries grew by considerably less (3·6 per cent per annum), despite the very rapid increase in oil exports. Without oil, the growth of their exports was only 1·9 per cent per annum.[1] In this period, apart from oil, the industrial countries (North America, Western Europe, and Japan) increased their exports of both food and industrial materials far faster than the primary producing countries. For instance, from 1953–60 the industrial countries increased their exports of food and materials by 44 per cent and 71 per cent respectively, against corresponding figures of 10 per cent and 24 per cent for primary producing countries.[2] Those ex-

[1] Source of above figures: *Towards a new trade policy for development*, Report of the Secretary-General of UNCTAD.
[2] *International Trade 1961*, GATT. Geneva, 1962.

ports from the USA, which were financed under PL 480, accounted for only 11 per cent of the increase in industrial countries' exports of primary commodities. But the primary producers include the rich countries, Australia and New Zealand. The poor countries did much better, increasing the volume of exports by 48 per cent between 1953–4 and 1960–1, i.e. by 5¾ per cent per annum.[1] That the poor countries' exports in this period did not grow even faster has not been due solely to a slow growth of world demand for primary products, or even to a slow growth of demand for imports of primary products. It has also been due to the competitiveness of exports of primary products by some of the rich countries, to a rapid growth of internal demand in the underdeveloped countries themselves, and in some cases to slow growth of output.[2]

The behaviour of the terms of trade of the underdeveloped countries over a very long period is uncertain, and whether or not they have deteriorated is controversial. But there is less doubt that they have deteriorated in recent years. Dr Prebisch puts the deterioration at 17 per cent from 1950–61, about three-quarters of the resultant loss of earnings being concentrated in Latin America,[3] the absolute figures being $13·1 billion for the whole underdeveloped world, and $10·1 billion for Latin America (the fall in coffee prices was the main reason why Latin America suffered so badly). Of course, 1950 was almost the peak for the terms of trade between primary products and manufactures, and there has also been a significant recovery in primary product prices in 1963 and 1964. So, a choice of different years, say 1953–64, would not show nearly such a large decline.[4]

As already stated, it is not clear that there is a long-run tendency for the terms of trade to move against primary producers. They were, for instance, the same in 1961 as in 1923. Since this book is about aid, not trade, we cannot here discuss the question whether there are good theoretical reasons for supposing that a long-run trend towards deterioration has now been established. Two remarks must suffice. First, in the long run, prices are much less important than volumes:

[1] cf. Bela Balassa, *Trade Prospects for Developing Countries*, Yale University Press, 1964, p. 10.
[2] For the influence of some of these factors on India's exports see Manmohan Singh, op. cit., Chapter II.
[3] op. cit.
[4] For a very full and recent account of both volume and price trends see Professor Bela Balassa, op. cit. Comparing 1960–1 with 1953–4 Professor Balassa estimates that the value of exports of poor countries rose by 36 per cent, with a fall in unit value of 8 per cent. For these seven years the value of exports thus rose at an annual rate of 4·4 per cent per annum.

it is vastly unlikely that the long-run relative price trend between primary and manufacturing production could be as high as 1 per cent per annum; thus fluctuations in the aggregate terms of trade are more important than trends, and this has implications for aid policy as we shall see below. Secondly, it is most misleading to aggregate the underdeveloped world. The major part of a fluctuation in the terms of trade may be due to relatively few commodities which are of major importance to only a few countries. We further deal with the problem of fluctuations below. Here it may be noted that a particular country can suffer for quite a long time; there is more risk that a particular commodity suffers a secular decline in demand and price than that commodities in the aggregate do.

The slow rise of the total value of the exports of the underdeveloped countries from 1950 to 1961 has given rise to some alarming estimates of the size of the balance of payments gap which will emerge. The most well known is the gap of $20 billion which the UNCTAD Secretariat suggested would emerge by 1970 if the underdeveloped countries were to grow at an average rate of 5 per cent from 1960–70. Leaving aside the validity of this estimate, it is almost certain that some increasing gap must emerge from any extrapolation of past trends.[1] We have seen that the volume of exports of the underdeveloped world grew at 3·6 per cent in the 1950s. During the same period its domestic product grew at 4·4 per cent, and its imports at 4·6 per cent. The difference between the 4·6 per cent and the 3·6 per cent was financed partly by aid, and partly by a loss of reserves which cannot now continue (these being partly offset by the deterioration of the terms of trade).

The theory which has emerged from contemplation of such figures, and for more general reasons, is that for many years, until indeed they are much more industrialized and can export manufactures on a large scale, the poor countries cannot hope to increase their exports as fast as one would wish to see their production increase (which is, at the very least, the 5 per cent postulated in the UN Development Decade). At the same time, it is held that even recent rates of development cannot be maintained without imports increasing faster than production, because of the need for imported capital goods to speed the development of the manufactures in which lies the only long-run hope of either expanding exports as fast or faster than the national income, or of getting the rate of increase of imports down to, or below, the rate of increase of production. Therefore, an increasing gap is inevitable for many years if satisfactory growth is to be achieved.

[1] cf. Balassa, ibid.

Is this theory valid, and does it constitute an argument primarily for more trade, or for more aid? How are trade and aid linked? The answers depend on three further questions. (1) How much can exports be expanded? (2) Can growth be maintained or accelerated with a lower rate of growth of imports? (3) Can the poor countries save enough to permit the amelioration in their position which might otherwise come from an improvement in the demand for their exports, or from a reduction in the demand for imports arising from an import-saving pattern of development? These three questions are much too difficult for any firm answer to be given. One can only indicate some of the relevant considerations.

Take exports. Ignoring the terms of trade, it is very difficult to believe that the growth of exports of primary commodities, however favourable the trading policies of the rich countries, will not lag behind a desirable growth of total production in the underdeveloped world. This is not to say that the position could not, and will not, be considerably improved. Some part of the reason for poor performance has been a failure to increase production or productivity. A large number of poor countries are, after all, net importers of food—and food imports have been rising. Thus growth itself, and also more savings, would have improved the position. To this extent it can be said that it is aid, not trade, that is needed. Furthermore, a more rapid growth of foreign demand for their principal exports would not have permitted most poor countries to raise their imports of capital goods by anything like the amount of the improvement in their receipts. Consumption would also have increased. Again, to this extent, it is more savings or more aid that is needed.

Nevertheless, taking account of the fact that the use of primary products by the rich countries may not grow as fast in relation to total output as in the 1950s, and that the rapid growth in the productivity of the rich countries' own primary production may well continue, it would seem highly unlikely that the growth of primary product exports from poor countries can increase by as much as 5 per cent per annum, from, say, 1960 to 1975. It is still highly unlikely even given the most favourable assumptions about the rich countries' policies and their rate of growth, and about the growth of productivity and production in the poor countries.[1] What hope is there for the problem to be solved by exports of manufactures? That no large

[1] Professor Bela Balassa estimates a rate of increase of 4·6 per cent per annum from 1960–70, given target rates of growth of income in the rich countries. On 'most likely' income growth assumptions, and allowing for some deterioration in the terms of trade, this reduces to 3·2 per cent (ibid., p. 44).

impact can be made for many years follows from the fact that, in 1960, exports of manufactures accounted for only 5½ per cent of the total exports of the poor countries to the rich countries.

This brings us to the subject of imports, because to date the growth of manufacturing in poor countries has been based far more upon import-substitution, that is manufacture for the home market, than it has been based upon exports. Only Japan and Hong Kong seem to be exceptions to this rule. Part causes of this have been the protectionist policies of the rich countries, and the natural difficulties of breaking into the latters' increasingly sophisticated markets. That there has also been very little trade in manufactures between the poor countries themselves is partly because of the protection which has been required to develop manufactures at all. The inhibiting effects of this on mutual trade have not been offset by common markets, or by subsidizing exports of manufactures.[1] Indeed, intra-trade among the underdeveloped countries has actually declined in relative importance in the last decade.[2]

It has been argued that the scope for import substitution is now more circumscribed than it was, and that exports must henceforth provide more of the stimulus to industrialization.[3] There is certainly an element of truth in this. The larger and more advanced of the poor countries already produce most of their manufactured consumption goods. India, Argentina, and Colombia, have gone furthest, and import very few manufactured final consumption goods, although semi-manufactured components of consumption goods still figure significantly. Further substitution has become more difficult and more capital-intensive. The investment required tends to have a higher import content and longer gestation periods; so that, for a more considerable time than with simpler manufactures, import-substitution actually increases imports as the required capital goods outweigh the import-saving on final products. But there are, in number, many more underdeveloped countries which have such small markets that they can go in for import-substitution even of simple manufactures only at very high cost. These constitute cases where more trade is complementary to more aid, rather than in any way a substitute for it. For more trade, both with the industrialized countries, and within the underdeveloped world, could considerably increase their absorptive capacity for capital, and would permit more useful aid.

[1] The logic of this counterpart to protective tariffs for import industries, which is contrary to GATT rules, has been little recognized.
[2] cf. Balassa, op. cit., pp. 74–6.
[3] *Towards a New Trade Policy for Development.*

The above paragraph suggests that there is a risk of circularity in the argument that foreign exchange is the major impediment to growth. Agricultural production is by far the major determinant of the growth of the underdeveloped countries. But investment in agriculture is relatively small, except in areas where irrigation plays a major part, and it is not import-intensive. So, it may be asked, 'why should it be assumed that the underdeveloped countries' imports must increase faster than their production?' The standard answer is, of course, that they have to import capital goods to industrialize rapidly. Why has it to be assumed that rapid industrialization is essential to rapid growth, when industry is, almost everywhere, a very small part of output? The circular answer is that industrialization is necessary to save imports of manufactured goods, and to expand exports, and so solve the balance of payments problem, which is caused by industrialization.

It can be argued, indeed it seems to be the truth, that the balance of payments problem of some underdeveloped countries, in so far as it does not arise as a mere reflection of the fact that they cannot save enough to finance the investment it is useful to undertake, arises from the fact that growth is concentrated too much in the small industrial sector, where it has little impact on the aggregate growth rate and adds much to the import bill, and too little on the primary sector. This, in turn, is probably due mainly to two reasons: (1) that it is very difficult to know how to stimulate agriculture, and (2) that some of the relatively more developed poor countries, with uncertain or dim export prospects, wish to make sure that they quickly acquire the industrial complex which will permit them to build their own capital goods, in view of the uncertainty as to whether capital inflows, including aid, will permit them to continue to import enough capital goods from abroad to absorb the savings which they expect to be able to make. Thus, the notion that growth must become self-sustained within a reasonably short time, say fifteen years, itself may add to their balance of payments problems within that period, and may distort the investment pattern too much in favour of capital-intensive and import-intensive industrialization. This consideration has certainly played some part in the pattern of Indian industrialization during the Second and Third Five-Year Plans.

With the import needs of growth dependent on so many factors, including the direction of growth policy in the recipient countries, it is impossible to make a valid future projection of the volume of imports needed to achieve various growth rates. Even more obviously than with exports it depends largely on savings. Even the supposedly objective projection of recent past trends can give rise to highly divergent estimates, which, moreover, naturally reflect past aid, itself partly related to past savings.[1] Finally, any balance of payments projection includes services, for which projections are particularly shaky, and can give rise to wide variations in estimates.

To sum up, we have come to the conclusion that it is wrong to base either a case for aid (or more aid), or for more liberal trade policies, on estimates of future balance of payments deficits. Let us elaborate on this a little. Quite generally, such estimates at best show only what would happen if a certain rate of growth were achieved while various policies and trends remain unchanged. But not only may it be the case that the target growth rate is unachievable without changes in policy which would upset the estimates, but also the target rate may be unachievable anyway, for lack of absorptive capacity. In practice, moreover, such estimates cannot even show a hypothetical gap with tolerable accuracy, except possibly over a very short period, because the identification of trends is a very uncertain matter, especially given that the figures themselves are no better than very rough estimates.

But let us nevertheless assume, for the sake of argument, that some estimate of the gap is not misleading, and that trade and aid are the only variables, and ask first how far trade can close the gap, and secondly whether aid can then be regarded as a residual need. Now more exports would certainly not reduce the gap to the extent of the apparent improvement, because one cannot assume that the extra savings required would be forthcoming: more imports would result. Nevertheless more trade would certainly help because an increased demand for exports of primary commodities raises national production without the need for much further investment. This is because resources in the underdeveloped countries are rather specific, and not easily transferable—indeed often not transferable at all without capital investment. Any such rise in national output will, in turn, increase savings. Thus, trade helps to reduce the need for aid, because it does part of the job of aid—i.e. it helps to raise the national income, and this in turn generates increased savings. Also, as we have seen,[2] it is possible that some countries would save more if they could import more.

As against this, in the medium run, an improvement in trade policies, particularly those which might lead to an expansion of intra-

---

[1] For instance, the UN estimate for UNCTAD gives an increase of 87 per cent between 1960 and 1970: the far more detailed estimate of Professor Balassa (op. cit., p. 81), suggests 54–61 per cent for the same projected growth rate.

[2] Chapter V, pp. 143–4.

trade among the underdeveloped countries, may increase recipient countries' absorptive capacity and so enhance the opportunities for effective aid, although this effect might be offset by the fact that greater trade in simple manufactures should lower costs and capital-output ratios. But, in the short run at least, the importance of these effects of trade should not be exaggerated. Thus, the agricultural exports of the underdeveloped countries in 1960 (and it is in agriculture that increased demand might have a favourable effect without much investment), amounted to under 6 per cent of their aggregate gross domestic product; and this may well be an overestimate, as it seems probable that the output of subsistence agriculture tends to be underestimated in the extremely shaky figures which underlie the calculation of the GDP of the underdeveloped countries.

Nevertheless, the considerations outlined above tend to imply that more trade destroys the basis on which trade gap estimates are based. Thus, if a gap of $x billion is projected, and improved trade could, say, result in increased exports of $y billion, it by no means follows that $x-y billion would be needed. Only for very short periods, during which trade and other policies could be expected to have negligible structural effects, can a balance of payments estimate be used as an estimate of aid needs. Even then, in the aggregate, this is to a large extent making a balance of payments estimate stand for an estimate of savings deficiency.

Nor does the case for improving trade policies, and enlarging the markets of the underdeveloped countries by common markets or preferences, ultimately rest on any balance of payments gap. Even if aid covered the gap, there would still be almost as strong a case for improved trade policies. Essentially, they are ways of helping to increase the growth of the underdeveloped countries: first, by improving the demand for primary products produced by non-transferable resources, and secondly by enlarging the market for exportable manufactures, thus making more economic production of relatively labour intensive goods more practicable. In the end such policies would reduce the need for aid, just because they would help growth. Moreover, the developed countries would help themselves in the process. But, in the short run, trade is only to a small extent a substitute for aid.

Finally, the aggregation implied in forecasts of the balance of payments deficits of the underdeveloped world, hides enormous differences in the situation of particular countries. In some, export trends of primary products are highly unfavourable, and the stimulation of primary production very difficult, and further import substitution costly in imported capital. These are the countries where foreign exchange may be the primary bottleneck. But, in some others, exports are already the leading factor of growth. Some even have more foreign earnings than they can usefully employ domestically. In many others savings, or the ability to use capital, are the bottlenecks.

We believe that the above discussion strongly implies that the proper way of making any quantitative aid estimate (and we attempt a very crude impressionistic estimate in Chapter X below) is via a country by country estimate of the gap between absorptive capacity and savings. Admittedly, in those countries where a shortage of foreign exchange seems the prior bottleneck, the productivity of both investment and savings may be affected (see Chapter V, pp. 143–4 above). But this can be allowed for.

2. FLUCTUATIONS

We turn now to the problem of fluctuations. We can treat this only very briefly, repeating the excuse that this is a book about aid, not trade.

Although instability of real export earnings is by no means confined to the underdeveloped world, it is more severe than for the rich countries.[1] Since quantities and prices are almost inextricably bound together, it is impossible to say that the cause of the instability is fluctuating prices, or terms of trade. Indeed, quantities exported showed slightly greater instability than prices in the period 1946–58.[2] Nor can one easily segregate, certainly not in the aggregate, the effects of variations in supply and demand. Furthermore, it is not a problem which should be treated in the aggregate, for it is certainly not true that all poor countries have particularly unstable exports. 'Australia, Finland and France, for example, have much greater export fluctuations than Brazil, Ceylon or Panama.'[3] It would seem that the likelihood of a particularly damaging effect is at its greatest when exports are concentrated on a few products which are particularly liable to price fluctuation, and when exports are large relative to GDP.[4] In such circumstances, planning for growth may be

[1] See J. D. Coppock, *International Economic Instability*, McGraw-Hill, 1962, and MacBean, op. cit.

[2] Coppock, ibid., quoted in MacBean, ibid., p. 324.

[3] MacBean, ibid., p. 324.

[4] We say this despite the fact that statistical investigation has shown a lack of significant correlation between indices of export concentration and instability. See MacBean, ibid., pp. 329–30, and for further references. Despite this, it would seem to us that the kind of country described in the text undeniably faces greater risks than other countries where foreign trade is less important and more diversified.

severely disrupted. Of course, this disruption can be avoided if sufficiently large reserves are kept, but for the countries most seriously affected they would have to be very large, and rather few underdeveloped countries are cautious and pessimistic enough to keep very large reserves (Israel, Spain, Taiwan, Ethiopia, Burma, Thailand, Sudan, Nigeria, and Malaya, were exceptions in 1962 with reserves equal to more than six months' imports), and it is difficult to blame them for this. Countries which appear to be specially vulnerable include Zambia (copper), Gambia (groundnuts), Senegal (groundnuts), Cuba (sugar), and Colombia (coffee). These all had 70 per cent or more of their 1962 exports accounted for by one potentially vulnerable commodity. Another sixteen countries had between 50 per cent and 70 per cent of their exports concentrated on one product. The commodities whose behaviour can be most upsetting for underdeveloped countries, by virtue of their importance and instability, include copper, tin, groundnuts, sugar, cocoa, timber, rice, bananas, cotton, tea, rubber, and jute. Coffee alone is the principal export of nine of the countries with export concentration exceeding 50 per cent. Coffee is next to oil in importance in international trade and it has been one of the main sources of instability in recent years. Between 1955 and 1962 nine countries suffered a decline in export proceeds of more than 20 per cent during some part of the period, and seventeen countries a decline of over 10 per cent.[1]

The question we must ask and answer is what are the proper roles of trade and aid in dealing with this problem of instability. There are two basic approaches, (1) the commodity or trade approach—smoothing out price and quantity fluctuations by trade policies which operate on the effective demand and supply of particular commodities, and (2) the country or compensation approach—varying the flow of financial resources to compensate for fluctuations in trade receipts. It is also possible to combine the two, and have compensatory financial arrangements based on a particular commodity.

Commodity agreements have a prima facie superiority because reasonable stability of prices is desirable for more reasons than stabilizing the export earnings of primary producing countries.[2] On the other hand, depending on their nature, they may have the disad-

[1] Uruguay, Bolivia, Sudan, Turkey, Colombia, Pakistan, Thailand, Nicaragua, and Ethiopia, over 20 per cent: Dominican Republic, Brazil, El Salvador, Costa Rica, Honduras, Ecuador, Argentina, Philippines, 10–20 per cent. Source: IBRD, *Economic Growth and External Debt*, Vol. I, 1964.
[2] Of course, excessive price stability can destabilize export proceeds.

vantage of preventing or anyway slowing down desirable changes in the production pattern, both between countries and within particular countries. Many economists favour buffer stocks, which do not interfere with the pattern of the long-run development of production. But for some commodities, like bananas, they are quite unsuitable.

It is possible to give aid through trade, via commodity agreements which deliberately maintain the long-run price of some commodities above the level that would otherwise prevail. This is not merely a matter of dealing with fluctuations (though it may do that too). It is a method of giving aid, much practised by the French, who have thus run farm-price support programmes for some members of the Franc Area, in coffee, wine, groundnuts, and other products. This system has grave disadvantages. First, it makes the distribution of aid between countries dependent on the accident of the distribution of production of those few commodities whose prices it is possible to support: the distribution of aid should be more rational than that. Secondly, unless extended to all countries which produce the product, or any closely competing product, others are harmed. Thus, Latin American and other African countries are harmed by the French support of coffee production in the Côte d'Ivoire. Thirdly, it tends seriously to distort the pattern of production and inhibit desirable long-run changes in it. Fourthly, it tends to perpetuate the concentration on one or a few export commodities. Fifthly, it is giving aid in a form in which the donor has no say over the disposal of the aid funds for development (and we have argued, and will argue strongly, that such a say is, in most recipient countries, desirable). Deficiency payments, or commodity compensation schemes, need not have the last-named disadvantage: but, in some measure at least, they suffer from the other defects.

We would thus argue that commodity agreements should not be a form of aid. They should not go beyond the point where they can be said to be ironing out fluctuations (of course, we know that in practice the distinction between a fluctuation and a more permanent adjustment cannot easily be made *ex ante*). Although it is true that resources are rather difficult to shift to alternative production in many underdeveloped countries (especially with tree crops and minerals), nevertheless aid should not be given in a form which must inhibit such shifts, or tend to perpetuate the problems to which monoculture gives rise. Nor, from the donor's point of view, should aid be given without clear development purpose. To put it bluntly, price support for an independent country may result in the aid proceeds being spent on destroyers and palaces.[1] Commodity-agreements should, therefore, be looked on as mutual assistance projects. On the other hand, while we think that the rich countries should try to see that they are not incurring subsidies, they should hardly insist on a strong chance that they themselves will gain.

Is there then a role left for aid in dealing with fluctuations? The answer is 'Yes', for two main reasons. First, even with goodwill, sound commodity agreements are difficult to negotiate and maintain : they will, for this and other reasons, certainly not solve the whole problem. Secondly, a country may suffer considerably for many years because one of its leading exports becomes particularly depressed, either in a rather long period fluctuation, or even for permanent reasons (it needs a long time to decide which is which). Such a country, if it was receiving a proper amount of aid before, will clearly need more during the difficult transition period when it is trying to develop alternative production. Now, with a rational distribution of aid by donor countries, one could argue that such circumstances will anyway be taken into account, so that a medium to long-term decline does not call for special compensatory finance. A short-term decline will. But, in this case, one can argue that this should not be in the form of development aid, and should therefore be financed either by IMF, or other medium-period, loans at normal rates of interest. Thus it can be argued that compensatory aid falls between two stools.

The underdeveloped countries themselves are provisionally in favour of some scheme of compensatory finance, on top of the three- to five-year balance of payments finance obtainable from the IMF.[2] Looking to a longer period, it was resolved at the UNCTAD that the IBRD should study and report on a system of compensatory finance to be administered by the IDA.[3,4] Having regard to the fact that the

---

[1] Strong support for this point of view is contained in René Dumont, *L'Afrique Noire est mal partie*, Paris, Editions du Seuil, 1962.

[2] Since February 1963, primary product exporters can draw up to 25 per cent of their quota almost automatically for this purpose, regardless of existing commitments. See *Compensatory Finance of Export Fluctuations*, Report by the IMF, February 1963. The UNCTAD proposed that this proportion be raised to 50 per cent.

[3] The UK's representative, Mr Heath, expressed UK government support for such a proposal at an early stage of the Conference.

[4] The idea is that the scheme should be on a country, not a commodity, basis. This seems entirely right. If a two-commodity country's shortfall in one is already compensated by a bonanza in the other, there is no call for compensatory finance. The rational basis of compensation must be countrywise.

distribution of aid, as it emerges from the differing policies of many donors, is sufficiently haphazard to give insufficient guarantee that recipients suffering from loss of export earnings would get extra aid, it seems, prima facie, a good idea that some special attention be paid to this problem. It is noticeable that the countries which have borrowed short excessively are mostly among those whose export prices have suffered. Moreover, the increased difficulty of economic planning, when faced with the possibility of large uncompensated shortfalls in export earnings, gives added weight to this view.[1] But further comment should obviously wait on the IBRD's study.

3. CONCLUSIONS ON TRADE AND AID

This concludes our survey of the relations between trade and aid. Obviously, we have not tried to deal more than cursorily with trade problems: the object has been to explore trade no more than enough to show the relation of aid to trade, and the extent to which they are substitutes or complementary.

Trade is a substitute for aid to the extent that it helps to make the underdeveloped world richer. This it can do both by improving the demand for primary products, and by helping to ensure more rational and lower cost industrial development in the underdeveloped world. It is only to a small extent a substitute for aid so far as the financing of balance of payments deficits goes. Aid is needed primarily because underdeveloped countries cannot raise the savings required to finance all the worthwhile investment that can be undertaken. So far as marginal aid goes, there are some exceptions to this—countries which could and would save more themselves if they could export more: but they are not typical, and even with them lack of savings is the rationale for most, even if not for all, of the aid they could well use.

[1] The shortfall need not necessarily be absolute to give rise to planning difficulties and financial set-backs. A country may reasonably have planned for increased earnings, which did not materialize because of price falls. For example, Ghana did not suffer a fall in export earnings from cocoa in the period 1954–64, but the volume of cocoa exports expanded by about 75 per cent! The UNCTAD resolution on this topic appropriately mentions shortfalls below reasonable expectations. On all this, see also *International Compensation for Fluctuations in Commodity Trade*, UN, N.Y., 1961, doc. E/3447.

CHAPTER VII

FORMS OF CAPITAL INFLOW

1. FINANCIAL AID

In Chapter V we discussed the limits to the effective use of foreign capital for economic development, and in Chapters V and VI, what determines, subject to these limits, the basic need for capital. We now turn to the effect on development of the forms which such capital takes. These also may limit the effective use of capital.

The simplest form of capital inflow is the provision of convertible foreign exchange. But very little foreign capital indeed comes to the underdeveloped world so conveniently. If any divergence from this form is described by saying that 'strings are attached', then almost all foreign public capital has strings.

First, much of the total flow is provided to finance specific projects. If such projects were exactly what the recipient would have chosen anyway, then project-tying makes no difference to anyone. If such were the case it would not, of course, exist. In this chapter we are not concerned with the merits and demerits of project-tying as such. That is discussed in Chapter VIII. But one of the reasons for project-tying is that it facilitates the tying of aid funds to expenditure in the capital-supplying country. It is this latter kind of tying with which we are concerned in this chapter.

The extent of aid-tying has been described in Chapter II. Formally or informally, a very high proportion is tied. While there are commercial reasons for tying, the primary purpose of most tying is the protection of the capital supplier's balance of payments. For reasons discussed in Chapter X, most donors feel they need to ensure that a major part of the capital supplied is used in such a way that their own exports are increased. To the extent that exports are increased, the capital outflow puts no strain on the supplying country's reserves.

Merely tying the funds supplied to procurement in the supplying country does not ensure the required effect. Thus one could formally tie by simply giving the recipient some inconvertible credits. But such credits could be used to buy imports which would have been bought anyway, and the convertible foreign exchange thus freed used to buy more from other countries. The point of tying is then lost. Inconvertible credits constitute effective tying only if the recipient would normally import less than the amount of the credit from the supplier. But they can be made more effective in two ways. First, the range of goods for which they can be used may be limited to exclude categories normally imported from the credit supplier. Secondly, the recipient can be asked for assurances that extra imports will result, and some check can be kept on this. But the most effective form of procurement tying is to finance only the import content of new projects. It is then only in the somewhat rare event that the recipient would anyway have bought that particular capital equipment from the supplier that the tying is not effective.

If a high proportion of foreign capital is thus tied to the import content of projects there may be some very damaging economic consequences. The basic economic distortion is that the pattern of the recipient's imports may be too biased towards capital goods for new projects. This can result in domestic resources, which could have been mobilized to create investments, being left unused. A country may be in such a position that if it accepts all the capital goods offered, then it cannot both meet the domestic cost of the projects for which these capital goods are intended, and carry out, without inflation, all the other desirable investments and current government expenditures for which no aid or foreign capital is forthcoming. If the foreign capital could be spent partly on consumer goods, then the country could carry out less investment with a high direct import content, and make other investments which would employ its own people and resources to a greater extent. Such greater employment of domestic resources would (assuming that taxation is already as high as is reasonable) result in an increased demand for consumption goods, which would, in the absence of controls, necessarily result in increased imports, either directly of consumption goods, or of materials or components which would permit a greater output of consumption goods from the recipient's own industries. Thus, making consumption goods, materials, etc., available to a country enables it to increase its investment. Not merely this; it may make the total aid given more effective in that a given amount of aid has a greater effect on the employment of the country's own resources. Food aid for example may be as effective in increasing investment as any other kind of aid. (Commodity aid is considered below.)

There is nothing merely theoretical about the above argument. Despite substantial commodity aid, India has in the past suffered from excessive projectization, in that the aid given for capital goods for projects could have been more rapidly and beneficially spent on increasing imports of components, raw materials, spare parts, and minor capital goods not required for specific new projects. Donors have increasingly realized this, and recently a large part of aid to India has not been tied to projects.[1] India is not the only country in which existing factories have been idle for lack of inputs only obtainable abroad. It has also happened in Pakistan, and several Latin American countries, including Chile and Colombia.

In countries such as the above which already make many or most essential manufactured consumption goods, and which can also contribute some manufactures to investment activities, and which control imports, the over-projectization of aid tends to result mainly in deficiencies of materials, components, etc. (but also in food at times). It is admittedly questionable whether, even if aid had been less linked to projects, the Indians would have started fewer projects and permitted more 'general purpose' imports. But at least the forms of aid should not be such as to encourage excess capacity in existing industries.

In other countries, what is essentially the same problem results in different symptoms. As we have seen, the governments of many African countries have not taken full internal borrowing powers. In such cases, if aid is too much tied to direct capital-goods imports, the government concerned literally cannot find the domestic currency to finance the domestic costs (wages, home-produced materials, etc.) of their investment activities and other expenditures. This is known as the 'home cost' problem. Faced with this problem, and assuming that they will nevertheless accept all the aid for imports of capital goods which they can get, they are forced to choose projects with a high import cost, and to maximize the import cost of others. Some donors have actively encouraged this, e.g. the British in Kenya. This has led to the absurdity of using imported goods and materials when these were available locally. Since such imported goods are often more expensive, not only are domestic resources left idle, but the cost of the project may be greatly increased.[2,3] The 'home cost' problem

---

[1] The USA, Germany, and Britain, the three principal non-Communist donors of aid to India, made nearly half of their 1963 commitments (excluding commodity aid) in non-project form. This amounted to about one-third of non-Communist aid (excluding commodity aid).

[2] For a specific example see Little, *Aid to Africa*.

[3] It is true in theory that if there are underemployed resources, and the government takes steps to employ them to create capital, then it can prevent consumption rising by increased taxation (until such time as the resultant greater output

has been recognized for some time, and has been studied in East Africa by a DAC consultative group. But very little appears to have been done to relieve it.

It may seem absurd that a developing country should tie its own hands financially. What happens if the government simply creates enough money to pay for the domestic costs of investment? It will then create an excess demand for consumption goods, which cannot be met from aid-financed imports of consumption goods. The other side of the coin of relatively excessive imports of capital goods is thus a combination of unused domestic resources, and inflationary price rises for consumption goods. Although the authors are too ignorant of Latin America to be sure, it may be that this analysis has some relevance to Latin American inflations.

The remedy for the defects of aid which result from tying is obvious. If the supplying countries have no sufficient reason for 'projectizing' their aid, then they should permit any kind of good to be imported from them (assuming they feel that aid must be tied).[1] The main objection is that this may make tying somewhat less effective, as the use of the tied credit is more likely to impinge on things that would have been imported anyway, and might be used for goods which have been merely shunted through the donor. This objection can be minimized by administrative action, and by excepting a few commodities particularly liable to shunting operations.

If, on the other hand, they wish to projectize their aid, then they should pay the domestic costs of the project as well as the import cost. Again, the objection is that it is difficult to ensure that the imports, which indirectly result from domestic expenditure on a project, come from the capital-supplying country. One possibility is to open a tied or inconvertible credit to the value of the domestic costs, which, as with the case of inconvertible credits for non-project aid, could be spent on a wide range of goods. The counterpart funds resulting from the sale of the imports would provide the recipient government with the domestic currency it lacked. As before, this is probably somewhat less effective tying than when aid is tied to the export of capital goods. Also, it is not as good as completely convertible currency from the point of view of the recipient. It is possible that the sort of non-capital goods which the recipient will want are not those which the supplier can economically supply. This, of course,

---

permits greater consumption). In practice, however, this is too much to demand of some countries with weak tax systems and with political problems.

[1] They may wish to make some exclusions for political reasons, e.g. armaments.

is particularly likely to be the case if it is food or raw materials which are demanded.[1] Nevertheless, such a provision would undoubtedly make things considerably easier for the recipient, especially as PL 480 aid is likely to be independently available from the USA if there is excess demand for food (see below).

An objection to projects being wholly financed by external funds is that it is likely that the recipient government will adopt a more responsible attitude to the selection, design, and operation, of projects if it has a direct financial interest in each project. Our experience does not suggest that much weight should be attached to this argument. But, even where it is valid, it is still often the case that the economically desirable domestic component of projects is much higher than the proportion of the cost which it may be desirable for recipients to bear for psychological reasons. Even if the capital-supplying countries want to insist on some recipient participation, they could still generally pay a considerable part of the domestic costs.

At this point it should be remarked that the IBRD, which, of course, has no tying problem, nevertheless until recently has felt bound by its charter to pay only the import content of projects. This provision of the charter was evidently based on the naïve view that only capital goods help development. The IBRD (and IDA) has become increasingly liberal in the interpretation of the charter, and its policy now is to finance domestic costs in cases where there is a problem.[2] This accords well with its new policy of expanding its interest in agriculture and education, sectors in which import costs tend to be low.

We have now dealt with the main distortion which may, and does, result from aid-tying, and with ways of mitigating it. But there are other reasons why tied aid is considerably less effective in promoting development than untied aid. First, there is the most obvious reason:

[1] The inconvertible credits could be made transferable to overcome this problem. Thus, e.g. Australia could be permitted to accept inconvertible sterling from India in payment for wool. This, however, would hardly satisfy the supplier's reason for making the credit inconvertible in the first place, because the third party would usually be able to use such inconvertible currency for its normal imports.

[2] 'The executive directors have agreed upon a restatement of policy with respect to financing local currency expenditures. It has now been made entirely clear that our criterion in the selection of projects is the extent of their respective contribution to economic development, regardless of the ratio of costs as between foreign exchange and local currency. We now stand ready to finance some of the local costs of high-priority projects in cases where financing for imports alone would not provide adequate support.' From 'Address to the Boards of Governors' by Mr George D. Woods, President of the IBRD, Tokyo, September 7, 1964.

that the recipient cannot buy its imports in the cheapest market. But, while this is prima facie a disadvantage to the recipient, it should be remembered that the whole point of aid-tying is precisely that the recipients should *not* buy in the cheapest market. Therefore if, in fact, the capital-supplying country dare not supply so much unless aid is tied—if, in fact, aid is tied for genuine balance of payments reasons— then the recipient must weigh this against the fact that the real value of such aid is reduced by tying. The terms on which the capital is supplied are important here. If the donor supplies the capital at 6 per cent interest, and it turns out that the equipment which the recipient wants to buy costs 50 per cent more than it would from some other country, then clearly the major benefit of such a transaction goes to the supplier. But if the capital is supplied on subsidized terms; if, that is, there is a substantial aid element in the loan, then the recipient has no cause for complaint, although the value of the aid remains, of course, less than if it were not tied.

Sometimes the prices which the recipient has to pay for imports are magnified by the fact that aid-tying may introduce a strong monopoly element. There may be very few potential suppliers—even only one— of the equipment involved in double-tied project aid (i.e. aid tied by project as well as to procurement in the donor country). There have undoubtedly been cases where the recipient was thus exploited. Even where recipients are not exploited, the consciousness of having to pay more than world prices is not good for aid relations.[1]

There are still further disadvantages of procurement tying. In particular, it puts a serious burden on already weak administrations. To quote: 'Even where there is only one donor involved, steps have to be taken to see that, for example, the contractor imports his door-handles and light bulbs from the USA. Where there are many donors involved the problem becomes nightmarish. Imagine trying to build the Niger dam from seven different tied loans (the UK offer of aid will not be fully taken up in this case, and may not be used at all— because the jigsaw puzzle cannot be solved!). It makes things very difficult for contractors who have to buy from sources they are not used to, and do not know. Some of the smaller local contractors have felt unable to tender for projects for this reason. It undermines the good principle of accepting the lowest tender, which may no longer be the best from the country's point of view, if its currency-mix is less appropriate to the tied aid than that of higher tenders. Lastly, aid-

[1] For a study of the subject of the above two paragraphs, in relation to USA aid to India, see J. P. Lewis, *Quiet Crisis in India*, Brookings Institution, 1962, pp. 278-85.

tying does much to create cynicism about the donor's motives. Donors struggle so hard to supply goods themselves that it is not surprising that recipients come to believe that it is a benefit rather than a sacrifice to them.'[1]

All in all, tying aid to procurement in the donor country greatly reduces its effectiveness, and also seriously affects the political impact of aid. We have shown certain ways in which its bad effects could be mitigated: but they all involve some reduction in the effectiveness of tying. But the question of how far it is likely to be possible to get rid of tying can only be answered, when, in Chapter XI, we have seen how essential it is to a continuance of aid at present levels, and to its growth.

We now turn to the discussion of two particular kinds of tied aid— commodity aid and technical assistance—both of which have special features, and to both of which most of what has been said above about aid-tying is inapplicable.

2. COMMODITY AID

Commodity aid is, of course, the most tied of all aid. The vast bulk consists of American surplus agricultural products. France, Canada, and Australia, have given food aid; but this is chickenfeed. From its inception in 1954, USA surplus agricultural commodity disposals have totalled $10 billion reckoned at market prices, and in 1963 totalled $1·8 billion. Not all has gone to underdeveloped countries: and not all of it represents a transfer of resources, since the USA uses some of the local currency proceeds for expenditures it would anyway incur. Of the total flow of financial resources to under-developed countries, the market value of the USA commodity aid (net of USA retentions for its own use) has amounted to about 20 per cent in the years 1962–3.

The main commodities concerned are wheat, cotton, fats and oils, rice, feedgrains, and tobacco. These account for 93 per cent of the total. Wheat is by far the largest, and alone accounts for 45 per cent of the total. The main recipients have been India, Pakistan, Yugo-slavia, Korea, Spain, Egypt, Poland, and Brazil. India and Pakistan together account for 27 per cent of the total from 1954–63, and the other five mentioned for 32 per cent. But, on a *per capita* basis, Israel has been far the largest recipient ($154 per head), with Yugoslavia and Korea ($45 and $27 per head respectively) poor runners-up. India has received $5 per head.

[1] Little, *Aid to Africa*, pp. 29–30.

Commodity aid can hardly be as useful as untied aid, which could anyway be spent on the given commodities if the recipient so wished. Nor, except as a limiting case, can it be as useful as tied aid which is not restricted to particular commodities, for exactly the same reason.[1] But there are also particular arguments to suggest that commodity aid is less valuable to the underdeveloped world than its normal market value suggests. First, if the USA had provided the same number even of inconvertible dollars, but with unrestricted use in the USA, the recipient countries would certainly not have wanted to spend it all on the commodities concerned. The prices of the latter would consequently have been lower, and the aid given would have been to that extent more valuable. Secondly, to some extent, commodity aid reduces the demand for competing products from underdeveloped countries themselves (even on the assumption that the alternative was no aid, rather than general purpose aid). Some part at least of the demand, satisfied in some underdeveloped countries by commodity aid, would have been effective anyway, and would have helped other underdeveloped countries. Thus wheat and rice aid must have reduced the demand for rice from Burma and Thailand, and cotton aid the demand for cotton from the Sudan and Uganda. These countries have thus suffered from commodity aid, getting little or none of it themselves.

The idea that commodity aid alone can permit faster development to the extent that sufficient extra demand is created to absorb the value of the aid commodities, so that there is no interference with the commercial demand for such commodities, is economic nonsense. This could be the case only if investments were created by labour alone, and if the extra wages were spent solely on the commodities concerned. For any given amount of commodity aid to be absorbed, there will be some extra demand for other things. If this extra demand for other things is not somehow accommodated, then commodity aid cannot be absorbed without displacing commercial sales. If commercial sales are displaced then there is no net extra consumption of the surplus commodity, and the surplus is shifted (to other countries, and possibly other commodities) rather than used.[2] But the underdeveloped countries continue to benefit in that the burden of the shift is borne mainly by other developed exporters, principally Australia and Canada.

[1] See below for this limiting case.
[2] We are not here speaking of an historical displacement. Commercial sales can be displaced without an actual fall. The comparison is with what they would have been if no commodity aid had been given.

As against the above, it is unfair to look at commodity aid alone. If it is looked at as a component part of all aid, then the picture changes. In many countries the extra development which aid in total induces will cause them to import more consumption goods, and some part of this extra demand may be satisfied by surplus commodities from the developed countries without there being any necessary distortion from an optimum development pattern. We have already seen that aid for non-capital-goods imports has an important role to play in the development of some recipients. Commodity aid can satisfy part of this, without there being any interference whatever with commercial sales, as compared with a situation in which no aid at all was given. To the extent that this approximates to reality, it can be true both that commodity aid reaches the limit of being as valuable to the recipients as convertible currency, and that other exporters of the commodity are unharmed. It is not in fact suggested that such bliss has quite been the case. If commodity aid is a high proportion of total aid, as with Israel, then it may be that even aid in total is insufficient to increase the total consumption of the commodities to the full amount of those supplied on aid terms.[1] But the underdeveloped countries themselves need not worry about bliss reigning. As a whole they have certainly benefited very greatly, and it is doubtful whether any single underdeveloped country has suffered from the American aid programme as a whole, and this is what in all fairness should be looked at.

Turn now to consider the position from the point of view of the USA's main export competitors in this field—Australia and Canada being the most important—who, prima facie, suffer a loss as a result of the USA programme. One has to consider the alternatives. Given USA production, the alternative, apart from burning the products which would nowadays one hopes be politically impossible, would be to sell the surpluses commercially. But this would (by lowering prices) harm the other exporters, especially the wheat exporters, more than present policies. In fact, given USA production, the losers by the surplus disposal policies are the UK and other importers. Countries like Canada do not lose by commodity aid, but by the USA farm support policies which create the surpluses. Similarly, given her production, it is doubtful whether commodity aid costs the USA anything.[2]

---

[1] Burma probably has the strongest claims to damage for it has received rather little American aid, and also does not benefit from the support for wheat prices which is implicit in PL 480 operations.

[2] Any such calculations based on demand elasticities is very chancy. But in 1960 T. W. Schultz estimated the cost to the USA as about zero, and the value to the

How far back do we take the argument? It is entirely unrealistic to suppose that either the USA or European countries will not continue to support the incomes and way of life of the farming communities. It is pointless to speculate as to the position if there were no such policy. But, of course, the USA both supports farm prices, and uses production quotas to limit output. It is possible to produce more or less. One can therefore ask what is the real cost of reducing or increasing the surpluses, given the policy of supporting individual farms or farmers. It has been estimated at about 25 per cent of the Commodity Credit Corporation's acquisition and storage costs.[1] This is the crux of the matter. With given political demands, the real cost of commodity aid is very low. This also implies that surpluses in the USA could be very considerably increased at low real cost, since present quota policies leave much land, labour, and other farm overheads, under-utilized. It is sensible then for the USA, given the political commitment to farm support, to be willing to increase commodity aid, mostly food, much more rapidly than other forms of aid. Add to this the fact that all experts expect large surpluses to develop in Western Europe, and one is plainly, for the future, faced with the problem of how rapidly and usefully the underdeveloped world can and will increase its consumption of temperate zone products.

This depends mainly on the rate of growth of incomes, and on the pattern of output and demand in the underdeveloped world, which will be partly in turn influenced by the import policies of the developed countries. Plainly, the greatest hope for the absorption of large quantities of surplus agricultural products, especially food, is if high population growth and sluggish agricultural output is combined with rapid urbanization, and industrialization of a labour-intensive character. This is an outcome which one cannot want, for it inevitably implies, for decades, a very slow growth of real income per head. Any reasonably rapid amelioration of the misery of the lives of the rural masses of the underdeveloped world can be based only on an improvement in their own output, and a reduction in birth-rates. But although the outcome may not be desirable, it is very possible, and the famine reserves implicit in the large unrealized potential food output of North America and Europe may prove a godsend. Also, it is by no means impossible that a rapid improvement of agricultural

recipients as 37 cents for every dollar's worth at market prices, in view of the price falls estimated to prevail if the surpluses were thrown on to the market. ('Value of Farms' Surpluses to Underdeveloped Countries', *Journal of Farm Economics, Proceedings Number*, December 1960.)

[1] cf. George Allen, 'Food for Peace', *Lloyds Bank Review*, July 1963.

output in the underdeveloped countries should be combined with increasing food shortages, provided that non-agricultural output can be increased fast enough, and, above all, much fuller employment be achieved. The fear that reliance on food aid might reduce recipients' own efforts to improve their agriculture is groundless; this has been shown in, for instance, both India and Pakistan.

But, whatever the longer-run outcome, which is so uncertain as to be almost idle speculation, there are opportunities in the present situation of actual and potentially greater world surplus, of which more advantage could be taken. The first opportunity may be only rather remotely connected with longer-run development: but is certainly desirable on humanitarian grounds. This is to increase the demand for food independently of incomes, both by dietary education, and by the provision of school meals and 'welfare' food distribution, including of course famine relief. This is already done under Titles II and III of the American PL 480. The second opportunity, which is closely connected with development, is the encouragement of labour-intensive investments. The matching of surplus food with putting underemployed or unemployed hungry men to work to create something useful (even if it is not very useful) is so obvious that there has been no lack of advocacy.[1] That performance has disappointed a number of critics has various causes: the emotional preference for twentieth-century ways of doing things; the difficult organizational problems involved in managing labour gangs, a lost art known to the Pharaohs, the Moghuls, and the great railway contractors, and refound only, apparently, by the Chinese; and, finally, the fear of an inflationary rise of food prices if too many hungry men are given work.

Food aid has direct relevance only to the last-named cause. Even here, the recipient country may require assurances of continuity of supply. But this has not been lacking. The USA has signed four-year agreements with India and Pakistan, and should be in a position to extend such assurances (if, in the event, the demand for food is overestimated, local stock-piles are themselves a desirable investment, and some part of recent food aid to India was envisaged for this purpose). There have been, on a small scale, direct attempts by the USA to encourage such developments, e.g. in Tunisia, by actually having wages paid partly in food. Liberal economists will have no truck with

[1] See, e.g., A. Shonfield, *Economic Growth and Inflation*, The Council for Economic Education, Bombay, 1961, and comment by I. M. D. Little in 'A Critical Examination of India's Third Five-Year Plan', *Oxford Economic Papers*, February 1962.

this! To quote Professor Viner's already well-quoted remark, ' . . . under the Food-for-Peace program it is planned to pay workers on development projects in part in American surplus food instead of money. It may be that several millennia after the introduction of the use of money as a medium of exchange we have found this to be a mistake.'[1] A clumsy device, indeed! But, on the other hand, it is not difficult to imagine that this might have been the only way to get the Tunisian Government to start such works programmes. A more serious difficulty—the sort of difficulty always implicit in bilateral barter—was that couscous cannot be made from hard wheat.[2] US wheat is also not popular with the consumer in India or Pakistan.

This points to a more general problem, that the surplus commodities are not always those best suited to the demands or needs of the underdeveloped world. If, for instance, grain is in excess supply despite all the food aid that can be arranged, some switch of the surplus to protein foods may be indicated. This, ideally, might involve multilateral arrangements between developed countries, e.g. the USA might give grain to European countries to process into dried milk for the underdeveloped countries. Such swops might be difficult to arrange, but the important point remains that if surpluses are to go on indefinitely, which is almost for sure, then it is worth paying some attention to producing the most suitable surpluses to give away.

The example of surplus agricultural commodity aid has led to the idea that the same principle might be applied more widely—are there not other things which could be supplied whose real cost to the donor is much less than their value? Where excess industrial capacity exists, so that marginal cost is much less than average cost, might not governments buy the goods cheap, and ship them on aid terms to underdeveloped countries? Where an area is depressed, could not the same thing be done? Is this not a good way of trying to increase aid, by making the donor country's sacrifice small, and by enlisting the support of the depressed commercial and other interests involved?

The difficulties are great. Agriculture is not really much of an analogy for here the excess capacity is chronic, and governments have no intention of letting farming decline to the extent that it would under the influence of free market forces. It is different with industries, which seldom suffer from long-period overcapacity: and if

[1] Jacob Viner, 'Economic Policy on the New Frontier', *Foreign Affairs*, July 1961, p. 568.
[2] cf. 'Policy for United States Agricultural Export Surplus Disposal', *The University of Arizona, College of Agriculture, Technical Bulletin* 150, August 1962, p. 64.

the period is short it is likely to be extremely difficult to marry the real needs of recipients to such excess capacity in time; furthermore, such sources of supply are too erratic for sensible planning in underdeveloped countries to take account of them, and there is a danger that some underdeveloped countries will accept supplies which do them little or no good just because they are suddenly made available on credit. Long-period excess capacity usually occurs in industries which are hit by competition from underdeveloped countries themselves, and so could play no role in such a scheme. Possible opportunities may occur where a whole area is relatively depressed, and likely to remain so for some time. Thus the UK has given some extra aid to be spent on goods from the North East of England. Such opportunities can occur, and make sense: where they do the goods should, like PL 480 aid and unlike the UK case, be supplied very much on aid terms in recognition of the fact that the cost to the donor is small. Despite this, we would not expect the scope for 'industrial surplus aid' to be very great.

We turn now to the financing of commodity aid. More particularly we discuss the practice of selling goods for local currency, which is now almost confined to PL 480 Title I aid (but previously other USA 'soft' loans were made against repayment in local currencies). The other forms of financing the movement of surplus commodities are not exceptional.[1]

The principle is that the local currency proceeds, or 'counterpart' of the sales of the commodities, which are disposed of by the recipient government through normal commercial channels, are USA property. The USA Government uses part for its own local government expenditures, e.g. Embassy expenses.[2] In 1962 and 1963 taken together, planned USA use of counterpart funds came to about 16 per cent of the total value of Title I agreements. Most of the rest is supposed to be either granted or loaned back to the local government for agreed projects, but in practice a high proportion just languishes in the bank.[3]

The only conceivable object, from the point of view of economic

---

[1] Title I, comprising about two-thirds of total PL 480, is sales for local currency. Title II provides commodities on grant terms. Title III provides food for donations through relief agencies. Title IV is against long-term dollar loans.

[2] In the case only of Poland has the whole of the proceeds been reserved for USA purposes.

[3] Some relatively small part has been used for common defence, and for loans to USA private enterprise in the recipient country (under the Cooley amendment of 1957). This last use is highly unpopular with recipients.

development, is to retain USA surveillance over part of the development fund of the recipient country. As we shall see, there are, in some countries, good reasons for supposing that such donor control is beneficial for economic development. But, where a country has proper banking institutions, it does not need to borrow or be given, with strings, its own currency from the USA. It can borrow it from its own banking system. It makes not the slightest difference from the economic point of view which it does. Therefore such a country will use these counterpart funds only for things it wants to do anyway, and only then in order to please the Americans. This is the reason why so much remains unspent. In fact, the control is largely a sham, and in any case AID administrators, conscious of the absurdity, do not exercise the same degree of surveillance, even in countries where such surveillance might be beneficial, as they do over new aid funds.

There are, admittedly, the countries with a 'home cost' problem, those still bound by currency board arrangements.[1] These need to make use of the counterpart funds, and therefore USA control can be made effective. But even here there are disadvantages. The food aid has a deflationary effect when it comes in—which usually counters an inflationary potential. There is then a long lag while use of the counterpart money is agreed. Its use then has an inflationary or reflationary effect which may be ill-timed. Certainly, it is in principle an extra impediment to sound budgeting and planning that some domestic funds can be used only when agreement is reached, especially as the best use of such funds may well be for non-project purposes. The main point, however, is that even if the balance of advantage lies with American-owned counterpart funds in a few countries, it is certainly a pernicious system in most,[2] and distinctions cannot easily be drawn.

There is in fact little or nothing to be said on the credit side for such arrangements. On the debit side, they cause misunderstandings (the USA is trying to make one aid song be sung twice over—indeed, in the case of loaned counterpart funds, many times over), and a great waste of administrative effort in shadow-boxing over the agreed uses for the counterpart funds. This clumsy device, which does much to offset the goodwill which should flow from commodity aid, was born from a belief in the economic obtusity of Congress and the American public, who might be gulled into thinking that the commodities were being sold and not given away. The latter is, of course, apart from the

---

[1] See pp. 162–3.
[2] See, e.g. Lewis, op. cit., pp. 315–26.

reservations of counterpart funds for USA use, the economic reality. Many economists have flogged this horse—but it still has not died.[1] There are many things to admire about American aid, but the creation of American-owned counterpart funds is not one of them.

To conclude, it is very hard to judge how far and fast commodity aid can be expanded in the long run. But it has been highly beneficial, and more use still could probably be made of it now, especially if recipients plan to use it, rather than using it merely when shortages develop. It has to be carefully fitted in with other kinds of aid, if third countries are not to suffer. Where the third countries are rich, it is not so much that one minds them suffering, but that their opposition may reduce the effectiveness of the programme, and they may be discouraged from giving aid themselves. The administration of aid does not obviously encourage this necessary co-ordination, since, no doubt for good domestic political reasons, PL 480 Title I is not administered by AID. For the future, the probability of substantial surpluses being generated in several European countries will make co-ordination harder and more necessary, if the best use with least recrimination is to be made of the excessive potential of Western agriculture. For this reason, the first attempt at a multilateral endeavour—the UN World Food Programme, administered by FAO—is much to be welcomed.

3. TECHNICAL ASSISTANCE AS TIED AID

We have said some harsh things about the practice of tying aid, but there is one form of tying which in present circumstances actually tends to increase the usefulness of aid. This happens when aid is provided in the form of the services which we are accustomed to call 'technical assistance'.

Technical assistance from the donor's point of view takes two main forms. First, people are recruited in the donor country for service overseas, partly, often largely, at the expense of the donor government; secondly, scholarships and training facilities are provided in the donor country. Why is technical assistance singled out for special treatment in this way, when recipient governments might equally well be given more financial assistance, and left to decide for themselves what fraction of their aid should be spent on the services of foreign experts, and on education and training overseas?

The reason why 'tying' aid to technical services is acceptable to

[1] e.g. Lewis, op. cit., and E. S. Mason, 'Foreign Money We Can't Spend', *Atlantic Monthly*, 1960.

recipients is that it tends to increase the value of the nominal amount of aid spent on technical assistance; technical assistance contrasts strongly in this respect with financial aid tied to procurement in the donor country, and with commodity aid, both of which tend to be worth less than their nominal value. The contrast exists because many of the services provided under technical assistance programmes are scarce or unobtainable on the world market, and can be secured by recipients only with the help of donor governments.

Donor government assistance in recruiting is most important when the experts (or training facilities) to be supplied can be found only within central government departments, or within organizations like the post office or the army which are ultimately subject to central government control. If an expert is needed to set up or reorganize post office services overseas, or if on-the-job training is needed in the post office, then clearly this can be arranged only through the central government. If technical assistance is needed in decentralized fields of government, like training town clerks, or in school-teaching, or even in non-government fields like university teaching or medicine, the central government can still be an almost indispensable intermediary; in school-teaching, for instance, the British Government has encouraged and helped representatives of the teachers' organizations and local authorities to work out a code of secondment, which enables a teacher to work overseas for at least five years, without losing his pension rights, and with the certainty that he will have a job to return to. Although these arrangements do not depend upon the donor government having a financial interest in the technical experts and training facilities that are provided for overseas governments, a donor government is likely to make a more serious attempt to recruit people, and find training places, that will carry a British (or German, or Russian) technical assistance label, than if it merely recruits on behalf of overseas governments.

A further useful attribute of technical assistance, when it takes the form of educational and training facilities in donor countries, is that since both donor and recipient governments take part in the choice of courses, and selection of candidates, the types of training offered can be more closely geared to the needs of the recipient economy (and the capability of the donor) than education which is paid for privately, or by the recipient government. Ideally, part at least of the training provided should be linked with technical assistance on the 'expert' side, and even with capital assistance. For example, if an expert is provided to reorganize and expand a recipient's postal services, training should be provided for the men to run the new service; or if financial aid is provided for a new oil refinery, both experts and training facilities should be provided in engineering, management, and the other skills needed to operate the refinery. Donors have found in the past that, left to themselves, recipients have been reluctant to spend enough of their own resources on the technical expertise demanded by a new installation, and offers of free or subsidized technical assistance are therefore extremely useful in persuading recipients to accept the necessary advice and training.

The independence of former colonies, especially those which were formerly British, has seriously reduced the supply of foreigners prepared or able to make their careers in developing countries. Under current conditions, advisers and teachers for work overseas are recruited on contract, for a maximum of three years (though with the possibility of renewed contracts in some cases), because neither donor nor recipient government wishes to be committed for longer periods. Recipient governments are afraid of barring promotion for local people by taking foreigners on career terms, and donor governments have felt unable to set up career services for expert advisers. The result is that expert advisory or even operational work overseas is regarded by the employee as a temporary interruption to his career at home, and he is not willing to stay abroad for more than a few years, for fear of losing promotion in his real career. For instance, a young and ambitious doctor, who works overseas soon after he qualifies, is more than likely to miss any chance of becoming a consultant, which he might have had if he had stayed in England.

However great the probability that foreign advisers, teachers, etc., will make mistakes, foreign influence cannot be avoided. Few societies are so isolated that they have been unaffected by contact with the products, ideas, and techniques, of richer countries; and most are already changing so fast, economically and socially, that they could not restore their traditional institutions even if they wished to do so. Population growth is perhaps the most obvious stimulus to continued change, but new material and social ambitions of all kinds are close competitors. Whatever the potential dangers of foreign influence, developing countries must import foreign skills and education at the moment, if they are to achieve economic progress. Isolation on the Russian or Japanese models would not be a feasible policy for any of the developing countries at this stage, because they do not yet possess the numbers of trained and skilled people, or the determination to introduce technical change, that the Russians and Japanese possessed in the late nineteenth century.

4. THE NEED FOR TECHNICAL ASSISTANCE, AND FORMS OF TECHNICAL ASSISTANCE

Technical assistance represents only a small fraction of the total transfer of skills from rich to poor countries. But, as we have said already, it is the form of transfer most amenable to selective control by the recipient government. It is important that governments and individuals in poor countries should learn to consider more carefully the likely effects of innovations that appeal to them, and should be more selective in their choice of foreign influences to be encouraged or discouraged.

This process of selection itself, however, requires a certain level of sophistication and understanding of the scientific approach to decisions, which is lacking in many recipient countries. Especially in Africa, there are many countries which need technical assistance not only to transfer new skills, but, temporarily at any rate, to operate the whole machinery of government, educational institutions, and that part of productive capacity which is on a scale larger than the family farm. This means that the process of selecting and adapting foreign influences to local conditions is very largely neglected, and that institutions are modelled very closely (if at times unsuccessfully) on the institutions of a European country, usually the former colonial power. This situation could hardly have been avoided, but unless the institutions of such countries are gradually adapted to fit local traditions and needs, they will continue for a long time to depend on foreigners or foreign-trained nationals for survival.

Technical assistance therefore varies in form and function, depending on the type of country receiving it. At one end of the scale are countries which can fill ordinary government posts, and many specialist appointments, from among their own nationals; but which occasionally have to import highly specialized skills for particular jobs, like designing an oil refinery or setting up an industrial research department. The most efficient of these countries can identify for themselves which jobs need to be done, and the type of experts needed to fill them, and are capable of arranging job specifications and recruitment: technical assistance for them means simply that they pay less for an expert, and are helped with recruitment; the latter may be especially useful if there are no consulting firms capable of doing the particular job needed. But few countries possess government machines efficient enough for technical assistance to be so simple. Most need help with 'pre-investment' surveys, feasibility studies, pilot projects and the like; and, pushing the process one stage further back, with economic planning and project selection in general.

Efficient donor administration of aid can help, by means of careful project selection, and by drawing attention to the need for surveys and planning.

But technical assistance can stop at the planning stage only if the government machine is capable of implementing the planners' decisions, and in many countries this condition is not fulfilled. In some countries the most essential form of technical assistance is providing people to fill 'operational' posts, including teaching, in the ordinary government establishment. While technical assistance comes up against political and personal difficulties at every level, filling operational posts presents by far the most delicate problem. Civil servants in a newly-independent country dislike taking orders from a foreigner. Citizens outside the civil service dislike dealing with foreigners. Ambitious subordinates resent foreigners who appear to stand in the way of their promotion. Sometimes the position can be made easier by appointing a foreign 'adviser' who will in effect do an operational job, but this may create personal difficulties with the titular 'operational' employee. An advisory appointment is of course appropriate, and preferable to an operational appointment, if there is a suitably qualified, but inexperienced, local man who can be trained 'on the job' by the foreign adviser, to fill the operational vacancy once the adviser has left.

The notion of absorptive capacity applies as much to the various types of technical assistance as to financial assistance. Specialists doing 'once and for all' jobs can be employed only to the extent that there are identifiable jobs for them to do, and when there are people capable of running the installations and services that these experts set up. Absorptive capacity for such specialists can be increased by appointing foreigners to help with economic planning, feasibility surveys, pilot projects, and professional and technical training for running new projects. Absorptive capacity for advisers on planning, and for professional training, is in turn limited by the capacity of government, and by the output of secondary and higher education institutions. It can be raised by appointing foreigners to government and teaching posts. The ultimate limit to absorptive capacity for technical assistance is therefore set by the acceptability and suitability of foreigners in government and teaching.

In the short run, the acceptability and supply of foreigners are the restraints which are obvious to all those who have been in contact with post-colonial governments. Many government departments in Africa would run a great deal more smoothly if they were not understaffed. Many more East Africans could be found places in higher education if there were more places for secondary school pupils. But in the longer run a more serious restraint, which may underlie some of the hostility to foreigners in the civil service establishment of these countries, is the difficulty of adapting institutions—from legal procedures to school curricula—to local conditions The more a government depends on foreign experts and foreign training courses to staff and teach its civil service, the more difficult adaptation becomes.

This brings us to the final function of technical assistance—research. As the above remarks suggest, not nearly enough is known about the degree to which the institutions and traditions of rich countries—their legal and social systems, their languages, philosophical systems, educational methods, etc.—are necessary for any society which hopes to achieve material prosperity, and how far they are merely accidental results of European history. Many other types of research are also needed, especially into the application of natural science to problems of developing better seeds, methods of husbandry, methods of birth control, and so on; and in the application of social science to finding ways of persuading people to adopt new crop rotations, fertilizers, etc. Much of the research needed can be done only in developing countries, and must often be specific to quite small areas, bounded by climatic or tribal differences.

Even more important than new research, at any rate in Britain, is the need to draw upon the experience of people who have lived and worked in developing countries. There is a great deal of knowledge and expertise among ex-colonial civil servants, consulting firms, missionaries, technical experts, and teachers, who have worked overseas on contract, which is exploited in an informal way by means of personal contacts and in conversation, but which could be used more systematically.[1]

5. TECHNICAL ASSISTANCE AND FINANCIAL AID

In Chapter V we said that technical assistance could help a recipient to increase its absorptive capacity, i.e. its ability to use financial aid productively. In this chapter we have shown that technical assistance is by no means an homogeneous activity, but that the usefulness of the various types of technical assistance may in turn be limited by absorptive capacity. In countries where this is the case, that is in countries which lack the educated manpower to staff government or

[1] But see also English edition, Chapter XVI, pp. 307-8.

teaching posts, or to take up offers of specialized technical and professional training, technical assistance in the form of teachers and staff to fill operational posts in government may reasonably be administered independently of financial assistance.

But other types of technical assistance—the supply of experts to carry out surveys and research, to design installations and services, or to staff planning departments—should usually be related to financial assistance. The main reason for this is that recipient governments tend to overestimate their own efficiency, and to ask for financial help with projects that are ill-chosen, badly designed, or wrongly located, and which they will be unable to run efficiently when they have been completed. Providing technical and financial assistance in a 'package' tends to increase the efficiency of both. It can ensure that a project for which a loan or grant is made is properly designed and costed, and is feasible. Conversely, a technical expert's or survey team's advice is far more likely to be taken if related financial aid can be made dependent on measures to follow such advice. When a donor government is supplying substantial amounts of money for a number of projects, it is also in a position to insist that the recipient employ well-qualified staff (not necessarily provided by the donor or of the donor's nationality) in government posts closely concerned with these projects: and if it thinks it necessary to insist on such appointments, it should do so. Combining technical and financial assistance in these ways is useful in combating corruption as well as inefficiency. To some extent, a donor's aid advisory staff can themselves provide technical assistance, as well as examine proposals and supervise expenditure. Britain's Middle East Development Division (MEDD), and some of the USA AID Mission staff, do just this; and the arrangement seems to work reasonably well.

The reasons for recommending that technical and financial assistance be more closely integrated, mostly arise out of the difficulty of administering aid effectively, and we shall therefore return to this question in Chapter VIII under the heading of Aid Relations.

PLANNING, PROJECTS, AND AID RELATIONS

1. DEVELOPMENT PLANNING

How can lenders and donors decide how much foreign capital a poor country should get? We have seen that they must at least assess the productivity of investment, the domestic average and marginal savings rate, the level of income per head, and the rate of population growth. Whereas the latter factors are more or less statistical, although often unknown, the first in theory demands a complete survey of the investment possibilities, indeed of the whole economy. It is usually only within the framework of an entire investment programme—that is an economic plan—that the productivity of a single investment project can be properly assessed. This is part of the reason why donors have wanted to see development plans. In addition, plans give some earnest of the intention to try to develop in a rational co-ordinated manner. Furthermore, of course, the production of a development plan should be a stimulus to a correct analysis of the obstacles to development, which we have discussed above, and to finding ways round or over such obstacles.

Let us first look at the ideal, whereby a development plan is an operational document laying down the course of investment and related policies for a number of years, and is also a call for foreign capital and assistance over the same period. This is the essence of any plan, although the document itself should also generally contain as full an analysis as possible of the developmental problems faced, and of the policies designed to overcome them, in order that the user of this document can see the rationale of the expenditure proposed.

First the plan, say a five-year plan, should be in the context of a long-run 'perspective' plan. To know best what to do in the next five years, one must try to peer ahead for some twenty years (much capital equipment put down now will be extant then, and some investment now in education and health will first be yielding its product then). Certainly, the broad lines of the succeeding plan should be known, because much capital investment whose output is needed in the next plan period must be started in this one. Secondly, the ideal plan must, of course, cover all government expenditure and revenue. Thirdly, whether or not government investment constitutes a major part of total investment, the plan must at least estimate private investment (it may or may not, in part, control it), not only in the aggregate, but in some detail: in the aggregate, because total investment and private capital inflow are among the essential components in any estimate of the aid needed; in some detail, because much private and public investment is complementary. Total investment should be related to some growth target, projecting the future course of both investment and consumption per head.

The investment plan must of course be feasible. Each item of expenditure must be capable of being spent in the period, after proper detailed planning. It must also be coherent: that is, supply and demand must be balanced in detail, except in so far as the demands of scale make it profitable to over-provide in the early years. Finally, and most impossibly, it should be optimal. Of all the possible coherent plans, there is one that will yield the best return. The best return has to be assessed over time. The government has to take a view on the competing needs of investment and consumption for many years ahead.

All this, and more, has been done, well in advance of the period to which the plan relates. The plan has thrown up a request for aid: this may take the overt form of a balance of payments gap, or a savings gap, or even a budgetary gap (but the form in which the gap is presented is not even prima facie evidence as to what constitutes the primary development bottleneck). The donors meet, and consider the plan. They may criticize, for if they are to provide some of the resources, on aid terms, they feel entitled to do so. There is a to-ing and fro-ing. The plan is amended, in the light of both the criticism and of the amounts the donors think they are ready to provide. There is a final meeting of minds, and the donors underwrite the amended plan. It will not, of course, be carried out exactly—for as it goes along it must be amended in the light of unforeseen events. But donors and the recipient keep closely in touch; the amendments are approved, and the necessary foreign resources flow on the proper terms. There is little delay in spending the aid which has been committed, because all individual projects have been planned in detail, and are ready to be started as soon as finance is available.

The ideal, as described above, is, of course, a gross caricature of reality. Most development plans come nowhere near being workable and economically well-integrated affairs. They always contain much that has not been planned in detail, and often much that is not feasible within the period. Donors do not come together to discuss the plans, meet the recipients, and jointly decide how thay can best help the plan, not even where 'consortia' have been arranged. Funds, mostly tied, are given largely for projects. There is frequent friction and rancour over the detail of projects. Certainly, no plan has yet been underwritten.

Some of the deficiencies in the manner of aid-giving were discussed in Chapter VII. Here we elaborate a little on the difficulties and deficiencies of planning: this is necessary because the role of the plan in aid-giving cannot be appreciated without some discussion of the nature of plans and their inevitable shortcomings.

There are great difficulties in the way of good planning in underdeveloped countries. First, there is ignorance of the most important macroeconomic facts. The size of the population is often not known to within 10 per cent. More important, the rate of growth of population is seldom known with sufficient accuracy. For instance, India's Second Five-Year Plan was based on a population growth rate of 1·4 per cent at a time when the population was growing by over 2 per cent. Consequently, the potential labour force and its growth rate is unknown. Also, very little is known about the trend of production in many countries. There are often more or less adequate indices of factory production, but this is a tiny proportion of the whole. Export crops, especially where there is little indigenous consumption, and plantation crops, may be well known: but this is not true of the quantity or trend of food production for domestic consumption, which normally constitutes the bulk of agricultural output. Extremely little is known of the output of services, handicraft production, traditional buildings, etc. In fact, many of the components of GDP, and hence GDP itself, and its trend, are often little more than poor guesses.

One may be lulled into a sense of knowledge by the now wide production of figures of GDP per head. But it is inadvisable to use such figures as more than rough indicators of 'orders of magnitude'. Such other key macroeconomic magnitudes as investment, and hence domestic savings, are also usually little more than guesses, inspired or otherwise. Trade figures are often inaccurate, and are even non-existent in a few very new countries. Very little is usually known of the non-trade components of the balance of payments, of invisibles and capital movements. If economic facts are ill-known, still less can be known of economic relationships, of the determinants of savings and agricultural output, and so on.

This ignorance implies that attempts to plan for some specific but general achievement such as full employment, or a certain rate of growth of output per head, are generally eyewash. The magnitude of the task is not known very accurately. Still less is known about the amount and type of investment needed to meet either general or particular targets. The Indian and Pakistani Plans come nearest to being coherent attempts to define ends, and stipulate the means required to achieve them. But when one allows for the window-dressing and the grave deficiencies of the estimates on which they are based, it is hardly surprising if outcomes, in so far as they are known, often bear rather little relation to design.

Generally speaking then, it is necessary to start with the means, and ask what resources can be made available for development, and then try to do the best one can with them. Assessing the means—and here the primary bottleneck may, as we have seen, be the ability to spend money well, or may be savings, or foreign exchange—is far from easy, and involves highly political decisions as to the level of taxation, and perhaps the degree of regimentation to which the economy should be subjected. Such an assessment is much harder than in a developed economy, where relatively excellent savings, investment, and balance of payments figures, are available for many years; and where particular real bottlenecks—an overstrained administration, lack of certain skills, or transport, etc.—are less likely to be obtrusive; and where export demand is less variable.

Among the many unknowns in assessing the means, the one with which we are particularly concerned is the level of foreign aid. How can a plan be produced if this is unknown? As things stand, it has to be guessed. In theory, if the guess is wrong, the amount of investment will have to be reduced, and this may mean that the whole pattern of investment becomes distorted.[1] It is not even as if a new plan can be made when the level of foreign support is known, for most aid commitments are made only annually.

Knowing the means is only the first step: the best use has to be made of them. Real resources lie behind the financial estimates. One should plan to reduce the strain on particular shortages, and to make the fullest use of resources which are not scarce. Then one has to take a broad view as to which are the promising sectors for development, and what are the obstacles; and devise means to overcome them. Then, in more detail, one has also to match supply and demand.

[1] But see also p. 187.

Excess capacity in some particular sector is waste: a deficiency, especially where imports cannot be brought in to break the bottle-neck (e.g. internal transport, and power), may mean that many other resources are wasted. Even where there is no problem (as in health, education, administration, and defence) of overt overproduction, or immediately disastrous deficiency, extremely difficult decisions as to the best balance of expenditure have to be taken: waste can be just as serious in fields where it is less obvious.

In thus attempting to use the means to the best advantage there is a further complication for the developing countries. As we saw in Chapter VII, foreign grants and loans do not just come in as foreign exchange which can be used for anything. Not merely is aid mostly tied to expenditure in the 'donor' country: it may also be tied to particular products. Most aid is also on a project basis, and often limited to the import content of that project. Moreover, donors have preferences as to the sort of project they will support. If account is taken of these preferences more aid may be forthcoming—but for things which the recipient wants less than others. On top of all this, and much besides, the expenditure has to be carefully phased so that all projects are efficiently and smoothly brought to conclusion, with no bunching of expenditure at particular periods, leading to over-strained resources at one time and excess capacity at another. This all has to be carried through by an administration, which is nowhere up to the standard of most developed countries; and in some countries is almost wholly inexperienced even at keeping things going, let alone in planning for economic development.

The above paragraphs make the problem sound impossible. So, of course, it is. No plan is optimal, or goes smoothly. We have also briefly presented the manner in which foreign aid comes, as an added complication, which, while providing some welcome resources, adds to the almost impossible problem of efficient utilization of resources. This will be further examined in the next section of this chapter. But first we must say something of the range and scope of different actual development plans.

About the only thing economic development plans have in com-mon is that they all constitute demands for foreign loans or grants. The Indian Second and Third Five-Year Plans have, with the possible exception of the Pakistan Third Plan, been the most com-prehensive and sophisticated. Here one finds attempts to balance overall savings and investment, and to predict all components of the balance of payments. The public sector is also relatively large (for an underdeveloped country), and large-scale fixed-investment in the private sector is closely controlled. The Government, and State Governments, in fact make themselves in principle responsible for almost all development, the Government being directly responsible for most output in several key sectors. Since Indian industry is among the more extensive in the underdeveloped world, and since India is a fairly closed economy, it is of some importance that particular outputs should be in balance with each other. Her exports (and aid, and reserves) are not large enough or flexible enough for any errors in planned output, or achievement, to be easily hidden by imports filling the gap. The degree of importance of coherence—production of just the right outputs—is relatively high. In food production, India is also sufficiently near the limits to make failure in agricultural advance perennially threaten hunger and famine. The Central and State Governments are closely involved in trying to stimulate agricultural production by all the usual means of co-operatives, community development and extension services, land reform, rural credit, fertilizer production, irrigation, land reclamation, etc. While India contains the skills which permit her, with little outside assistance, both to attempt some relatively sophisticated overall economic planning, and to design many projects and programmes in detail herself, nevertheless the complexity and magnitude of her problem is so great that these skills are overtaxed, and many failures occur.

India is a Federation of sixteen States with a population of over 465 million people. Certain of the most important development sectors, especially agriculture, but also health and education, are the responsibility of the States. India is not only a highly democratic country, but also one in which heterogeneity of outlook, through linguistic, religious, and caste differences, is much more obvious than uniformity. That central planning of economic development, with quite strong elements of rationality, can exist at all in the face of essential political compromise, and without much force in the presence of abject poverty, seems something of a miracle, especially when one considers that the strength of the Indian Administrative Service, which constitutes the administrative *élite*, is only a little over 2,000.[1]

At the other end of the range of the seventy-five independent underdeveloped countries, there are a number of the smallest newly-independent African States. Here certainly no macroeconomic plan is as yet possible. There are not enough facts. Working very much in the dark, the typical government can do no more than estimate the

[1] For a very full description of Indian Planning, see A. H. Hanson, *The Process of Planning: A Study of India's Five-Year Plans, 1950–63*, Oxford University Press, 1965.

revenue it can and should raise, make proposals for current expenditure, and then make a list of the investments it would like to undertake. In a number of cases the government cannot cover its current expenditure, and is therefore dependent on foreign capital for all the development it undertakes. The plan, no doubt, will also contain some history, some survey information, and discussions of general policy: but this is background material. What counts, if the plan is to be used as a basis of aid-giving, is that there should be a firm expenditure plan, which could be efficiently and economically carried out if the foreign aid were available. For this to be the case, the projects and programmes must have been designed and costed in some detail, and shown, so far as is possible in the current state of ignorance, to be worthwhile. Further, there must be an order of priority if the total aid required is likely to be in excess of that obtainable.

To speak of an order of priority may make economists raise their eyebrows. In an ideal plan, it may be argued, everything hangs together. If the plan is to be reduced in size, then everything has to change. Fortunately, this is true only of an 'optimum' plan, which is certainly never attainable. In reality, in many economies, the degree to which projects and programmes are closely interrelated is limited. In any case one does not know exactly what the proper relation, or balance, is. Consequently, one may be able to reduce the size of a plan by simple weeding out or pruning, without thereby arriving at something one knows to be inferior to what one would have planned if one had started with a smaller total expenditure in mind.

It is, indeed, fortunate for planning at all that this is the case. It is a general rule of planning, that it has to proceed in ignorance of the total funds available. Thus, state governments in a federation must make plans without knowing what subventions they will get from the centre; ministries without knowing their vote; and so on. This must be the case, because the higher authority cannot allot funds to the lower in a vacuum without knowing what it can use them for. Planning is an iterative process, of guesswork and revision: but without much iteration, for time does not permit it. The optimum could be achieved only if each lower planning authority could produce a whole range of different plans to suit the different amounts of money it may finally obtain. Time alone makes this impossible. Thus too much should not be made of the fact that recipients do not know how much aid they will get when they make their plans. There is no getting round this difficulty. The best that can be hoped for is a rough idea of the order of magnitude, so that time is not wasted in putting together a rather inflexible plan that cannot possibly be financed. Of course, there will be parts of the plan which do necessarily hang together, and are inflexible in this sense. Such strictly complementary expenditures must then be treated as wholes: the point is that, in practice, if not in theory, the plan does not and cannot constitute a single fully inter-locking whole. It comes more or less close to this ideal, but some-times, in the least developed and most open economies, hardly close at all. In the poorest and least developed there is thus little problem of coherence, the number of feasible projects being rather few and often not essentially dependent on each other.

2. AID FOR PLANS, PROGRAMMES, OR PROJECTS

Economic plans have been discussed above. A project is any unit of expenditure, which, for reasons of administration, accounting, or purpose, it is convenient to define as such. It may range from a grand river-valley scheme to a school, or a small team of experts. A 'pro-gramme' is used in the sense of a set of projects which are linked to-gether in that they are economically so complementary that if one is to be carried out then all should be; or that they are all intended to be carried out in a certain period by the same administrative unit. In what follows programmes can be equated with projects.

There has been much argument as to whether aid should be given on a project (or programme) basis, or on a plan basis.[1] Our discussion of economic planning was meant to show that this must depend on the kind of plan which the recipient government can produce, or wishes to produce (a number of underdeveloped countries do not have plans at all). It may also depend to some extent on the nature of the economy. We saw in Chapter VII that many of the disadvantages of project aid flow from the fact that aid for projects is mostly tied aid. Here we are concerned with the advantages and disadvantages of project aid as such.

If a country can and does produce a good tightly-knit plan, in which everything depends significantly on everything else, and where the timing of projects and programmes is also therefore of impor-tance, giving aid for projects may be harmful for a number of reasons. Even supposing that the donors simply pick projects from the plan, and that the total of aid can be absorbed by the projects they approve, difficulties and delays can arise. They may arise from indecision on the part of the donor, and also from disagreement between donor and

[1] To confuse matters, 'programme aid' has sometimes been used in the sense in which we use 'plan aid'.

recipient as to the best design, or method of carrying out, the project. This is very common. Also, expenditure on projects is often delayed for unforeseen reasons. In that event, with project aid, the funds cannot be switched to another project which may be wilting for lack of money. Also, where there are many donors, it may be very difficult to marry the projects in the plan to donors' preferences. Some may be left high and dry, and others may be too big for a single donor, in which case difficult problems of co-operation arise. Administrative difficulties for the recipient (and good administration is everywhere scarce) are certainly increased. Furthermore, if most aid is given only for projects, the result may be that either the aid cannot be absorbed or that too many projects get started. Not all development activity consists of expenditures which can be turned into projects. This is particularly likely to arise where there is already considerable industrial capacity, and where, therefore, there is a high demand for replacements, minor extensions of capacity, and so on.

Finally, such aid in practice has tended very much to go to large infrastructure projects with a relative neglect of the final productive sectors, and of small projects. This can be doubly harmful in that it may tie up a disproportionate amount of domestic funds, since donors seldom subscribe the whole cost. This emphasis has occurred for various reasons, the most important of which are (1) the attraction of the fact that infrastructure projects are usually politically neutral, (2) that donors, for administrative economy, dislike small projects, (3) that donors dislike financing recurrent expenditures, which often comprise a large part of small projects, (4) that for obvious reasons aid is given almost entirely to governments, and many donors dislike financing things in the public sector which private enterprise might undertake, (5) that small industrial and agricultural projects demand and require much more intimate working with the recipient administration, and this is full of pitfalls, and (6) that aid cannot so easily be tied to supplies from the donor country. However, none of these reasons can be reckoned as disadvantages of projects as such. It is rather that donors, to some extent, prefer the wrong kind of project.

Economists, often intellectually obsessed with optimum planning models, tend to overestimate the disadvantages of 'projectizing' aid, and to underestimate its advantages from the point of view of economic development. If a country's plan consists of little more than a list of projects, with no priorities attached, and with no indication of the preparedness of such projects, then the prospective donor cannot assess the rationale of the plan, for it will give little indication of how the money would in fact be spent. More fundamentally, the donor may have little confidence in the recipient government's ability to design or administer projects, and little confidence that the recipient government will spend the money with developmental intent. Alternatively, it may have little respect for the recipient's views as to what constitutes development. If such is the case, then to give money 'in aid of the plan' is little different from simply giving money without caring how it is spent, whether on palaces or schools, on improving the administration, or on bribing voters. If aid is given for development, because the electors of the donor countries believe that aid should be for development, then the donor governments often have no choice but to projectize their aid. It is only thus that they can try to see that the money they give, or the capital they provide, is economically spent in ways which promise to be beneficial for the development of the recipient country.

It can be objected that this may merely mean that aid funds are diverted to the sensible projects, while the recipient concentrates its own funds on the sort of things donors dislike, so that the supervision and policing of aid funds makes no difference. This might be true where aid is rather small relative to total investment. Even where this is so, however, it can be the case that insistence on a good economic and technical appraisal, and on sound financial control in carrying out aid projects, will both set an example and in itself contribute to the knowledge of how things should be done. At its best, insistence on such standards, especially when they can be mutually enforced by donors and recipients, helps to transfer planning and executive skills to the recipient, and therefore serves as a form of technical assistance. Moreover, aid is often not small relative to total expenditures on development. Sometimes there could be no development without aid. In these cases, the objection clearly has no validity.

If the bias in favour of the big infrastructural projects, which are easy for donors to plan—ports, roads, runways, power stations, dams, university buildings, etc.—can be removed, then project-tying should be, for many poor countries, an advantage from the point of view of development. This is not to say that infrastructure is not needed. Of course it is. But much has been provided, and in many countries the priorities now lie with improving agricultural credit, extension, and education; with the processing and marketing of agricultural products; with encouraging small-scale indigenous industry; with technical education and industrial extension; with improving various administrative services, and so on. It is becoming more generally recognized that more aid should flow into such fields. But there are many difficulties. Often ignorance of the best way to proceed is common both to the recipient government department, and to donors. Projects and programmes in such fields are likely to cause tension, and it is admittedly more difficult—though not usually impossible—to map what needs to be done in such fields into projects or programmes, over the realization of which the donor retains some control. Nevertheless, if aid has to keep out of areas which are crucial to development, and if there is no confidence on the part of donors that the recipient could and would of itself put sufficient emphasis on such improvements, then the role of foreign aid in economic development is all the more limited.

The argument that in many countries the only good approach to aid-giving is via projects, does not in the least imply that such projects should not be chosen in relation to some strategy for development. If the country's own plan does not map out a coherent and feasible strategy, both overall and in particular sectors, or if there is no confidence that the strategy would in practice be followed, then it may be best for donors to form a strategy of their own. Otherwise, there is too much risk that projects yield little return either because they are themselves of low priority, or because, as so often happens, complementary investment or complementary organization and administration is not undertaken. This implies an element of planning by donors, both in selecting sectors which seem to them to be of high priority, and within sectors to ensure that what they instigate does not fail through lack of complementary action. This in turn raises difficult problems both as to political and working relations between donor and recipient, and for co-operation between donors. These problems are discussed at greater length in the next section.

3. AID RELATIONS

There can be no denial of the fact that aid-giving would be much easier if the recipient countries planned, both overall and in detail, with sufficient competence, realism, and economic sense, for donors to feel that they need do no planning themselves. This is, undoubtedly, the objective to aim at. Encouragement and help, via technical assistance, towards this end is essential, and perhaps the highest priority. But, in some countries, there is little desire to employ foreigners in planning offices, or departments, and in some also the planners carry little or no weight. It is highly tricky, politically, for foreign governments effectively to influence the balance and detail of development spending. This should not, however, blind one to the fact that, with many recipients, donors cannot otherwise feel any confidence that their money is not going to be put to very poor use. Nevertheless, such interference will often lead to friction and accusations of neo-colonialism. Indeed it *is* neo-colonialism, but neo-colonialism in the cause of development. Occasionally, in some quarters, this is welcomed. But it is more usually resented. This is perhaps the basic dilemma of aid, at its most perplexing where the recipient administration is either highly incompetent, or corrupt, or is not really interested in development.

If the necessary people can be supplied from abroad, it is relatively easy to ensure that enough expert advice is available to recipient governments. If necessary, the amount of financial aid offered can be cut down until it bears a reasonable relationship to the recipient's ability to spend money effectively, given the maximum technical advice that is available or can be absorbed. More difficult is the problem of preventing large-scale corruption, and of ensuring that the advice is followed, or at least considered seriously. Surveillance of this kind is possible only if an aid donor has considerable detailed knowledge of the recipient's economy, and of its monetary, fiscal, and other economic, policies.

The threat to withdraw or reduce aid may give the donor wide implicit powers of interference for the purpose of imposing sensible economic solutions to development problems. But interference in a recipient's economy, however clear the donor's apparent right to intervene, and however helpful the intervention may be for the recipient's development, is almost bound to be resented as an affront to national independence. Even so, few recipients would deny that donors have some right to choose how their own resources should be used. A donor's right to influence the use of the aid it gives is not often questioned in principle by recipients. In the extreme case of a gift in kind—whether of a factory, sports stadium, hospital, tractor, or anything else—it would be impossible to deny that a donor has the right to choose what it should give, and embarrassing (though sometimes justifiable) to point out that some alternative gift would have been more useful.

Difficulties arise when aid is used together with a recipient's domestic resources in a project or programme, or when the money is lent and has to be repaid. When both donor's and recipient's resources are thus involved in a project, it becomes necessary for both parties to be satisfied with arrangements for selection and supervision. Recipients tend to feel that the degree of donor supervision should vary with the amount of donor subsidy; if aid takes the form of a grant covering a large proportion of the cost of a project, more supervision will be acceptable than if the so-called 'aid' is lent at 6 per cent, or covers only, say, 10 per cent of project costs. In countries where donors feel that considerable supervision is necessary, they should therefore see that their loans are cheap, and also that they pay for the major part of particular projects, even where this involves them in financing local expenditure. Countries which are very poor are usually those where most supervision is required, so there is a double reason for the use of cheap loans and grants.

More complex problems arise where a single donor provides a fairly large proportion of a particular recipient's total development budget. In such a case, the donor is likely to adopt various expedients for influencing planning and general economic policy. This is justified, from its point of view, because only rational planning can ensure that development funds (including aid) are spent in the really important sectors of the economy, and on projects which are compatible with one another. But interference with planning, unless help is actually asked for, is likely to be resented. A recipient's view is put in an article written in 1962 by two Pakistani students,[1] who think it very wrong that 'In the economic sphere the US Government has the right to receive information about all projects on which even a small proportion of aid money is being spent. The agreement providing for commodity assistance grants that the American Government has an interest in the monetary stability of Pakistan, thus enabling it formally to have a say in our development policy. . . . Thus US experts are associated at all levels of policy making. This means in effect that the USA interpretation of what is "sound policy" prevails.' The article criticizes the whole of USA and Pakistani policy, and ends with a plea for 'the restoration of national independence'. Our point is that the authors feel USA interference in planning to be out of proportion to the volume of USA aid.[2] Incidentally, in the past few years, Pakistan has progressed beyond all expectation.

[1] Alavi and Khusro, 'Pakistan: the burden of US Aid', in *New University Thought*, Autumn, 1962, published by the New University Thought Publishing Company, Chicago. Reprinted from *Pakistan Today*.

[2] An added complication is that a large part of USA aid to Pakistan consists of surplus commodities. These are valued in USA estimates of aid at world market prices, and Alavi and Khusro believe that they should be valued at prices little more than zero, especially as the commodities are not formally given to the Pakistani Government, and the proceeds of their sale are used in part to pay for the expenses in Pakistan of USA diplomatic and military staff. (Cp. Chapter VI for our discussion of commodity aid.)

The above may be an extreme view, but is nevertheless common. Interference beyond the project level is often fiercely resented, above all when a donor's right to supervision, as measured by its contribution or by its sacrifice, is shaky. There are people who argue that grant aid is the right of all poor countries, and should be provided 'without strings', but on the whole it is accepted that providing grants or subsidized loans gives a donor some rights as to the projects on which his aid will be spent—provided the aid is not spread too thinly.

But even when it is agreed that, as a general principle, donors have a legitimate interest in project selection and to some extent in general economic planning and policy, differences of opinion between donor and recipient are bound to occur from time to time. The most serious are those which arise from basic differences of purpose; if a donor uses his influence to promote his own export industries, or if a recipient government is more interested in military exploits, or finding jobs for ministers' relatives, than in developing the economy, it becomes virtually impossible for donor and recipient to collaborate.

A second source of differences of opinion is the question whether particular sacrifices—in the shape of accepting a foreigner as director of a new government department, or reforming a particular ministry and thereby offending certain established civil servants—should or should not be made for the sake of more rapid development. Such differences may involve matters of priority different only in degree from the basic issue of whether development is among the recipient government's most favoured objectives. On the donor's side, prejudices about state versus private operation of certain industries may fall into the same category, since they may be very important to the donor, but irrelevant to development.

A third class of disagreements, again different only in degree from the second, lies in the field of politico-economic policy. There may be genuine disagreements between donor and recipient, based on economic theory but often coloured by political prejudice, about whether greater emphasis should be placed on industrial or agricultural investment; whether economic growth in backward regions should be promoted at the expense of a lower rate of growth in the economy as a whole; whether certain industrial or agricultural projects should be undertaken by public or private enterprise, and so on.

Disagreements of all these types are bound to occur. When they occur, donors may find great difficulty in balancing their own interest in development against the legitimate exercise of sovereignty by the recipient government. At times a withdrawal, or at least reduction, of aid, may become advisable on economic grounds, especially when it appears that the recipient government is not really interested in development. But for political reasons, since withdrawing aid can cause more hostility than almost any other action, donor governments are loath to go to this extreme, and may prefer to continue giving aid in the knowledge that it is not thereby doing much for development. If, more happily, donor and recipient are united in caring about development, then it is up to both sides to be as understanding and flexible as possible on the political side (strategic matters apart), and for the donor to avoid building any political prejudice into its aid agreements.

What are the possible methods of supervision? The simplest, which is now ruled out in all but a few small recipient countries, is by means of colonial administration.[1] This degree of interference by foreigners is clearly out of the question in an independent state, and other more limited types of supervision must replace it. There are three basic methods of supervising the use of aid; they may of course be used in conjunction with one another.

First, specially appointed staff of the donor government, based in the recipient country, can keep a close check on the accounts of the departments using aid funds. They may of course hire accountants to do the work, but the important thing is that they should know whether the various goods and services on which money is spent (cement, haulage, building contractors' services, etc.) are entered at correct prices, and that the corresponding operations are actually being carried out as alleged in the accounts. No large-scale corruption should pass unnoticed if supervisors on the spot are reasonably vigilant. This kind of supervision is expensive, if it is to be at all thorough, and is appropriate only if large sums of aid are involved, if aid is not dispersed over too wide a field, and if corruption is known to be serious. Otherwise, the check on expenditure is likely to cost more than the amount of money saved. If aid is given in the form of general budgetary support, the amount of work involved in checking the whole of government expenditure in a meaningful way would be not only impossible, but also intolerable to an independent recipient government. But if aid were provided for a certain type of government service—say agricultural extension or technical education or land settlement—the job of supervising expenditure effectively should be manageable.

The second possibility is to have technical assistance people working in ordinary operational posts in government. This would resemble

[1] See Chapter I, pp. 30-3, for a brief description of the British system.

the supervision of colonial days, since the British employees of colonial governments had close informal ties with Whitehall, and were in an excellent position to influence policy, and supervise expenditure, along lines acceptable to the British Government. But this kind of arrangement can no longer be so effective, since the informal but close ties that British expatriates working for overseas governments had with the CO have now been replaced by more formal but looser ties with the ODM, and with the FO and CRO. A further change is that expatriates even in operational posts tend increasingly to be concerned with technical matters,[1] rather than with the general administration of a department, and are therefore less able than their predecessors to keep an eye on expenditure. Nevertheless, an overseas government that still employs a large number of British expatriates inspires more confidence in British aid administrators than a more completely indigenous government. This is reasonable in so far as, in these circumstances, large-scale corruption is less likely to go undetected by the British Government. However, as the number of expatriates in operational posts is falling, this method of keeping track of the use of aid will soon become obsolete unless backed up by other more formal methods of supervision.

The third possibility is for aid donors to take primary responsibility for a project or programme; they will provide the necessary surveys, staff to set up the project, money to pay for it, and training courses for local people who will later take it over. The extent to which the recipient will provide men and money towards the project must depend on local capabilities; as many local staff as feasible should be involved from the earliest stages. This kind of approach can be varied to suit the needs of a wide range of developing countries, from the very primitive which will be unable to provide much beyond the unskilled labour and some raw materials, and will be unable to take over running the project for a long time, to the relatively sophisticated who can acquire the necessary new skills quite quickly.

Whatever is done about supervision of both accounting and planning, it is important in some countries that donors should take more initiative in proposing financial and technical assistance projects. In a country where there is a serious and comprehensive plan (i.e. one

[1] Recruitment of operational personnel under the OSAS illustrates this point. 41·3 per cent of personnel actually in service at December 1963 came within the category 'Public Administration, Economics and Finance, and Social Services', compared with only 8·8 per cent of 1963's new recruits. New recruits in Education, Industry and Technology, and Health and Sanitation, accounted for 55·9 per cent of total recruits, whereas only 30·2 per cent of those in service fell within this group of specialisms. See *Technical Assistance*, ODI, Table 15.

which relates projects to one another in some detail) donors should try to base their proposals on that plan. But where not even the recipient government takes its plan seriously, donors should have enough knowledge of the recipient's economic needs to make their own suggestions for things to be done. Even where there is a plan, donors should know enough to be able to see which projects are the most important to the recipient's economy. If donors went to the trouble and expense of building up their knowledge of recipient's economies, this in itself would help to improve the standard of planning, since their professional advisers would sometimes be able to influence it, and could normally give technical assistance in their own professional fields. This is precisely what happens in the Middle East, where the British Government's MEDD has built up unrivalled knowledge of the economies of Middle Eastern countries, in most fields from general economic planning to individual sectors like industry, forestry, and agriculture. This type of advisory service, which can both assist the donor's aid administrators, and give advice to recipient governments about economic policy and all aspects of aid, and can in addition perform some of the functions of short-term technical advisers, is unique among British institutions. As the MEDD is an advisory, and not a policy-making, body, its members are able to have less formal and more fruitful contacts with members of governments in the region, than is possible for ordinary embassy staff in the direct line of responsibility for actual decisions about aid.

The effect of more determined attempts by donors, in co-ordination, to influence recipients' policies depends on many factors. Perhaps most important is the recipient's assessment of donors' sincerity about development; if, for instance, donors who believe that agricultural and rural development is of great importance, behave in such a way as to lend colour to the belief that they oppose industrialization for selfish reasons, then satisfactory aid relations are less likely to be established. Other factors include the calibre, both technical and personal, of donors' professional advisers and aid administrators, and the amount and terms of the aid made available.

If donors are to take more initiative and responsibility in the spending of aid, and if they are to have teams of professional advisers stationed permanently in the main areas, and sometimes in single countries, their relationships with other donors will become even more important than they are at present. Otherwise there would be unnecessary and expensive duplication of advisory services, and, worse still, donors might attempt to force conflicting policies on the recipients. The problems posed, now and in the event of more donor advice and interference in recipients' policies, will be discussed in the next section.

4. THE MULTI-DONOR PROBLEM

Developing countries attach great importance to political non-alignment. One way of demonstrating non-alignment, to their own citizens and to the rest of the world, is to make sure that aid comes from many sources. Even if there were no Cold War, and no decision to be made about alignment or non-alignment, a country which received all its aid from one source would almost certainly resent the dependence implied in such a relationship, and try to widen its contacts. Finally, most recipients feel that there is scope for playing off donors against one another, and for extracting more aid in total from a number of donors than they could hope to acquire from any one of them.

Despite the strong incentives for diversifying sources of aid, most developing countries still receive a high proportion of their aid from a single source. The most conspicuous are probably the French-speaking countries of West and Central Africa, whose aid comes almost exclusively from France. Sentimental ties apart, they have reason to accept this arrangement because their chances of getting more by appealing to America, Russia, and possibly China, are so slight that the risk of damaging their relationships with France is not worth running. A further reason is that the French discourage other donors from entering the field, and the only other donor of any significance in the area is the EDF, which co-operates fairly closely with the French Government.

Latin American countries are in a position similar to the ex-French African countries in certain respects. A very high proportion of their aid comes from the USA, and is likely to do so for a long time, since the USA is the only important donor with a strong enough foreign policy interest in Latin America to be willing to give or lend on a large scale. The main difference between Latin America and French-speaking Africa is that both the Latin American governments and the USA would like to attract aid into the area from other sources (i.e. Europe), and are likely to meet with some success. A second difference is that Latin American governments probably have rather more scope for flirting with the East in order to attract more aid than has been the case in French Africa; USA aid to Latin America has increased remarkably since Cuba's revolution and new relationship with Russia.

Other countries that rely heavily upon one donor are those whose aid is closely linked with USA military strategy—Taiwan, South Korea, South Vietnam, etc.—and those which have until very recently been British colonies. It seems likely that the latter—e.g. East and Central Africa—will follow Nigeria and Ghana in establishing a pattern of aid in which no single donor predominates. Whatever their own preferences in the matter, and it is undoubtedly true that they would like to reduce their dependence on Britain, the UK Government is not willing to provide the amount of finance that would be needed to establish the kind of relationships that France has with her former colonies.

Even in the countries most dominated by one donor, there are usually several minor donors; in ex-French Africa, for instance, the AID, various UN agencies, and the EDF, also provide some aid. Thus, for these countries as well as for those that have arrived at, or are moving towards, the position occupied by India, Pakistan, Turkey, or Nigeria, of receiving substantial amounts of aid from many sources, there is some need for co-ordination. An extreme case is India, which by 1963 had received commitments of aid from nineteen governments, seven UN bodies, and two private foundations. The largest donor, the USA, had contributed less than one-third of the total (excluding surplus commodity aid).

Countries receiving aid from many sources are faced with a number of problems which would not arise if, like colonies, they looked to a single donor. It is useful to classify these problems into those which are unavoidable, those which are created by donor's policies, and those which arise out of the recipients' weaknesses.

The first group of problems arises from handling aid negotiations, and receiving technical assistance, tied aid, and aid in kind, from a variety of donors with different languages, technical standards, and systems of education. Short of reverting to a single-donor single-recipient system, there is very little that can be done to remove these problems, though it might be useful to try to arrange technical assistance in such a way that no recipient received experts from more than, say, three or four countries.

The second group of difficulties, those caused by donors' policies being directed at some end other than development, are not peculiar to the multi-donor situation, but are special cases of more general problems. The first such policy is procurement tying: however efficient the recipient government, it is exceedingly difficult to allocate a large number of tied currencies between various imports for various projects, taking into account price differences and the future availability of the same currencies for replacements and extensions. Mistakes will tend to result in unfinished projects, idle capacity, and expensive retraining of technicians and mechanics. Tied aid from a single source may be more obviously wasteful, in that goods are more likely to be bought at prices above those quoted elsewhere: but if the aid can be relied upon to continue in the future, its administration is less difficult, and mistakes less costly.

The second policy that may make multi-donor aid less efficient than single-donor aid is project-tying. We have said that project-tying is often appropriate as a method of surveillance and of providing technical and financial aid in a 'package'; but this is the case only if the donor's priorities are determined by the recipient's needs and the donor's capabilities. Where project-tying is too heavily influenced by a donor's political or trading policy, its effects on development are usually harmful. Ideally, project-aid from many donors should improve a recipient's hope of covering all the important projects in its plan, since several donors are more likely than a single donor to possess between them the know-how for, say, constructing a hydro-electric power project, a steel mill, a textile factory, a railway extension, and an improvement in agricultural extension. When, however, donors are more interested in prestige or future exports than in the recipient's development, they may compete vigorously for a few favoured, import-intensive, prestige projects, and be unwilling to look at the smaller less glamorous projects which tend to involve the use of a high proportion of local materials and manpower, and to be more important for development. When there are many donors, so that the contribution of each to development is difficult to trace, there is a greater temptation to concentrate on prestige, than would be the case if there were a single donor whose contribution to development was expected to be significant, and whose interest in the recipient's development was therefore more intense.

The donor policies discussed above will tend to have an adverse effect on development in a multi-donor situation however efficient the recipient's administration, and however well-planned and well-executed its policies for economic development. When a recipient's administration and planning machinery is weak, and donors who genuinely wish to promote development are therefore obliged to take an intimate interest in its policies, and to supervise the use of aid in some detail, a third group of problems arises. It is quite clear that if, as we believe, most donors ought to supervise more closely the use of aid in many countries, an enormous amount of waste and duplication would be the first result. If every significant donor to countries like Nigeria, whose sources of aid are already well diversified, were to set up an aid office in Lagos, with permanent professional advisers and supporting staff on the AID model, there would be an intolerable waste of very scarce manpower, which would anyway not be available to extend such a system to many countries. Recipients would also find their own scarce administrators spending too much time on discussions and negotiations with the donor agencies. If each donor, in these circumstances, were to attempt, without consulting other donors, to impose on the recipient its own ideas about what development policies should be followed, the result would be chaotic.

This situation has not yet occurred because so few donors at present administer their aid adequately. What is clear is that better administration of aid, however desirable in itself, cannot contribute very much to development unless better co-ordination is also achieved.

The most obvious solution to this problem, superficially at any rate attractive to recipients, would be for each to accept aid from a single multilateral donor. Whether that donor were organized on a world-wide or regional basis, it would in principle be able to pursue a consistent policy in each recipient country, and to refrain from selecting projects for reasons not determined by the recipient's needs. It would probably be able to keep within bounds the number of languages, technical standards, and tied currencies, that each developing country had to handle. Politically, however, such an organization or group of organizations is almost inconceivable. The chances of persuading the USA, USSR, and all other aid donors, to pay money into a common pool—or failing that, to set up regional multilateral organizations with the undertaking that no country would offer aid except through the organizations to which it belonged—are negligible.

In spite of this, it is worth asking what recipients would think about such an arrangement, because many of them claim to prefer multilateral to bilateral aid, and there is still widespread support for the idea that a large part of financial aid should be channelled through a SUNFED.[1] If the organization were donor-controlled (like the IBRD) recipients would probably not like it at all. Even if it were controlled by recipients themselves (like the UNEPTA and UNSF), decisions made by a single monolithic agency, without appeal, would be resented. Many recipients would believe, correctly, that they would have attracted more aid through bilateral channels, even if the total of aid were the same. Moreover, if the agency failed to attract as much aid from its donor members as they would have given bilaterally, almost

[1] See Chapter I, pp. 46–7,

all recipients would probably acquire less. Finally, the recipients would inevitably quarrel about the criteria for allocating aid.

As regards development, a donor-controlled agency that really aimed for development would probably be effective in promoting it; it would almost certainly be more effective than bilateral donors working independently of one another. On the other hand, a recipient-controlled agency would almost certainly find it more difficult than a donor-controlled agency to apply economic criteria firmly. This might please recipient governments in the short run, but it would not be to the long-run economic advantage of the people.

It is thus obvious that no full multilateralization of aid is acceptable to all parties. The Western donors would not dream of multilateralizing most of their aid unless the Eastern donors agreed to do likewise. If this improbable agreement were reached, aid would certainly be reduced, unless donor control were established, and neither of these outcomes would please the recipients. It is therefore plain that one can look for some limited solution of the multi-donor problem only in a closer co-ordination of bilateral aid, where the co-ordinating agency might well be a multilateral organization. Even if the co-ordinating agent were above suspicion, e.g. the UN Resident Representative, some fear of the mere existence of co-ordination is to be expected in some recipient countries. But one may hope that such fear and suspicion will die down, or can be overcome: for co-ordination can certainly help greatly to improve the development-efficiency of aid, by preventing waste, improving planning and project selection, and speeding up the usage of aid. The initiative in promoting such co-ordination, and choosing the means of achieving it, lies primarily with the donors. The problem is discussed again from the donors' point of view in Chapter XIII.

CHAPTER IX

THE TERMS OF AID, AND THE DEBT PROBLEM

In Part I Chapter III we stressed that interest rates must be subsidized if a capital flow to an underdeveloped country was to rank as aid. The arguments used were essentially moral, political, and semantic. But in this part of the book we have been considering the flow of financial resources regardless of terms. We shall now deal more fully with the economic rationale of charging interest, and requiring capital repayments.

First, consider the matter as if there were a single donor and a single recipient of public capital, and as if the capital were provided because the donor considered that the recipient could not develop satisfactorily without some net receipt of funds. Now it could happen that this situation would continue for ever: one country being always sufficiently richer than the other to justify this. In that case it is clear that charging interest on loans, or insisting on repayment, would be futile from the lender's point of view. Any repayment, whether of capital or interest, must itself be more than covered by further loans.

It can be argued that loans should be made at full rates of interest, even if more aid must be given to cover both interest and repayment, for the sake of financial discipline in the receiving country. Some think that cheap money is more likely to be wasted by governments than dear money. It is very doubtful whether there is anything in this argument. Observation suggests that governments which waste money through bad planning and administration, corruption, or sheer extravagance, do so regardless of whether interest rates are high or low. Certainly many of the most foolish projects are financed from very high-interest loans. Assessment and supervision by the donor is a far more effective way of improving end-use. The further point that the final recipients of loans, the productive units themselves, should pay normal interest rates is better founded. On the other hand it is irrelevant, because there need be no connection between interest rates paid by a government and internal rates charged.

After this digression let us return to the point that charging interest and asking for repayment presupposes that, at some time in the future, the recipient country will be deemed not to need any new transfer of official capital. Indeed, it must in addition be deemed to be in a position both to pay interest on the past inflow of capital, and to make repayments. It will have to be more than capable of a self-sustained growth of income per head (if it is to be presumed that the donor will still want the country to grow).

Let us then trace the official capital importing phases of such a country, which receives loans on each of which it must pay, say, equal annual amounts in redemption, and also interest. Since, *ex hypothesi*, this country will pay back one day, it must be presumed that it eventually saves more than enough to sustain its own growth, and to pay interest on the aggregate outstanding amount of capital borrowed in the period before it reaches this point. What determines this aggregate amount? This depends on the whole preceding history. But, to simplify a little, we shall first suppose that it receives enough foreign capital during this earlier period to make the ratio of investment to domestic product high enough to sustain the growth of domestic product at the desired rate. How high this rate is depends, of course, on the productivity of investment.[1] Secondly, we have to assume that, as the country grows, its savings rate increases to some rate higher than the required investment rate. Otherwise, plainly, its need of foreign capital never ceases: if the savings rate became equal only to the desired investment rate, there would still be a deficiency equal to the interest charges on the accumulated debt, and these would grow indefinitely at compound interest, because the country would still always have to borrow enough to pay the interest. Thus the amount of capital it must borrow depends on the marginal savings rate, which determines how quickly it reduces, and finally eliminates, the need for foreign capital.[2] It depends on the initial savings rate as well, for that determines how far the average savings rate has to rise. But it also depends on the interest rate the country is charged. Thus, during the whole period when it must borrow net, the aggregate amount it owes mounts not only by the net borrowing each

[1] For simplicity we assume that this does not change during the debt cycle. We further assume that the desired rate of growth is possible throughout. These are highly unrealistic assumptions, but the essential nature of the story of the debt history would remain the same given less stringent assumptions.

[2] Of course, the marginal savings rate need not be constant. It may rise as the country develops. A low initial marginal savings rate cannot necessarily be taken as a sign that the country will never be self-supporting, or even that it will take a long time. This is also true of the productivity of capital.

year for investment purposes, but also by the interest on the outstanding debt. This is quite regardless of the fact that it actually pays interest, for it is necessarily borrowing the sums required to pay the whole of the interest right up until the time that its own savings exceed its own investment.

It is possible that a country never reaches the stage when it can pay back capital. We have already seen that if its own savings rate rises only to equality with the required investment rate, then interest payments will increase annually at a rate equal to the rate of interest. Provided the rate of interest is less than the rate of growth of output, this would not be disastrous because the interest payments would then slowly decline as a proportion of GDP.

If a country can go on borrowing indefinitely, it can still grow without interest payments increasing continuously as a proportion of domestic product (which certainly implies disaster in the end), even if the marginal savings rate is less than the required investment rate, provided that interest rates are low enough. Obviously, it could do this with interest free loans.

There is in fact an interest rate below which interest payments do not 'explode' as a proportion of domestic product, which is a function of the initial and marginal savings rates, the capital output ratio, and the desired rate of growth. The lower the two former, and the higher the two latter, the lower is the critical interest rate. For instance, with an initial savings rate of 5 per cent, a marginal rate of 20 per cent, a desired growth of 5 per cent, and a capital output ratio of three, the critical interest rate is $7\frac{1}{2}$ per cent.

But with the same initial savings rate and desired growth rate, the critical interest rate would be only $3\frac{2}{3}$ per cent if the capital-output ratio were 4 and the marginal savings rate were only 16 per cent (less than the required investment rate of 20 per cent). In this latter case the country would require outside capital for ever at the subsidized rate of $3\frac{2}{3}$ per cent (i.e. aid for ever, and ever more aid) in order to be able to grow at 5 per cent. But the low interest rate would prevent the service payments rising indefinitely as a proportion of domestic product.[1]

[1] With these figures, if domestic product were 100, the debt would be 300, giving an interest charge of 11 at $3\frac{2}{3}$ per cent. This interest charge plus the required investment of 20 gives a total foreign and domestic savings requirement of 31. Since domestic savings is 16 (assuming that a very long period has elapsed so that the marginal savings rate equals the average savings rate), borrowing from abroad is 15. This raises the debt to 315 in the next year. But domestic product is then 105, so that the same ratio is preserved, and all magnitudes can continue to grow at 5 per cent per annum.

However, this last case is rather uninteresting, for if aid has to be given for ever then there is no sense in charging interest at all. In fact, if a country's productivity of capital and its marginal savings rate are not high enough for growth to become self-sustaining, charging interest is futile. If it can just become self-sustaining, then the critical rate of interest equals the rate of growth, but it is still pointless to charge interest. In other words, unless a country can do better than just become self-sustaining, so that the critical rate of interest is higher than the rate of growth, there is no sense in charging interest at all, because all it does is raise greatly the level of debt which will never be repaid (but remember we are still considering the artificial case of there being only one donor).[1] Suppose we accept the minimum UN growth target of 5 per cent, and assume that capital output ratios lie between 3 and 4, that the initial savings rate is only 5 per cent but that marginal savings rates lie between 16 and 24 (at least 15 is necessary for self-sustained growth on these assumptions), then the critical interest rates range from $3\frac{3}{4}$ per cent to $9\frac{1}{2}$ per cent.[2] Less than this rate must be charged, otherwise self-sustained growth, and debt repayment, becomes impossible. The goose would have been killed by expecting too much.[3,4]

But the above formal argument presents high interest rates in much too favourable a light. To quote the report on which the above is based: 'the calculations assume that countries can continue to borrow and service debt in perpetuity on whatever scale the calculations may imply, without breakdown of the process so long as condi-

[1] Taking the example of the previous footnote, if no interest were charged, the debt would stabilize at four-fifths of domestic product instead of three times domestic product.

[2] These interest rates must be regarded as including the effective rates paid on equity capital, which may be quite high.

[3] The above three paragraphs are derived from Essay No. 4 in Vol. II of the IBRD study, Economic Growth and External Debt, prepared by J. P. Hayes, assisted by Hans Wyss and S. Shahid Husain. The interpretation is, of course, ours. The formula for the critical interest rate is $\dfrac{g(s-S_0)}{kg-S_0}$, where k and g are the capital-output ratio and growth rate, and S_0 and s the initial and marginal savings rates. The proportion of debt to national product becomes $k-\dfrac{S_0}{g}$.

[4] This paragraph might seem like an apologia for the UK policy (now somewhat eroded) of making either hard loans, or grants, with nothing in between. But this is not so, for the UK gives both loans and grants to the same country. Taking the paragraph without qualification would imply rather that some countries can grow with hard loans, while others should have only grants. We certainly would not advocate this.

tions of viciously cumulative debt can be avoided.'[1] If a rate of interest just below the critical rate were charged, the debt and interest payments could become enormous, before the position began to improve. Thus, for a 5 per cent growth rate and initial savings rate, and a capital output ratio of 3–4, and marginal savings rates of 15–20 per cent, interest charges alone would eventually swallow up around two-thirds of domestic savings. Borrowers would not tolerate this.

Lenders too have their rules of thumb. A common one is to look at the proportion that debt service (interest and capital) bears to export receipts. Given the vulnerability of the exports of many underdeveloped countries[2] this is a crude indicator of the probability of a country running into a debt-servicing crisis. Even making rather more favourable assumptions than reflect achievement in the last decade (assumptions which imply a critical rate of interest as high as 10 per cent),[3] and assuming that export receipts grow at 4 per cent per annum (a higher rate than recently achieved by many if not most underdeveloped countries), from an initial level of 10 per cent of GDP, the IBRD study shows that if all aid were in the form of hard loans at 6 per cent with repayment over fifteen years, then the servicing of the loans would rise to over 50 per cent of export receipts before the situation began to improve.[4] A typical country, exhibiting these figures, would not be considered eligible for loans, though Israel may be the exception which proves the rule.

This brings us to the subject of amortization. Unlike interest, amortization is irrelevant so far as the ultimate burden on the recipient is concerned. From the donor's point of view (still assuming one donor), if the object of aid is to promote self-sustained growth, then no net repayment can be expected until the savings rate in the recipient country has risen so far that it exceeds both the domestic investment required, and payment of interest on the accumulated debt. In the last-mentioned example of the previous paragraph, this would take twenty-five years. Such an exemplary country would have obtained a net addition to its resources for fifteen years. After fifteen years its savings rate would have caught up with the required domestic rate of investment, but it must needs go on borrowing to pay, at first,

[1] op. cit., p. 74, para. 72.
[2] See Chapter IV, pp. 125–7.
[3] The assumptions are: growth rate 5 per cent; initial savings 10 per cent; marginal savings 20 per cent; no initial debt; gross capital/gross output ratio 3 :1. Actual growth in the 1950s was only 4·4 per cent, and the observed capital/output ratio about 3½.
[4] op. cit., Vol. I, p. 54.

all the interest, and later only part of it. This period would last another ten years, after which it could repay capital. The logic of the situation suggests that even such a fortunate country should have a twenty-five-year grace period both for capital repayment and interest (which would accumulate at compound interest, but be deferred).[1]

The figures of the example are reasonably similar to the kind of figures on which India plans, and has planned since 1956. Now, even if India achieved by 1981 a position in which she could grow at 5 per cent, and service her debt without further aid—and this would constitute a miracle—would one want her to receive no aid? Her income would still be less than $150 per head! Self-sustained growth is conceivable, albeit improbable, in conjunction with extreme poverty. But, poverty apart, it seems wildly optimistic to suppose that there will be more than a handful, perhaps two handfuls, of countries which will be free of the need for aid, even if it is calculated solely on the basis of self-sustained growth, within 25 years, especially as this implies a net addition to resources for a period of only fifteen years. There are the overpopulated areas of Asia, where, since there is no surplus land, the capital output ratio can be expected to be high. There is Africa, where the indigenous level of skills is low, and the map is badly drawn for economic growth. These impediments will take a lot of time, and a lot of trouble, in all senses of the term, to cure. The greatest hope may be in an easing of the population explosion. But, again, it would be optimistic to expect much within twenty-five years. Amortization, without very lengthy grace periods, can in these circumstances be interpreted only as a lack of seriousness and commitment on the part of the donor countries. The donor country might change its mind, and want to withdraw its capital. But then it would be, in all probability, fooling itself. The recipient would probably abrogate its debts, and all would be lost.

But, before coming to any conclusion, we must consider the fact that there are many donors—not one. What difference does this make? First, take amortization. The presence of other donors means that in theory one donor can get paid back out of others'

---

[1] The whole of the preceding analysis has been made in terms of using foreign savings to supplement a deficiency of domestic savings. We recognized, in Chapter V, that there may be some countries where a deficiency of foreign currency may be the overriding problem. But the savings/investment model here used can always be applied if one makes allowance for the influence of a foreign currency deficit on the productivity of investment, and on savings. This was discussed in Chapter V, pp. 139–46.

loans, before the recipient becomes capable of repaying capital. The donor country is not quite so committed. The loan can be regarded as a better investment, for there is some probability that others will continue to lend, and so permit repayment. This raises problems which we refer to again in Part III of this book.

From the recipients' point of view there is obviously less security in short-term loans. The debt may be 'rolled over' all right: but the recipient cannot be certain of this. The volume of repayment of debt is already high. It was reckoned by the IBRD to be about $2·2 billion in 1963 (including private, government guaranteed, repayments). A high proportion of this must have been on private account, since the DAC figure for amortization of public debt for member countries in 1963 was only $0·5 billion. However, this figure will certainly rise rapidly from now on, as it comes to reflect the rapid rise in gross aid which began in 1958.

A high level of repayment raises the level of gross aid which a country must receive for any given amount of net aid. Unfortunately, however, donors still tend to think in gross terms. Thus, for instance, aid commitments at consortia meetings are always quoted gross, although it is only the net figure which is significant. The hard donors consequently appear to be more generous than is the case. Thus thinking in gross terms must tend to reduce the net level of aid for those recipients whose repayments have become, or will shortly become, large—for such countries as Chile, Brazil, Argentina, Turkey, and India.

Furthermore, the presence of many short-term lenders, including private lenders, is a temptation to incur too much badly-phased short-term debt, with the result that repayment obligations get concentrated into a few years to an extent which creates an impossible problem. Some of the lenders are then forced to relend if the debtor is not to default. But not all will be willing to do so, especially private commercial lenders. This situation causes difficulties among the lenders. It also, of course, constitutes a serious set-back to the borrowing country's credit, which makes a further crisis all the more likely. Yet the country's resultant bad reputation may bear no relation whatever to its capacity for economic growth, or to the question of whether or when it will eventually become capable of repaying debt.

It can be argued that this is the borrower's fault. On the other hand, the borrowers who have borrowed short excessively have often done so to alleviate the strains set up by falling export prices. Many countries have a high proportion of public debt repayable over a short period. The IBRD report cited shows twenty countries with 40 per cent or more of their 1962 debt repayable within five years,[1] and this excludes any repayments due to the IMF. Most of these are countries which suffered from declining export prices in the late 1950s. It may be thought that it is right that a country should borrow short in the face of a temporary fall in export earnings, and repay on recovery. To some extent this is valid. But it is also true that a country needs more development aid if the adverse fluctuation extends over more than a year or two: and there is no reason why such extra aid should be short-term. This takes one back to the schemes for compensatory development finance discussed in Chapter VI. Any such scheme should help to alleviate the excessive piling up of short-term debt. So also, of course, would a further lengthening of the amortization terms of development aid.

Let us now consider interest rates again. We saw that the long-term burden of debt is governed by the level of interest rates rather than by repayment terms. So far as recipients go, little difference is made to the argument by the fact that there are many donors—not one, as was assumed in the argument. Of course, recipients might turn down offers of loans from some potential creditors on the ground of excessive interest rates. We believe this is seldom done, although there are certainly more than a few cases when it should have been done. Unless the real yield of the project for which the loan is to be used (which is not, of course, necessarily the same as the financial return)[2] is greater than the rate of interest charged, then the loan harms the recipient, and benefits only the lender. Where the lender's interest is genuinely in development it will not, of course, lend in such circumstances. In that event, the flow of funds is limited by the interest rate. It is possible that this has been a limitation on IBRD lending (for years the IBRD has lent less than its available funds), although it is questionable how far precise estimates of economic return have governed, or limited, IBRD decisions.

Widely differing interest rates on official loans (from ¾ per cent to about 7 per cent) raise a different problem for donors. We saw that until a country's growth is more than self-sustained, the interest on loans must itself be paid from loans or grants. The generous creditor

[1] Argentina, Brazil, Burma, Ceylon, Chile, Colombia, Costa Rica, El Salvador, Ethiopia, Guatemala, Iran, Israel, Mexico, Peru, Philippines, Spain, Taiwan, Turkey, Venezuela, and Yugoslavia. Not all of these are likely to be in trouble. For some the debt, though concentrated, is small—e.g. Spain and the Philippines. Others have high reserves and a high export growth rate, like Israel and Taiwan. But the positions of Brazil, Argentina, Chile, and Turkey, are all very difficult.
[2] See p. 132 above.

may be assisting the recipient to pay high rates of interest to the mean creditors. This arises if the mean creditor gives less gross aid than the total of the interest and amortization which flows back to him. This is a donor problem, in the sense that only the donors can solve it. We refer to it again in Chapter XII. But it is also of concern for recipients, for it has been used as an anti-aid argument in the USA, which gives very cheap loans to countries which are also in receipt of expensive loans.

After this general discussion let us look at the actual average rates charged. Public aid in the aggregate is not expensive by conventional standards, and there has been a great improvement in this respect in recent years. In 1962, the average rate of interest for OECD bilateral lending (commitments) was under 3½ per cent. Moreover, over 60 per cent of the total bilateral official flow was grant aid. Multilateral loans also were, on the average, at about 3½ per cent, with grants forming about 45 per cent of the total. Eastern loans are generally at 2½ per cent, with very little by way of grant.

With well over half of all official aid in the form of grants, and with an average charge on loans of, say, 3½ per cent, one cannot say that the flow of financial resources is, in the aggregate, unreasonably expensive in the sense that it approaches any critical limit of the interest rate as discussed on pp. 205–7 above. This probably remains true even after allowing for suppliers' credits and equity investment. On the other hand, one can well ask the moral question of whether one ought to expect countries which will still be very poor, even although they have become capable of self-sustained growth, to repay.

However, it makes little sense to speak of the average rate of interest on loans, and the average proportion of grants. The terms which a country can stand, and still grow without trouble to maturity, depend very much on the country. A few very promising countries can probably borrow at 6 per cent or even more, and ultimately pay back the capital and accumulated interest—if the world demands this of them. But with many underdeveloped countries, whose income per head is low, and is unlikely to grow fast, the burden of debt will surely become excessive, unless they are given a very high proportion of grants, and the rates on the loans which they receive are kept low. The present terms of loans may not be intolerable, from an economic rather than a moral or political point of view, provided that the least promising get the cheapest money while the expensive loans are channelled to the most promising. The period of time during which a country is likely to be in receipt of aid is a very important factor in the relative burden of loans at different rates. Table 18 shows the relative amounts which a country can borrow this year, which will give the same absolute burden of accumulated debt at the time when it becomes self-sustaining. A glance at the power of compound interest is always salutary!

TABLE 18

Amounts which give the same liability as borrowing 1 for 50 years at 6 per cent

		Rate of Interest		
		$\frac{3}{4}$%	$3\frac{1}{2}$%	6%
Years elapsing during which	10	17·1	13·1	10·3
liability accumulates at	25	15·2	7·8	4·3
compound interest	50	12·7	3·3	1

Aid terms must be suited to the recipient. We shall refer to this matter again in Chapter X. Here it may be said that, if aid is defined in terms of the degree of subsidy for interest rates, plus grants, then it becomes quite rational that the most promising developers should get a large flow of resources—they can use it—but very little aid: while those in an earlier stage of growth, or those with particularly difficult problems, may properly get a relatively small flow of resources but a lot of aid. In addition to this need to tailor rates of interest to the longer-run economic prospects of recipients, there is also the shorter-run problem of those very promising countries which have, or shortly will, run into liquidity problems because of export difficulties or an ill-balanced debt-structure. So far as these latter are concerned, debt-maturities and grace periods are of more pressing importance than interest rates.

CHAPTER X

THE NEED FOR CAPITAL, AND THE
DISTRIBUTION OF CAPITAL FLOWS

Let us first consider the need for capital irrespective of the extent to which it is given on aid terms. (For the moment, we shall refer to public capital as aid, whether or not it is subsidized.) The problem has been deferred until this late point, because one cannot approach an answer, until one has discussed the purposes of supplying capital, the trade problems of the underdeveloped countries, and the problem of absorptive capacity and all that affects it. We assume that capital is given or lent for development, or to prevent decline, and we shall deal only with such flows.[1] Thus, as usual, we are not concerned with military aid. Nor do we attempt to assess needs on the basis that money should be given or lent without distinction between consumption and investment. Clearly, there is virtually no limit to the amount needed, or that could be usefully given, if we counted direct contributions to the consumption of the underdeveloped world. In fact, it is only within the context of development, that needs can be quantitatively discussed.

In producing a total of aid 'needs', it is further necessary to de-limit the recipients. This, as we saw in Chapter III, can be done either by the principle of self-sustained growth, or on the principle of utility. In either event some political weight must be attached, if only to rule out the Communist countries. We prefer the principle of utility, since we do not regard an apparently satisfactory growth rate as a reason not to assist an extremely poor country. Moreover, if a

---

[1] But USA 'supporting assistance' is included in the OECD figures we use. It is given primarily to prevent the economic decline or chaos which would otherwise result from the exceptional military commitments of the main recipients. In 1962 it totalled $499 million, but the figure proposed for the USA fiscal year 1965 is $349 million of which 80 per cent is to go to S. Korea, S. Vietnam, Laos, and Jordan. No sharp economic distinction can be made between such supporting assistance and the budgetary support given by the ex-colonial powers, e.g. that of the UK to Jordan.

rather rich country fails to grow satisfactorily then it is likely to be the case that aid would make little difference. Having agreed on the utility principle, we need to lay down arbitrarily some limit of income per head beyond which a country will not be aided. We shall assume that a country should be assisted until its income per head is $500–600, with aid being reduced when the first figure is reached, and eliminated at the higher figure (of course, it may continue to receive private capital).

This may well seem harsh. After all, should not the rich always give to the poor until equality is reached? Maybe. $500–600 is admittedly arbitary, but in fact raising it would make very little difference, because there are very few richer countries which would like to receive public assistance. Only three countries with GNPs greater than $500 per head in fact receive any significant aid—Trinidad, Venezuela, and Israel (and, of these, Israel is a very special case, as we shall see)—and we do not know of others who would want it. Japan with an income per head of less than $600 is a net giver of aid. Nor does South Africa with a GNP of less than $500 receive aid, while Portugal with a very low *per capita* income provides loans on a substantial scale to her dependent territories. The utility principle has to be overridden by the principle that one cannot aid those who do not want aid, nor those with whom political relations are such that no satisfactory aid relationship can be established.

Having delimited the countries, we next assume that those with incomes below $500 per head should receive as much capital as is necessary to supplement a reasonable level of indigenous savings plus any inflow of private capital, so as to raise their investment to the level of their estimated absorptive capacity for capital (or, alternatively, to the level which seems required to produce at least a 5 per cent per annum growth rate—whichever is the lower).

As already noted, any quantification of absorptive capacity, and hence of needs, presupposes that there is a rather rapid decline of productivity to zero from a worthwhile figure when a certain level of capital inflow is reached.[1] A slow decline over a wide range would make it necessary to specify the target level of productivity which is regarded as worthwhile. This would have to be rather lower for the poorest countries than for the better-off, bearing utility in mind. Furthermore, having regard to the great uncertainty surrounding any estimate of the productivity of capital in poor non-industrialized countries, it would mean that any estimate of the amount of capital that could be absorbed before productivity fell to the target figure

[1] Chapter V, p. 132.

would have an extremely wide margin of error. No estimate of needs could really be made on this basis: or, to put it in another way, all estimates of needs assume implicitly that the productivity curve becomes nearly vertical at some level of investment per annum.

Some may indeed argue that productivity curves are such that no quantification of needs has the slightest validity, even for individual countries (if estimates are valid for individual countries, then, in principle, so also is a global estimate). While admitting the force of this argument, we do not fully accept it. We think that the concept of 'absorptive capacity' has enough validity for very crude estimates, especially for countries with a very serious dearth of administrative and other skills. Admittedly, it probably has less validity for the more sophisticated of the countries with which we are concerned. But most of such countries are likely to be near the upper end of the income range. Near this upper limit, it is reasonable that the judgment of 'needs' begins to be influenced by considerations of income per head, or, in a few cases, by the fact that growth is already rapid, and in a few more cases by the fact that the country may not want aid.

Using the method outlined, can a quantitative estimate of aid needs be produced? Such an estimate requires an assessment of absorptive capacity country by country. It requires also an assessment of how much internal savings can reasonably be expected to contribute, also country by country (these estimates, as already explained, can make allowance for special balance of payments problems). In principle, therefore, to arrive at an estimate of aid needs one must conduct a searching analysis of the administrative, political, and economic, potentiality of every one of over a hundred countries and dependent territories. This is a formidable task, which by its very nature must contain a great deal of judgment and guesswork. It is far beyond the resources of the present authors.[1] But we do not believe that any short-cut is very valuable. We have already dismissed aggregate estimates based on projections of long-run trade trends as worth little.[2] The nearest published approach to a country by country estimate, made on the right general principles, is that of Professor Rosenstein-Rodan.[3] The author first posited a rate at which a country was inherently capable of growing, this being a reflection of

[1] But it should be done. If the knowledge of the IBRD, as well as a number of development institutes and experienced individuals, could be effectively mobilized, much better estimates than are now available should be possible. Of course, the US A AID must have the most extensive knowledge: but it is hardly in a position to make a non-political estimate.
[2] Chapter VI.
[3] Rosenstein-Rodan, op. cit.

his judgment of its absorptive capacity. Then he assumed a capital/ output ratio (uniformly $2 \cdot 8/1$, relating net national income to net investment). These together determined a required ratio of net investment to national income. Next, an initial domestic savings rate was estimated or guessed, and a desirable or reasonable marginal rate posited. These, together with an estimate of the initial national income, yielded estimates of needed investment and domestic savings over a period of years. Foreign capital required is, of course, the difference.

Professor Rosenstein-Rodan's estimate has been much criticized. Certainly, the assumption of a uniform capital/output ratio is hardly defensible, except on the ground that not enough was known to vary it. Furthermore, the savings figures taken or guessed, are highly unreliable. Finally, the whole estimate rested on the author's personal judgments about countries' capabilities of growth. Some of his projected growth figures seem eccentric, and many of them now look too low. Since the author himself would now change much[1]—the estimate is three years old, and there is considerably more knowledge now—we shall not pursue it.

What then can we do? Having discussed the principles, shall we abandon the reader with the remark that we cannot apply them? This might be the wisest course, but not the one we choose. If nothing else, some interesting points emerge from even the crudest survey of aid needs. Moreover, it would be dishonest to pretend that we have no opinion as to whether aid is too much or too little, and as to whether it is well or badly divided between recipients.

First, let us look at the facts. Here we have to introduce something new, for the amount of public capital a country needs obviously depends on the amount of private capital its gets. We have no comprehensive figures for net private capital movements for individual poor countries. But some guess can be made on a continental basis. In 1962, the total outflow of private capital from OECD countries to poor countries and multilateral institutions was estimated by the OECD at $2 \cdot 5$ billion. This makes no allowance for what we shall call the 'return flow'. The OECD figures are supposed to be for net investment in underdeveloped countries initiated by OECD residents. There is doubt about whether sufficient deductions are made from the gross figures in respect of return flow initiated by such residents.

[1] The author's present view is that, while his article underestimated the growth in Africa, and while some countries elsewhere also appear to be growing faster than projected, nevertheless, the order of magnitude of the total aid needed (as defined in the article) does not appear to require substantial revision.

But they are not even intended to be net of investment in OECD countries by residents of the underdeveloped countries, or returning colonials. This latter is what should be meant by the return flow: but as we use it, it probably includes some disinvestment by OECD residents.

In principle, the long-term capital flow to underdeveloped countries should be equal to the current deficit in their consolidated balance of payments, after allowing for any change in their reserves or other short-term finance. But it is extremely difficult to draw up a balance of payments account for the underdeveloped world. The details of such difficulties need not concern us. Professor Balassa has published an estimate for 1960 of a current account deficit for the underdeveloped world of $4·7 billion,[1] while recorded long-term capital movements to the underdeveloped world amounted to $6·5 billion. This implies that there were net errors and omissions or short-term capital movements of $1·8 billion, resulting in an apparent loss to the underdeveloped world of this amount:[2] to put it in another way, the apparent current deficit of the underdeveloped world was not nearly as large as the known capital movements would lead one to expect. By 1962 this overall 'errors and omissions' figure would certainly have grown, for 'errors and omissions' in estimates of the balance of payments of the OECD countries alone with the underdeveloped world have increased greatly between 1960 and 1962.

It is possible that the current account deficit of the underdeveloped world has been underestimated, through genuine statistical errors and omissions. In addition there are various forms of cheating to be reckoned with. One form, smuggling into poor countries, which in some parts of the world is quite prevalent, would result in an underestimate of the current deficit. On the other hand, another form of cheating which one might expect to be quantitatively more significant, for countries which exercise exchange control, is under-invoicing exports or over-invoicing imports in order to transfer money abroad. This would both be a capital flight and also worsen the recorded current deficit, although it would produce no error or omission if the corresponding capital movement was also unrecorded. Thus, to offset smuggling, there may be capital losses to poor countries which do not even appear as 'errors and omissions'.[3] All in all it seems

[1] op. cit., p. 106.

[2] The change in reserves of developing countries in 1960 was very small.

[3] On the other hand, imports may also be under-invoiced, to avoid tariffs. See J. Bhagwati, 'On the Under-invoicing of Imports', *Bulletin of the Oxford Institute of Economics and Statistics*, November 1964.

reasonable to suppose that a large part of these 'errors and omissions' consist of unrecorded capital flows from the underdeveloped countries. There are various scraps of evidence to support this.

There has certainly been in recent years a large withdrawal of capital from Africa by colonials. Since there is no capital control in the French Franc Area, and few non-French African countries exercise any effective control, almost all of this is unrecorded. But, for instance, the inflow of capital into Metropolitan France from Algeria in 1962 has been officially estimated at $1 billion, and the total such flow into France was almost certainly significantly larger than this.[1] There have also been flows, albeit of much smaller magnitude, from the Congo, Rwanda, and Burundi, to Belgium, and from East and Central Africa to the UK. In total, one and a half billion dollars would not seem an unreasonably high guess for Africa in 1962, and it could well be an underestimate. While most of this was a withdrawal of capital on the part of Europeans, it is also no secret that many African nationals have built up considerable fortunes abroad.

A study of Latin America by ECLA for the UN suggests that the capital outflow may have averaged $300 million in the 1950s, and have increased since.[2] $400 million might be a good guess for 1962. Information for Asia is even more scanty, but there has certainly been a significant outflow from the Middle East, resulting mainly from unrecorded investment of oil profits and royalties abroad. Mr R. Porter, who has an unrivalled knowledge of Middle East statistics, has made an estimate for us, using published Middle East sources, of $225 million. A figure of $600 million for Asia as a whole (leaving $375 million for South Asia and the Far East) seems consistent with 'errors and omissions' figures. The bulk of the reverse flow from South and Central America, and Asia, must have been initiated by nationals of these areas. It stems from various causes, political unrest, inflation, and also in some cases an apparent lack of profitable investment opportunities in the underdeveloped country itself.

In total then, in 1962, the reverse flow may have been about $2½ billion, more than equal to the entire recorded flow of private capital (including government guaranteed export credits) in the opposite

[1] The 'errors and omissions' item *vis-à-vis* the Overseas Franc Area in the French national accounts for 1962 was over $2 billion, so there is plenty of statistical room for this statement!

[2] *External Development Financing in the Economic Development of Latin America*, UN document E/CN. 12/649, April 1963.

TABLE 19

1962 flows of finance to developing regions

$m

	Africa	America	Asia (incl. Oceania)	Europe	Unallocated	Total
Public						
Official OECD bilateral[1]	1,573	876	2,233	470	229	5,381
Multilateral[1]	145	69	194	-3	7	412
Communist[2]	91	200	100	0	0	391
Other[3]	0	0	56	0	0	56
Total Public	1,809	1,145	2,583	467	236	6,240
Private						
Export Credits (OECD, over one year)[1]	182	233	35	1	97	548
Other private (OECD, bilateral)[4]	638	760	200	70	0	1,668
Return flow[5]	-1,500	-400	-600	0	0	-2,500
Total private	-680	593	-365	71	97	-284
Total	1,129	1,738	2,218	538	333	5,956

[1] From OECD, *The Flow of Financial Resources to Less-Developed Countries, 1956–63*, Table V.2.
[2] Total from OECD, ibid., Table II.14. Regional allocation guessed by authors.
[3] Australia and New Zealand, OECD estimate. Other non-OECD donors (South Africa and Finland) give aid only through multilateral organizations.
[4] Total from OECD, ibid.; Table IV.16. Regional allocation guessed by authors.
[5] See text.

direction, and equal to almost half the total of aid. This is a little known, but obviously important, part of the total picture of capital flows, and must modify to some extent one's ideas about the function of aid.

Table 19 brings together official public capital flows to Africa, Asia, America, and Europe, with private flows as estimated above. The allocation of these private flows, both the outflow and return flow, are of course extremely rough. But if the orders of magnitude are right it can be seen what a large difference private capital makes. In total, Africa may have lost some $700 million, and Asia about $400 million—while Latin America gained $600 million, and Europe about $100 million.

Table 20 presents some figures relating to fourteen different areas of the world. Aid is there given both as a proportion of GNP, and on a *per capita* basis, including and excluding private flows and non-OECD aid. Population and GNP are given as alternative measures of the size of the areas. Size has to be taken into account, although we do not suggest that aid should be given on a *per capita* basis, or as a proportion of GNP.[1] Since GNP figures are most unreliable, generally we use 'aid per head' as a measure of the level of aid. The differences in the receipt of foreign capital are very marked. Even after allowing for the return flow, Africa gets nearly twice as much per head as Asia, whether as a proportion of population or of GNP. Southern and Central America, which is much better off, gets rather more than Asia as a proportion of GNP, and about three times as much per head. The five aided European countries are comparable to Southern and Central America, getting just a little less both per head and as a proportion of GNP. In these tables we have given aid levels for 1962, rather than as elsewhere the average of 1962 and 1963, because we could make an estimate of the reverse flow of capital only for 1962. Single year figures are sometimes unreliable as marked variations occur. But where 1962 seems unrepresentative, or where there have been important later developments, we remark on it in the text.

Let us now briefly discuss the four continents in turn. Taking Africa first, we note that a large part of the official flow of funds, especially to Africa north of the Sahara, is merely compensating for the withdrawal of private capital. Indeed, in the case of Algeria, there must have been a large net capital outflow. Some of the 'aid' was directly connected with the outflow since it induced and permitted the recipient government to buy rather than confiscate property.

While capital flight may justify the very high levels of aid per head

[1] See Chapter III, pp. 92–7.

TABLE 20

1962 flows of finance to developing regions relative to population and GNP

	Population millions	GNP per capita	Official OECD 'aid' ($ millions)	Other aid plus net private capital flow ($ millions)	(3) per capita (to nearest $½)	(3)+(4) per capita (to nearest $½)	(3) as per cent of GNP (to nearest half per cent)	(3)+(4) as per cent of GNP (to nearest half per cent)
All Africa[1]	262	102	1,573[2]	−444	6·0	4·5	6·0	4·0
Africa north of Sahara[3]	57	172	755	—	13·0	—	7·5	—
Africa south of Sahara	177	77	816	—	4·5	—	6·0	—
French and Ex-French Africa S.S.	39	86	349	—	9·0	—	10·5	—
British and Ex-British Africa S.S.	106	97	206	—	2·0	—	2·0	—
All America[3]	220	283	876	862	4·0	8·0	1·5	3·0
North and Central America	59	291	145	—	2·5	—	1·0	—
South America	156	280	618	—	4·0	—	1·5	—
All Asia[1]	910	95	2,173	−15	2·5	2·5	2·5	2·5
Middle East[4]	51	231	257	—	5·0	—	2·0	—
India	463	81	675	100	1·5	1·5	2·0	2·0
Other South Asia[5]	157	77	454	—	3·0	—	3·5	—
Far East[6]	234	105	776	—	3·5	—	3·0	—
Europe[7]	89	304	470	68	5·5	6·0	1·5	2·0
World[1,8]	1,500	140	5,500	600	3·5	4·0	2·5	3·0

[1] Includes territories excluded from regional totals.
[2] Slightly overstated since French aid to overseas departments not in Africa included.
[3] Algeria, Egypt, Libya, Morocco, Tunisia.
[4] Iran, Iraq, Israel, Jordan, Lebanon, Saudi Arabia, Syria, Yemen.
[5] Afghanistan, Burma, Ceylon, India, Nepal, Pakistan.
[6] Cambodia, Indonesia, S. Korea, Laos, Malaysia, Philippines, Taiwan, Thailand, S. Vietnam.
[7] Cyprus, Greece, Spain, Turkey, Yugoslavia.
[8] Roughly rounded totals.
Sources: Columns (1) and (2): AID
Column (3): OECD
Column (4): Table 19, or authors' guess.

to Africa north of the Sahara, this is not so true of Africa south of the Sahara. Here, there has certainly been some capital flight, notably from the ex-Belgian countries and Kenya. For instance, as with Algeria, some British aid to Kenya has been to permit the purchase of settlers' property.[1] The aid figures also contain items, which are perfectly justifiable uses of money, but have no direct connection with development and are unrelated to the concept of absorptive capacity. Such are Belgium's payment of interest on the Congo's debt, and Britain's 'aid' for the compensation and pensions of former expatriate civil servants.[1] Nevertheless, the main statistical reason for the high level of aid to Africa south of the Sahara, is that the French-speaking republics get the exceptionally high amounts of around $9 per head, and around 10 per cent of their GNP. A few like the Côte d'Ivoire also receive considerable private investment. This is in great contrast with the ex-British countries and territories whose aid level was about one-quarter that of the ex-French ones. The extremely small size of most of the ex-French countries, and their poverty, probably results in a disproportionate amount of their GNP being spent on maintaining them as countries. But as, in fact, among these countries there appears to be little relation between 'aid' per head and either size or wealth, too much cannot be made of this. It could be suggested therefore that the high level of 'aid' to the ex-French territories indicates that the rest of Africa could absorb more capital.

On the other hand, the French-speaking countries are at present capable of absorbing enormously more technical assistance than the other parts of Africa, as a result of the still continuing French orientation of their governments and *élites*. Thus in 1963 France had no less than 51,000 technical assistance personnel abroad, the vast majority in Africa. This compared with a UK total of 14,000.[2] To some extent anyway, this in turn must help to increase the capacity to absorb capital. It is impossible to tell as yet whether as a result the French-speaking countries will do better. But it is undeniable that there has been great waste.[3]

Despite the high level of aid to French-speaking Africa, our belief is that, of recent years, there has been as much capital available to non-ex-French Africa south of the Sahara as it could well use. The limitation is, of course, one of absorptive capacity in the broadest sense. Certainly, much capital has been used in ways that do little or

[1] See English edition, Chapter XVI, p. 298.
[2] See Chapter I.
[3] See, e.g., Dumont, op. cit.

nothing for development. Many factories have been started with no reasonable hope of economic use. There are many buildings of excessive splendour which cannot be fully used for lack of demand, or of staff or pupils (e.g. hotels, hospitals, universities, and polytechnics). Economic as well as social overheads have been constructed which are well in advance of the demand, which could have been catered for in less capital-hungry ways. Some people are quick to insist on the development value of such things as television and luxury hotels, but the authors remain unconvinced. We have no doubt that the resources of Africa are such that lack of capital will eventually become the chief impediment to development. But at present almost every way of spending money for development, which looks promising, suffers from some non-financial difficulty—lack either of knowledge, or of administrative and other skills.[1]

Thus until ways are found of improving the usage of public capital in Africa, and of spending money to advantage in the productive sectors, especially agriculture, our judgment would be that aid levels to this continent are probably excessive. Despite the fact that some African countries have until recently been able to draw down reserves which they no longer have, we very much doubt whether development would suffer if aid were reduced as the capital flight from Africa dries up, so that the present net level of capital inflow would be maintained. It is more important to try to improve the usage of capital than to increase the volume.[2] Among African countries, Egypt probably presents the strongest case for more aid for development. All this, of course, applies only to the next few years. One must hope that Africa's absorptive capacity will rapidly increase.

Turn now to Asia. The relatively high figures for the Middle East are due to Israel and Jordan. Israel received the exceptional amount of $49 per head, despite the fact that her GNP per head was over $800. But 60 per cent of this is reparations from Germany, to which criteria for aid-giving can hardly be applied, while most of the rest is PL 480 commodities, which are not a scarce form of aid. Finally, Israel herself gives aid. Jordan's aid is largely, in effect, defence support. Iran also receives considerable aid in view of the fact that she has oil royalties of about $20 per head. But Iran is another country where aid cannot be divorced entirely from military expendi-

[1] See Little, *Aid to Africa*, for elaboration of the views expressed in this paragraph.
[2] Ignoring reverse flows, net aid to Africa fell slightly in 1963; this was more than accounted for by a fall of $100 million in aid to Algeria, which may have been more than counterbalanced by a reduction of the capital flight.

ture, and is thus difficult to discuss purely in terms of development. If there are anomalies elsewhere in the Middle East, where the level of aid is fairly low, they are not likely to be very large. Syria, which lacks oil, possibly has a case for further aid, but this would not amount to much.

The Far East is often used as an example of excessive aid, little of which is really for development. Certainly, Laos, South Vietnam, South Korea, and Taiwan, receive a lot of aid per head (respectively about 13, 12, 9, and 7, dollars per head in 1962). But we are not here concerned with such questions as whether American military aid and supporting assistance in South Vietnam or Laos makes sense, or will pay off in the end. If one removes USA supporting assistance, contingency fund expenditure, and part of commodity aid, some of which is also probably in the nature of defence support, one is left with figures for development aid which do not appear to be excessive.[1] Moreover, some countries in the area, such as Malaysia and the Philippines, receive very little aid per head ($1-1½). Malaysia, at least, is now, or may soon be, in a position to spend more on development, and absorb more aid. Indonesia also receives little per head from Western sources, but probably fairly large amounts from the USSR and China, though little of this is for economic development. Certainly, for political and other reasons, the USA has found it very difficult to promote any development in Indonesia.[2] But, all in all, it is now doubtful whether aid in this area could be further reduced without detriment to economic growth, unless military expenditure can be reduced by abandoning parts of it to Communist care, or somehow else.

It is South Asia[3] which constitutes the main apparent aid anomaly of the world. In terms of population, it is over 40 per cent of the underdeveloped world, with a population of 620 million people. It is the poorest area of the world, despite the fact that GNP statistics suggests that parts of Africa are poorer.[4] It receives less aid per head from the OECD than any other area, only $1·8 per annum in 1962.

The four smaller countries of the area, Afghanistan, Burma, Ceylon, and Nepal (total population 65 million), receive relatively little

---

[1] Furthermore, aid to Taiwan is now being rapidly reduced. The AID considers that Taiwan has 'taken off'.

[2] *Indonesia: Perspective and Proposals for United States Economic Aid. A Report to the President of the United States.* Yale University, South East Asia Studies, 1963.

[3] Afghanistan, Burma, Ceylon, India, Nepal, and Pakistan.

[4] GNP statistics per head can be taken only as very rough guides to poverty. See Chapter IV above.

aid per head from OECD countries.[1] But they either receive a lot of aid from others, or have very limited absorptive capacity. Afghanistan is heavily assisted by the USSR, and Nepal also receives aid from India and the USSR. Burma and Ceylon seem to get less than one might think them capable of absorbing: but in both cases there are political difficulties, Burma being notably reluctant to take aid.

Pakistan alone in the area is now receiving a high level of aid per head from the West. In 1962 it was $2·8, excluding the Indus Waters Scheme: including the scheme it was $4·0.[2] Since 1962, Western aid to Pakistan has increased very rapidly. In 1963 it was about $4·2, excluding the Indus Waters ($4·9, including it). In 1964 there will have been a further rise.[3] A very high proportion of Pakistan's investment is financed by aid. Thus in 1963, of a gross investment level of 17 per cent of GNP, gross domestic savings accounted for only 9·6 per cent.

After a long period of very slow growth in the 1950s, Pakistan has begun to grow rapidly—by rather over 5 per cent per annum since 1959/60. Agriculture, which grew by only 1·3 per cent per annum in the 1950s, shows a rate of increase of 3·5 per cent since 1959/60 (about the average rate of growth of Indian agriculture), and higher rates still are confidently expected.

Pakistan's improved performance has been accompanied by considerable liberalization, especially of imports of materials and components, which has permitted more use of existing capacity, and of agricultural inputs, especially fertilizers and tubewells. Her

---

[1] But there was a considerable increase in 1963.

[2] The Indus Waters Scheme (organized by the IBRD, and one of the most shining examples of aid, since it contributed not only to development but also to the solution of an international dispute) compensates Pakistan for the diversion of certain river waters to Indian usage, which prior to partition irrigated parts of what is now West Pakistan. It is, primarily, as things now stand, aid to Pakistan: but for the Pakistanis it is not development aid, but replacement aid following one of the exigencies of partition. Thus, on the one hand, excluding it from the figures of aid to Pakistan has a certain justification: indeed Pakistanis may claim it is aid to India. On the other hand, if one attempted throughout the world to exclude items counted as aid to a particular country, which there was some justification for excluding, one would have to exclude far more than the Indus Waters Scheme (some examples are given in the English edition, Chapter XVI). The reader is left to make his own choice. In the text we give aid to Pakistan figures, both excluding and including the Indus Waters Scheme.

[3] Pakistani figures give an estimate of $660 million gross for 1964/5, excluding Indus Waters aid (see *Preliminary Evaluation of Progress during the Second Five-Year Plan,* Planning Commission, Karachi, March 1965), i.e. $6·5 per head gross, and probably about $6·0 net. This includes a small amount of 'bloc' aid.

willingness to learn and accept advice, and her recent pragmatic economic policies, especially greater use of the price mechanism, have pleased donor governments and her Western advisers. Such policies have been greatly facilitated by increased aid, but have also been a cause of that increase. There is no doubt that increased aid has made a major contribution.

It is early to say whether a solid foundation has been laid for a continuance of the recent good growth rates, and for a gradually increased reliance on domestic resources, for some part of the recent growth is of a once-and-for-all character. But confidence is now high in planning circles, and it is plain that at least present levels of aid should be continued for some time. Pakistan is still a very poor country, and still has very difficult problems to face.

India is a very different case, and is the major enigma, and anomaly, of world aid giving. The people of India are among the poorest in the world—only Pakistan and a few other countries are comparable. At the same time, and exceptionally for so poor a country, India has one of the most competent administrations in the underdeveloped world, and also has a very considerable endowment of technical skills of all kinds. Her macroeconomic planning is among the most sophisticated in the underdeveloped world. She has a considerable industrial base, and an unusual amount of entrepreneurial talent. Capital is austerely used for economic development, with little or no emphasis on the prestige projects which are so common elsewhere. India 'helps herself' more than most underdeveloped countries. She has raised taxation considerably in a number of courageous recent budgets. She has reasonably effective exchange control. There is not much capital flight, and virtually no inessential consumption goods imports. If any country has a structural balance of payments problem, India has a strong claim to membership of this category. Corruption exists of course, but it is less than in other more aid-favoured areas, and does less to distort economic planning. Of undeniable political importance, and the subject of a recent Communist attack, India should prima facie be the darling and not the Cinderella of world aid. What is the explanation? Has India, despite all this, a remarkably low absorptive capacity? Or is there something very wrong with donors' aid policies?

Let us look at some figures. The Indian Third Five-Plan Plan's own calculation (for a projected growth rate of $5\frac{1}{2}$ per cent per annum) was for an average of $1·3 billion per annum gross, this being based on balance of payments estimates rather than on savings/investment estimates. Many foreign observers believed this to be an

THE NEED FOR CAPITAL 227

underestimate, if the investment programme was to be achieved.[1] OECD sources suggest that India actually received $664 million, $736 million, and $973 million net aid from OECD countries and multilateral institutions in 1961, 1962, and 1963.[2] (These figures represent *per capita* aid levels of $1·5, $1·7, and $2·1.) According to Indian sources,[3] total gross aid use in the first three years of the Third Plan (1961/2, 1962/3, 1963/4) was $712, $941, and $1,235—of which non-OECD aid (almost entirely 'bloc') was $52 million, $69 million, and $105 million respectively.

The shortfall of aid below estimated requirements was thus large in the first two years. This was probably more because the plan got off to a slow start (as did the Second Plan) than because aid was not available. India entered the period of the Third Five-Year Plan (April 1, 1961) with about $1·4 billion of undisbursed foreign official loans (excluding commodity-aid, and grants which, in India's case, are confined to technical assistance). In the first three years of the plan another $3·0 billion was authorized by all lenders (the Consortium committed $3·4 billion in this period), but utilization was only about $2·0 billion, so that the amount of undisbursed but authorized loans had grown to $2½ billion. The ratio of utilization of loans to the balance of funds whose use had been authorized at the beginning of the year has remained at 35–38 per cent, as shown in Table 21. Can one infer from the apparently low ratio

TABLE 21
The Use of Loans to India,[4] 1961-4 ($m)

Date	Authorized and undisbursed (carry over)	Used in following year	(3) as percentage of (2)	Total gross aid used (i.e. including commodity-aid, and grants)
March 31, 1961	1,384	483	35	712
1962	1,751	652	38	941
1963	2,333	822	35	1,235
1964	2,465	468 (half-year)	19 (half-year)	716 (half-year)
October 1, 1964	2,432			

[1] e.g. P. N. Rosenstein-Rodan (op. cit.) estimated $1·6 billion on a savings/investment basis. G. D. A. MacDougall wrote: 'Even if foreign aid is forthcoming on the large scale envisaged in the Draft Outline of the Third Plan, this may not be enough; for the import needs seem to have been substantially underestimated, as they were in the Second Plan.' op. cit.
[2] OECD, *Flow of Financial Resources, 1956-63.*
[3] Government of India, *Economic Survey*, New Delhi, 1964-5.
[4] Source: Government of India, ibid.

of utilization, and the excess of authorizations over disbursements, that India's use of aid has been governed by her own absorptive capacity? No such simple influence is possible. Until recently, most loans have been tied to projects, and this makes a high carry-over of aid inevitable. For instance, if all loans were tied to projects which take five years to finish after the expenditure is authorized, the ratio of use to carry-over would settle down to 40 per cent, but it would be much lower during any period in which authorizations were increasing.

It was only in 1963/4 that India began to get considerable amounts of non-project assistance (apart from PL 480), which can be more rapidly spent. For 1964/5 about half the aid committed by the Consortium is on a non-project basis, which is a great improvement. Even so, some of the non-project aid available is still limited to capital goods. Thus, although India by 1963/4 had built up to a total aid usage of $1¼ billion, which by 1964/5 probably reached $1½ billion, the use of loans did not catch up with authorizations until 1964/5. A large part of the rise in total aid use was due to heavy PL 480 imports, which amounted to $227 million in the first half of 1964/5, and was consequent on poor harvests in the previous two years.

Despite the higher aid level in 1964/5, India, at the beginning of 1965/6, was suffering one of her worst balance of payments crises, and there was at the same time considerable excess capacity in some industrial sectors, for lack of imported raw materials and components. The inference is plain: that aid, and planning, was still too much devoted to the creation of output capacity, and not enough to promoting current output, and to as rapid completion as possible of the schemes started. India has been asking for more non-project aid for some time, and many donors have responded: but the process has not gone far enough yet.

The low level of aid to India is partly a mere function of her size:[1] but it is also partly because India herself has consistently under-estimated the amount of aid needed for her plans. The other side of this coin is that she has consistently overestimated the amount of industrial and infrastructural investment which she could under-take with the foreign exchange resources available. This tendency has been buttressed by planning to do without aid in too short a time; with the consequent determination to build more capacity for import-substitution, in a somewhat indiscriminate manner, than was possible with the aid available in the period. This has resulted

[1] See Chapter III, p. 94, f. 1.

in costly interruptions to schemes initiated, and a low productivity of capital.

Recently the IBRD and AID have started to probe sectoral and project planning in more detail than previously, and have become discontented with what they have found. Previously aid had been given very much in support of the plan, and several missions of eminent persons had blessed the plans. But 'vetting' a central macroeconomic plan in a federation of India's size does not take one very far. As much or more depends on the coherence of sectoral planning, on project design and selection, on the execution of the plan, and on general economic policies. One cannot ignore the fact that central and state administrations are overstrained, and the management of public enterprise inadequate, lacking the numbers of skilled staff required to carry out, with speed and efficiency, the heavy burden of public control and ownership which has been assumed.[1]

Having said all this, we still believe that India can effectively absorb much larger quantities of aid.[2] So far as industrial and infrastructural projects go, no rapid increase of aid disbursement in the near future should be looked for. There is certainly a need in some sectors for improved planning and execution, and donors should in our view concern themselves with this, despite the resistance that is inevitably to be expected in certain quarters, and despite the fact that such concern may temporarily slow up aid disbursements.

But much more money could be quickly and effectively spent on imports of materials and components, especially inputs for agriculture—most notably fertilizers. Insufficiency of general purpose aid, which can be used for such things, not only means that the economy operates below capacity, but also increases the amount of control and administration required. India is, at present, forced to keep stringent investment and import controls in operation. This is something of a vicious circle. Some of the controls, as operated, undoubtedly reduce the efficiency of the economy, without helping to achieve any basic objective of policy.[3] This in turn slows up the usage of aid (sometimes even when the money is earmarked for a particular project), and is a heavy burden on the over-extended administration. If general purpose aid were increased, India could relax some controls over investment and machinery imports; and, still more important, import controls on some high-priority current

[1] See Hanson, op. cit.
[2] It should perhaps be said at this point that I. M. D. Little alone takes responsibility for what is said about Pakistan and India.
[3] See, e.g., Government of India, *Report of Steel Control*, October 1963, Ch. II.

inputs. There is little doubt that much more aid could then be absorbed, and that output would respond. Even if there was a once-and-for-all element in this, we believe that more rapid growth for a few years would greatly help morale, and itself lead to improvements in policy and planning. It would also lead to more aid later, because nothing succeeds like success when it comes to eliciting aid.

The Indian Government will probably ask for aid for the Fourth Plan at about the level of the Third Plan, $1·3 billion gross per annum.[1] This is below the level which will be reached in the last year of the Third Five-Year Plan (probably $1·5 billion), and not much above the average level of aid during the Third Plan period. In net terms, it would constitute an aid level of $1·1 billion per annum, against approximately $1·0 billion during the Second Plan period. Since the Indian population is growing at 2½ per cent per annum, this would constitute no increase in the extraordinarily low level of aid per head which India has been receiving. Furthermore, without doing any elaborate calculations, one can say that there is nothing in the history of Indian development to date which would suggest that a much larger plan can be mounted without more foreign assistance.

We believe that the Consortium should pay little attention to the Indians' own estimates of aid requirements for the Fourth Plan period. Having regard to the present level of aid absorption, and to the fact that, undoubtedly, $300–400 million of extra imports of materials and components, especially fertilizers, would be highly desirable, we believe that India can absorb an average level of net aid over the next five years of $2·0 billion gross per annum (including commodity and technical assistance), or $1·8 billion net, at the very least. It would, indeed, be incredible if she could not. Since India's population will average 500 million people during the Fourth Plan, this would represent an aid level of $3·6 per head, still far below the current level of aid to Pakistan.

If we allow $300–400 million for non-Consortium aid, this implies that Consortium commitments should now rise to something over $1½ billion per annum (since some increase in the pipeline of aid is inevitable if the disbursement rate is to be stepped up). We would

[1] The first adumbration of the Fourth Plan is the *Memorandum on the Fourth Five-Year Plan*, Government of India, Planning Commission, October 1964. This document suggests a balance of payments deficit of Rs 3,200 crores for the Fourth Plan period, after meeting amortization payments of Rs 500 crores. If we allow, say, Rs 200 crores for an inflow of private capital, this leaves Rs 3,000 crores, i.e. $6·3 billion, or about $1·3 billion per annum, which is much the same as the estimated requirements for the much smaller Second Five-Year Plan.

THE NEED FOR CAPITAL

regard this as the bare minimum target. Even so, such an increase in aid may require some change in Indian policies. But, in the context of a really significant increase in the aid level, these should be negotiable. Without such an increase, it is questionable whether very much influence can be exercised. The general policy of Western donors should be to satisfy themselves about project and sectoral planning (while offering all possible assistance towards improving such planning), and at the same time to ensure that the economy can be provided with the intermediate goods required to increase current production, together with the miscellaneous capital goods needed for 'balancing' capital structures and completing projects.[1]

India has absorbed a lot of space—although probably not more than 30 per cent of this chapter. But India is 30 per cent of the developing world. Even this does not sufficiently underline the full measure of her importance. This vast and poverty-stricken country, troubled with internal problems of a grave and potentially divisive character, but nevertheless maintaining one of the most democratic systems of government in the world, is proudly struggling to transmute her traditional culture into a progressive economic system. Many developing countries will be influenced by the outcome. The rest of the world is watching India, but it does little to help her. In the context of world aid, the low level of aid to India is a disgrace. The fault lies both with the Indian Government, and with donors. It should be a challenge to both parties to set this matter right—a challenge set by the poverty of the Indian people.

The Alliance for Progress estimated Latin America's needs (excluding Cuba) at $2 billion net per annum. This ought to have taken account of capital flight but does not appear to have done so. Table 19 does not give Alliance countries separately, but they probably received in 1962 about $1·6 billion net before allowing for capital flight.[2]

There are wide variations in aid levels in Latin America. Aid per head is very low (under $2) in Haiti, Guatemala, Peru, Paraguay, and Mexico. These countries range from the very backward to the well advanced (Haiti to Mexico), and also from poverty to relative riches (Haiti to Uruguay). The authors have insufficient knowledge

[1] There is still some feeling in India that it is imprudent to use loans for importng goods which are currently used, and do not increase capacity. We do not believe this is justified. But the cost of aid to India is relatively high. There remains an urgent need for donors so to improve terms, especially by reducing interest rates, that this consideration is seen to be unimportant.

[2] In 1963 this probably increased to about $1·8 billion.

to judge whether these low levels are fully explicable on grounds of
varying absorptive capacity (or unwillingness to take aid from the
USA).

At the other end of the scale come Bolivia, Venezuela, Costa Rica,
Panama, and Chile, with aid levels of over $8 per head. These also
range from the very poor (Bolivia) to the rather rich (Venezuela). Of
these, Chile's aid level was exceptionally high in 1961 and 1962
(averaging $16 per head), but this was due at least partly to the
earthquake of 1961. Bolivia appears to be a case of budgetary support for political reasons. Venezuela is an interesting case, as a
matter of principle. For her GNP per head at over $700 is higher than
that of Italy, and much higher than Japan. Yet she got nearly $9 per
head in aid in 1962 having earlier got nothing.[1] This, of course, was
the result of the nearby Cuban revolution. Venezuela's political
importance to the USA is obvious. It seems to us that no one can
really quarrel with assisting development in such relatively rich
countries, if the donor believes that it is in its political interest. We
did not quarrel with Marshall aid!

Thirty-five per cent of the population of South and Central America
is in Brazil, and over half in Brazil and Mexico together. If one adds in
Argentina, Colombia, and Peru, three-quarters is accounted for.
But these five countries got only 44 per cent of OECD and multilateral
aid to America.[2] On the other hand, they got 80 per cent of
IBRD/IDA/IDB/IFC/EEC loans, these being concentrated in
Colombia, Mexico and Peru, which together received over 100
per cent of loans from these sources to America.[3] Taking both
sources together, the five still received only about 46 per cent of aid.
Of the five, Argentina and Colombia both receive more than the
average for the area: and of these two, Argentina is a relatively
rich country. It could be argued that both have some additional need
for aid for structural reasons. Exports have been very sluggish for
both, and partly in consequence imports form a low proportion of
national income (about 8 per cent). Moreover, only a tiny proportion
of their imports consists of consumption goods. They may therefore
be faced with the 'structural' problem of transforming savings into
useful investment, and in this respect (though not in any other!)

---

[1] In 1963 the aid level fell to $6·6.
[2] The same percentage also held true for 1963.
[3] In 1963 loans from these sources increased enormously, from $44 million to
$256 million, thus more than accounting for the whole of the rise in aid to
America, Mexico, Colombia, and Peru, still received over half the total; but
Argentina, Chile, and Venezuela, also became large recipients ($89 million).

resemble India. On the other hand it is partly supply rather than demand which has prevented Argentina's exports rising.

Thus, of this group of larger countries, Brazil, Mexico and Peru seem to present the strongest prima facie cases for more assistance. The first two at least should have a high capacity for using capital, and all receive very low levels of aid ($2·4, $1·4, and $1·4, per head respectively in 1962). So far as Brazil is concerned, recent decisions indicate that USA aid there will increase substantially. Mexico succeeds in growing rather fast (recently at about 6 per cent per annum) without much aid. She attracts a lot of short- and medium-term private capital from the USA, which may be leading to an unbalanced debt structure. But she is probably unwilling to accept USA aid, except Export/Import Bank loans, which she does not (with some justification) regard as aid. She recently accepted some offers of loans from France, and may be a good example of a relatively poor country for which some diversification of the sources of capital is desirable.

There are also the West Indies, a particular British interest. They receive a high level of aid per head—about $8·0—very high considering that the UK is virtually the only donor, and that Jamaica and Trinidad are relatively well off. The high level is partly accounted for by their very small size, and in this respect they are somewhat comparable to the countries of French Africa.

All in all, it seems reasonable to say that Latin America might effectively absorb nearly another $½ billion, over 1962 levels, even allowing for possibly excessive aid in a few countries.[1] It seems likely that much of this suggested increase is on the way. In 1963 in fact, aid increased by about $200 million.

In Europe, Cyprus receives an exceptionally high level of aid (which is usually the case with small countries with a troubled history); Yugoslavia and Turkey also both receive fairly high levels, probably enough to sustain fairly rapid rates of growth. Greece now gets rather little aid, but receives a lot of private capital, and is sustaining a very high rate of investment. Relations with Spain are probably too difficult for any proposal for significantly increased aid to make sense. Portugal is an anomaly. With a standard of living little higher than that of Turkey, she gives a higher proportion of aid to GNP than any other donor country (almost all in loans to her overseas possessions). In total, and taking account of certain political difficulties, the

[1] CIAP estimated in November 1964 that OAS countries needed aid of $3·3 billion gross. Such is the debt position that this would amount to only $1·9 billion net—an increase of $300–$400 million over 1962 levels. (The very high amortization is almost entirely accounted for by Brazil and Chile.)

total level of aid to underdeveloped countries in Europe looks about right.

Let us now recapitulate in the form of a global survey, crude and ill-informed as any such survey must be. It would be very surprising if the world distribution of development aid looked reasonable in view of the largely uncoordinated efforts of over twenty different donor countries and agencies, and in view of the differing motives which impel their assistance. Nevertheless, surprisingly, some experienced observers take the view that there is nothing much wrong with it. This is not our view. It seems to us that, in Asia, India is grossly under-aided, and that to a much smaller extent Africa is over-aided. Probably Latin America could do with more, although mutual trade and internal reform is in many countries probably a more important desideratum for rapid growth than more aid.

Within these broad regions, the figures certainly suggest anomalies as between countries, although more detailed knowledge than the authors have is required to be sure whether such differences are not justifiable on development grounds. The authors themselves have detailed first-hand knowledge only of India, and more sketchily of Africa south of the Sahara, although they have of course drawn on the opinions of others (detailed written comparative assessments of absorptive capacity are almost non-existent). Thus this survey is admittedly jejune, and intended to be suggestive rather than weightily informed.

Apart from the heavy concentration of French aid, it seems to us that the greatest single factor making for a maldistribution of aid is that donors fail to divide aid given by the number of heads. Of course, one should not expect aid per head to be equal. But to put it on a *per capita* basis is a first approach to allowing for the size of the recipient. One meets many people who believe that India is the most heavily aided country. It is much more reasonable to say she is the least heavily aided. Brazil is another country which probably suffers by being big.[1] Nigeria, again, gets little aid in comparison with other African countries, and their respective capacities for development. In contrast, most very small countries are heavily assisted—although the high cost of government per head may be some justification for this.

In quantitative terms, and relative to 1962, we would suggest that probably India can use another net $1 billion per annum, and Latin America maybe $½ billion. Pakistan is already using $¼ billion

[1] Brazil may also suffer in another way—from her existing heavy debt. This we have seen should not be a consideration (see Chapter IX, p. 209).

more than in 1962. If, as seems likely, most of the capital flight from
Africa dies away, it should be possible to reduce aid by $½ billion,
without making any difference to economic development. In total,
therefore, we suggest that the underdeveloped world might usefully
absorb for development about another $1–1½ billion per annum,
an increase of around 20 per cent. This would be a fleabite for the
donors, well under £1 per head per annum.

The further future is still more problematical. In many of the more
backward countries, which suffer at present from lack of organization and a severe shortage of educated people, but possess some
natural economic advantages, the ability to use capital will, one
hopes, grow much faster than their wealth and hence their ability to
save. In other developing countries, which have a longer tradition of
education, the reverse may happen.

Whichever way the sum works out, it must be remembered that
we have been discussing the problem from the austere angle that a
country which has reached the income level of about $600 per head
should be able to save enough to finance either all the investment it
can undertake, or, if not that, anyway enough to give it a rate of
growth of about 5 per cent per annum, and that countries below this
level should be encouraged to save as much as possible. But this
austerity can be relaxed. There is no reason why aid should cease
just because a country becomes capable of self-sustained growth. Its
people may still be extremely poor. We would certainly hope that aid
is here to stay, for ever.

This chapter has thus far been about the world distribution of
public capital flows (despite the fact that we have used the word
'aid'). This is by no means the same thing as the distribution of aid
proper. A country may need to import a lot of capital, but not have a
strong claim for much aid. Another country may be able to use little
capital, but should get it on highly favourable terms. The principles
governing the amount of interest charged, and repayment terms, have
already been discussed in Chapter IX.

Unfortunately figures are not available for the terms on which
recipients borrow, so we cannot adequately survey how far the
distribution of aid is appropriate. We could discuss the proportion of
grants and grant-like contributions to the total flow of public capital.
This is not however a very good indicator, first because of the
existence of cheap loans from the USA and IDA, and secondly because
commodity aid, which is 'grant-like', cannot be expected to be distributed in line with recipients' ability to repay.

All we shall therefore do here is to emphasize some of what was said in Chapter IX. If a country can use more capital effectively, but cannot be expected to save enough, then the receipt of public capital should never be inhibited by its debt position or its repayment obligations. These are irrelevant as criteria of aid-giving. Given that few donors are willing to provide really long-term capital (since each individually hopes for the possibility of repayment—even though this can only be at the expense of other donors), the danger of a repayment crisis is always present. This risk, almost inevitable so long as loans are the media of capital flow,[1] is merely exacerbated by high interest rates, which moreover fulfil no positive function.[2] The poorer the recipient, and the greater therefore, with few exceptions, the volume of net aid likely to be needed before self-sustained growth is possible, the more essential is it that only very low interest rates be charged. But it can be argued that all public capital should be very cheap—for why should one want to increase the amount of debt that any country is to have as a kind of inverted legacy at its coming of age? It is, after all, still poor.

But given the fact that much so-called aid is expensive, it should clearly be concentrated on the countries which are relatively wealthy, and apparently close to self-sustained growth. Of recent years, the AID and the IBRD/IDA have given recognition to this principle—other countries much less, and the UK's policy of extending credits at more than 6 per cent to the poorest countries is reprehensible. Despite recent improvements, India, and Pakistan, and many African countries, which are a long way from being capable themselves of sustaining a high rate of growth, are still receiving public loans at high rates of interest. Although we have argued that Africa needs less public capital, it is also true that it needs more aid.

---

[1] Grants are, of course, a complete solution to the problem. But many recipients do not want grants, because they dislike the feeling of being recipients of charity.

[2] See Chapter IX, p. 203.

PART THREE

DONORS' PROBLEMS

CHAPTER XI

WHAT DETERMINES DONORS' AID LEVELS?

---

1. RATIONAL CALCULATION

We have seen that the flow of public resources to the underdeveloped world is only a very small proportion of the GNP of the developed world, and well under 1 per cent for most developed countries. But this proportion is not a magnitude which is very relevant to decision-making for individual governments, except in so far as, since the inception of DAC, it is spotlighted in international discussions, and some pressure may thus be brought to bear. From the point of view of an individual donor government, public money lent or granted to the underdeveloped world is one of many items of government expenditure. An increase has to be weighed either against a reduction in other government expenditure, or against the disadvantage of increasing taxation, or taking other measures to reduce other demands on output. In addition, it is government expenditure abroad, and so involves the balance of payments. This latter aspect is discussed in the next section.

It may be asked why, if a loan abroad is actually financed, as it may. be, by borrowing, it has to be weighed against other government expenditures or increased taxation. The answer is that developed countries are all in a position to maintain full employment of resources without having to invest in the developing world. This being the case, any increased government expenditure results in some extra demand for real resources which must be released from other uses. If other government expenditure is unchanged, then either private consumption or investment must somehow be reduced, normally by taxation. Of course, part of the demand created by a loan abroad will be spent abroad (possibly the major part if the loan is untied) and to that extent there is no need to free domestic resources from other uses: but in that event there will be a loss of monetary reserves which might have been spent for the benefit of the developed country. Thus public lending abroad is just like public investment at home in that, unless excessive reserves are held, room has to be found for it by reducing other demands, whether for investment or consumption: and similarly with grants to overseas countries except that, here, there is no prospect of the outflow being reversed. The only exception to this would be if the rich country could find no outlet in investment at home for savings which its citizens insisted on making: which is hardly likely to arise.

To the government of the rich country then, the proportion that public investment and grants abroad bear to total public expenditure may seem a more significant magnitude. Even this is fairly low. For instance in the UK it is 1·7 per cent; in the USA 2·3 per cent; and even in France only 4·0 per cent. (Defence expenditure in the same countries constitute 21 per cent, 35 per cent and 15 per cent respectively of public expenditure.) What determines these amounts? The formal answer is that the government (supposing for simplicity of exposition that the level of taxation is inviolable) must weigh the advantages to its own citizens of assisting other countries, against more domestic education, roads, defence, etc. In so doing it will normally to some extent be guided by the public's own views, which express themselves in various ways. But the government may be the leader or the follower. It may spend more on some things than expressed public opinion would seem to warrant, and try to get people's views to shift: or it may change its own pattern of expenditure more in reaction to public opinion.

There is little doubt in which category aid falls. Governments have made the running. This is notorious in the USA, where Congressional opposition to AID expenditure is persistent and often effective. In France, there was, until French aid figures were disclosed as a result of the formation of the DAC, little public realization of the extent of French aid: since then some opposition has manifested itself.[1] In Germany, opposition to German loans abroad has also developed. In the UK, public opinion is mute. There is certainly no pressure on the government to lend or give more to poor countries: but equally there has been no opposition. This apparent apathy may be partly due to the fact that British aid has been split up between several ministries, so that it has been difficult to focus parliamentary or public opinion on the subject.

Thus it seems broadly true to say that Western governments—anyway the four that really matter from a quantitative point of view—have gone about as far as they have dared in the light of public opinion, with the possible exception of the UK where Ministers' con-

[1] Known as 'Cartierisme', see Chapter I, p. 42.

sciousness of other possibly more attractive modes of expenditure has been more of a factor than any public awareness of the real cost of aid.

It may sound shocking to say that public opinion is an obstacle to any greater effort to help develop the underdeveloped world. But this seems to be the case. The only significant lobbies in favour of aid—apart from a handful of intellectuals—are those businessmen and farmers who, suffering from particular deficiencies of demand, stand to gain by it. For those who want to see more aid, a successful education of public opinion seems to be a necessity. In the USA, the only country in which the administration has so far had a recurrent need to 'sell' aid, it has been sold on the basis of self-interest, with just sufficient success to hold the line at, recently, about $0 \cdot 75$ per cent of the GNP and $2 \cdot 3$ per cent of public expenditure. What the ultimate political determinants of the aid level are, and where this level may be, is beyond our competence to judge. Certainly, few if any observers believe that it can be successfully sold at near the current level on a purely disinterested or humanitarian basis. In Europe, the underlying currents of opinion which ultimately limit the freedom of action of governments in this sphere have been still less tested.

2. THE BALANCE OF PAYMENTS INHIBITION

If a country wants to spend abroad, it is, of course, quite irrational that the balance of payments should be a limitation. It implies a disequilibrium, in effect an excess demand for other currencies, which is certainly curable by letting one's own currency depreciate, or by devaluing it, in relation to others.

But in fact, two of the 'big four' donors have genuinely felt themselves limited both as to the quantity and quality of their aid by balance of payments problems, although it sounds rather like a rich man refusing to give to charity because he has nothing in the bank. The USA has, since 1959, increasingly tied its aid, and a very high proportion is now tied. The UK has moved the same way,[1] but, despite this, explicitly claims that the balance of payments is the limiting factor to the amount of loans and grants extended. Whether this claim is justified is another matter, which is examined below.[2] It is notable in contrast that the USA has greatly increased aid since it first became conscious of balance of payments difficulties in 1959, despite the fact that the balance of payments has been a persistent

[1] See Chapter II, pp. 57 and 61, for an account of the extent of tying.
[2] See English edition, Chapter XV.

242 INTERNATIONAL AID

argument in Congress's endeavours to keep the total down. 'Moreover, there is increasing pressure to compromise the objectives of foreign aid for balance of payments reasons.'[1] Other minor donors, such as Japan, have also been probably inhibited at times by balance of payments problems.

It is impossible to examine fully, in a book about aid, exactly why it is that balance of payments problems should exist at all. In brief, the UK has found it difficult to take effective action which is consistent with full employment and healthy growth at home, to rectify its international accounts when they go wrong, within the period permitted by its reserves and quick liabilities plus its ability to borrow abroad. It has been inhibited from devaluing, the obvious quick mode of adjustment, for various reasons. First, the very liabilities which help to make its short-term position precarious are felt as an impediment to devaluation since they constitute the reserves of other countries, so that devaluation would be politically damaging, and might result in a longer-run capital flight. Secondly, the devaluation of sterling would have caused further difficulties for the USA, and hence would have damaged international relations. Devaluation is, for good or ill, a highly political event as well as a means of economic adjustment. Lastly, there is the fear that the tendency for costs to rise too fast would be accelerated.

The USA's position is rather different. Its difficulties have been caused to a much greater extent by heavy investment abroad. It has been relatively unwilling to use Keynesian budgetary policies at home, and has pursued relatively cheap money policies, which have contributed to the capital outflow. Its need to tie its aid to poor countries is thus partly a result of investing in rich countries. Its reserves position, and ability to borrow abroad, have, unlike the UK, been great enough for a very leisurely adjustment, mainly by tying aid and taking special action to make other investment less attractive. It is not at all clear that devaluation would be an appropriate remedy. But in any case it is unlikely that the USA could devalue vis-à-vis many other countries, for they would follow suit. The main effect of USA devaluation would be an increase in world liquidity—an almost world-wide devaluation against gold—with probably little effect on its balance of payments.

The long period of USA deficit has added greatly to the liquidity of the rest of the developed world. Without this, a shortage of liquidity, from which only the UK has in fact been chronically suffering, would

[1] W. S. Salant et al., The United States Balance of Payments in 1968, The Brookings Institution, Washington, 1963, p. 245.

have been widespread. But this period of increasing liquidity must end, as the USA is unwilling to lose more gold, and other countries to gain more dollars. It is obvious enough that there is something wrong with the world's international payments system, as far as both adjustment mechanisms and liquidity are concerned (the two hang together—the slower are countries to cure deficits and surpluses, the more liquidity is needed). Devaluation is difficult or undesirable for the main deficit countries, and the surplus countries have shown great reluctance, despite the small German and Dutch revaluations, to assist the former by increasing the value of their currencies. Any full analysis of how to put matters right is impossible here. We must break through the tangle of the long international argument on this subject, by expressing controversial views. Our belief is that an essential element in an international monetary mechanism more conducive to the achievement of both stability and growth is a reduction in the use of national currencies as reserves. Only this will permit a more free use of exchange rate adjustments. This in turn requires the substitution of the liquidity thus eliminated by internationally created reserves, which can then be more or less rationally adjusted to permit a balance between the time a deficit country needs to adjust its accounts, and the natural reluctance of the creditors to allow it to live on credit for too long.

While we still seem rather far from achieving the reasonable national behaviour required to eliminate, or at least reduce, balance of payments problems, one must suppose that we shall soon see at least a greater element of creation of international liquidity. As world income and trade expands this will need to go beyond the substitution of international money for some of the USA and UK debts which are at present used as reserves. Some countries will have to be given reserves, rather than earning them by running balance of payments surpluses or digging up gold. This brings us to the question of how such new international liquidity should be shared out, and therefore of the position of the underdeveloped world in all this.[1]

Obviously, some formula would have to be found which would include the underdeveloped world. But here we have to recognize a widely-accepted distinction between the developed world and the underdeveloped world. The new international money would in the

---

[1] Of course, one way of continually increasing international liquidity is to permit repeated increases in the price of gold. This means that the new international liquidity is given to the gold-producers, which is so illogical and unethical a method of 'sharing out' new purchasing power that one trusts world opinion will never permit it.

aggregate have to be created roughly in line with the felt needs of countries to hold reserves (if world inflation is not to be encouraged). But the belief is that only the developed countries want to hold reserves. This is of course over-simplified. There is nevertheless at least an element of justification in the belief that the underdeveloped world would in the aggregate quickly get rid of any such new purchasing power as they got. In fact, they would spend the new money, rather than treating it as a reserve. Most of the new money would therefore find its way into the reserves of the developed world. Let us, for simplicity of exposition, assume that all of it would do so. Then, since the new money creation can be equal only to the felt needs of countries to hold more reserves, that is the need of the developed world to hold more reserves, it follows that the developed world would have to *earn* that part of the new money initially given to the underdeveloped world, if world inflation is to be avoided.

As things stand at present, the above fact is sometimes raised as an objection to the creation of international credit. For instance, some opposition to the enlargement of IMF quotas springs from the tendency of some underdeveloped countries to treat an IMF loan as capital to be expended rather than as the medium-term reserve supplement intended.[1] But, at the same time the developed world extends cheap loans and grants to the underdeveloped world, and it would regard it as a reason *not* to give such aid if it was thought that the recipient would not spend the money but use it as a reserve! So why not let the new international money be deemed to be aid, in which case it becomes only proper to spend it, and everyone is happy?

This brings us to the brilliant suggestion of Mr Maxwell Stamp.[2] The principle of his suggestion is that newly created international money should be channelled to the underdeveloped world by crediting it to the IDA, which would lend it, on development criteria, to the underdeveloped world. It would then mostly find its way into the reserves of developed countries. Too much could not be handled in this way, if the IDA is to be able to apply it properly for development purposes. If too much were available, the IDA would have to distribute it without development strings, and according to some distribution formula, based probably on population and income per head. This, in effect, would destroy the IDA. But, probably, the

[1] Argentina, Brazil, Chile, Colombia, India, Indonesia, and Egypt, have all been in debt to the Fund continuously for more than five years, generally for increasing amounts.

[2] See 'The Stamp Plan—1962 Version', *Moorgate & Wall Street Review*, Autumn 1962, for the latest version of Mr Stamp's scheme.

IDA could in time handle $1 billion per annum—and there is no reason why total IDA funds should not be thus financed.[1] UN technical assistance funds and the UNSF might be similarly financed.

Thus new international money could take the place of existing subscriptions to multilateral agencies, which would reduce developed countries' fears for their reserves. The greater part of the increase in the desirable flow of funds to underdeveloped countries could be found in this way, which would be entirely painless to the developed countries so far as their balances of payments go. Indeed it would relieve them, and so not merely provide a considerable amount of untied resources, but would encourage the untying of existing bilateral programmes. Of course, since the developed world, unlike the underdeveloped world, would have to earn the new reserves, and since therefore they would constitute aid, the developed world would be justified, and have the right, to control their creation, and to insist that they be distributed for development.

Thus the scheme at one blow does three things. First, it contributes to the increase in international liquidity, which is needed and which, sooner or later, must come about. Secondly, it solves the very awkward problem of how this increase can be rationed out. Thirdly, it could provide most or all of the increase in the flow of funds to the underdeveloped world which is needed, and moreover do it in a way which ensures as far as possible that these funds make the best contributions to development. All that is needed for such gold certificates to be acceptable as a reserve currency would be agreement between the big four, the USA, UK, France, and Germany, to accept them.

It is not suggested that the amount of new annual world liquidity which is desirable, necessarily coincides with the amount of development capital which it is desirable for a multilateral but donor-controlled institution such as the IDA to spend in the underdeveloped world. But that does not matter. Something like the Stamp Plan may not be the whole answer, since more liquidity may need to be created than one would want to create through the Stamp Plan. But it has a very strong claim to be a component of the answer.

[1] The principle is Mr Stamp's. But the qualifications and interpretation, with which he might not agree, are ours.

CHAPTER XII

THE NEED FOR CO-OPERATION
AT DONOR'S CAPITAL CITY LEVEL

1. AID-TYING

The more rational world payments and adjustment mechanisms, discussed above, depend on international agreements which are very difficult to reach. It may be that the underdeveloped world will have to live for quite a long time with a developed world which fears for its balances of payments, and which uses various expedients in the field of payments, trade, and aid—most of which are harmful to the underdeveloped world—to regulate its external accounts.

Most such expedients are the subject of international rules, under the IMF or GATT, or of more restricted agreements like the EEC, EFTA, and the OECD. Curiously, manufacturing countries fear export subsidies more than import restrictions. Export subsidies are anathema, and the rules are not broken, although the letter of the law may be strained. The international rules, which permit import restrictions when there are serious balance of payments deficits, curiously again, favour quotas rather than use of the price mechanism. Thus the UK's measures of October 1964 were in defiance of the GATT and EFTA. It is an historical accident—for aid was unimportant when IMF and GATT rules were drawn up—that export promotion by means of aid-tying is not the subject of regulation. While 'dumping' is regarded with horror, countries show no effective concern with competitive export promotion by 'aid-tying', even when the 'aid' consists of expensive export-credits. Nor does the IMF show concern over the fact that much aid money is, in effect, inconvertible.

The underdeveloped world has some cause for complaint that the laws are made by the rich, for the rich. Import restrictions, which are instituted normally because the deficit-developed country is losing reserves to other developed countries, generally hit them too. They do not accumulate reserves, but nevertheless pay the price of being in surplus. And, as we have argued at length, aid-tying greatly reduces the value of aid. The developed currencies are generally convertible to rich countries, whether loaned to or earned by them; but are generally convertible to poor countries only when earned by them.

But, in the present state of the world, it is difficult to argue that aid-tying should be outlawed. If it had been, in the last five years, what would have happened to USA aid? It is fairly certain that the great increase from 1958 to 1962 could not have occurred. While for the present we can no more outlaw aid-tying than, say, import quotas, we can still argue that, like general import restrictions, it should be resorted to only when a capital-supplying country is in serious balance of payments difficulties. This has been argued, especially by the Americans, in the OECD. The two important surplus countries (France at times, and Germany) have argued in reply that their aid is untied.

The truth of the matter is that it is very easy to extend loans (or grants) which have no formal restriction against usage in third countries, or domestically, but whose use in the lending country has nevertheless been ensured. The method appears to operate rather differently in France and Germany. In the French Franc Area formal and informal agreements appear to operate to ensure that a very high proportion of all imports come from France. The result is that France can extend aid which can be used in the first instance for domestic costs, and nevertheless ensure that no strain is put on the French reserves. As usual, France is a special case. The worst disadvantages of aid-tying result if it cannot be used for domestic costs,[1] and this disadvantage does not appear to apply to French aid. So strictures against de facto French aid-tying cannot be as strong as in the case of other developed countries: moreover the total of French aid is too great for them to carry much weight. The possibility that France might enter into any OECD agreement to restrict aid-tying, in the manner that trade and payments restrictions are restricted by GATT and the IMF, seems at present remote. Such an agreement if effective would seem to the French to offend against the whole tightly-knit principle of the French Franc Area.

So far as the main donors are concerned this leaves only Germany to discuss, since it is reasonably clear from past behaviour that both the USA and the UK would be willing genuinely to untie aid whenever they felt reasonably secure as to their balance of payments situation. German aid is rather effectively tied in a quite different manner from French aid.

[1] See Chapter VII, pp. 160-6.

If aid is really to be untied, first a loan must be extended, and then its detailed use agreed without any threat or tendency to slow down authorization, or disallow projects, merely because they would or might contain a high proportion of domestic costs or third-country procurement. In the reverse case, the lending country may wait until a number of its contractors have in effect agreed projects with the recipients, subject to a public loan agreement being worked out. The recipient knows what it must do to get the loan: the 'aiding' government in turn knows what it must do if its business men are to get the business, and will of course be under pressure from them. This is a cosy way of pretending that an export credit is untied aid. It is also possible first to agree an untied loan, and then to back out of projects which do not promise a high proportion of procurement in the lending country. We believe that both these practices are extensively operated by Germany, although it is also true that we know of instances (e.g. in East Africa and the Sudan) where some local and even third-country procurement has genuinely been permitted. The reasons why a persistent surplus country like Germany, whose Government and bankers are afraid of too much foreign demand ('importing inflation'), should permit such procedures, is partly that the commercial lobby is too strong to resist, and partly that the donor country may get more kudos from constructing a project than from merely giving the money. For instance, the Germans evidently felt that the Italians got the credit for building the Roseires dam in the Sudan, although it was financed by German aid.

All countries now tie aid very closely, both those which make no pretence, and those which do. The kind of practice discussed in the above paragraph makes it clear that an agreed international code of behaviour on aid-tying would be extremely difficult to achieve and make effective. It is not surprising that the DAC has made no progress on this problem. A change of heart on the part of some donor governments, with greater emphasis on and belief in the importance of development, is really required, together with greater recognition of the harmfulness of aid-tying. In the absence of this, it is questionable whether much can be achieved by attempts to draw up a code of good behaviour. Nevertheless, in the hope that some improvement along these lines will be achieved, it may be worth suggesting that the best initial line of advance might be to try to reach agreement that, *regardless of the state of developed countries' balances of payments*, the only restriction on procurement for projects should be that initial expenditure of the loan should not be for procurement in developed countries other than that of the lender.[1] This would remove the worst feature of aid-tying,[2] and would retain by far the greater part of the effectiveness of aid-tying from the point of view of deficit developed countries. Admittedly, the result might be that a rich country would give rather less aid when its balance of payments looked unhealthy, than it would have done if fuller aid-tying were permissible. But our belief is that this would be a price worth paying from the point of view of the developing world.

2. AID TERMS, AND EXPORT CREDITS

We saw in Chapter X that, while the aggregate of loans and grants cannot be said to be any longer cripplingly expensive to the under-developed world, it made little sense to speak in terms of aggregates. The important thing is that countries which are likely to need aid for a long time should have very cheap aid, with very long waivers on capital repayment: while the more expensive aid should be reserved for the relatively rich and promising. This principle was generally accepted at the UNCTAD.

As we also saw in the previous chapter, there are few figures published on aid terms by recipients. While the OECD has done ex-tremely useful work in building up a picture of the 'flow of financial resources to developing countries' (without which this book could hardly have been written), this is an important gap which one hopes it may be able to fill.

Filling this gap would be a useful, perhaps even necessary, prelude to an attempt to getting international co-operation in suiting the terms of loans to the recipient. Individually, as we have seen, most donors of course do this to some extent, particularly the USA. Other countries do it more by varying the proportion of grants and loans, but this is less flexible, since most give grants only for non-self-liquidating purposes and projects. The IBRD can do it by mixing IBRD and IDA loans. But since there is no apparent co-ordination (and since some donors simply do not give cheap or very cheap loans), those recipients for which very cheap loans are deemed ap-propriate by the USA and IDA, also take very expensive loans from other governments (and also from private sources). Here the soft lenders can justly complain that the hard lenders are demanding quick

[1] This form of restriction has been adopted for part of AID funds, although most AID funds are for procurement only in the USA (but it should be noted that AID classified Hong Kong as industrialized, and hence not eligible for third-country procurement!).

[2] See Chapter VII, pp. 162–3 above.

repayment plus interest at their expense: and, further, that the main
object of soft terms—not to condemn the 'long-haul' recipient to a
humiliating and possibly damaging debt-position—is being under-
mined.

One cannot advocate that hard lenders should lend only to the
wealthier and more promising underdeveloped countries. Therefore,
all lenders should reach agreement to lend to any particular recipient
on the same terms. Since there are undoubtedly many recipients which
will soon be suffering from intolerable debt positions, unless further
gross aid is given only via soft long-dated loans, this means that
all donor countries should be persuaded to follow the lead of the
USA (so far as bilateral aid goes), and be prepared to match the USA
terms in appropriate recipient countries. But, further, agreement
would have to be reached as to what terms are appropriate to which
countries.

Where a donors' consortium exists, this can be used as the appropriate body in which to agree terms. But since consortia are never
likely to be manageable for more than a few countries, the DAC is the
obvious forum in which such agreement should be arrived at for a
much wider range of countries. Any government which lends to
India at high rates for short periods should, for instance, be regarded
as a blackleg, and the greatest possible pressure be exerted at DAC
'confrontation' meetings. The DAC has already tried to get aid terms
improved: but there is quite a long way to go yet. So far as Latin
American countries go, the Inter-American Committee for the
Alliance of Progress (CIAP) may turn out to be a more effective body
in defining suitable aid terms for particular recipients.

The problem is further complicated by private export credits, which
may or may not be donor-government guaranteed (they also may or
may not be recipient-government guaranteed). If a poor country,
deemed by the rich to need cheap credit, gets from them less than it
wants, it may, and often will, resort to short-term private export
credits at high rates of interest. This too can undermine the purpose
of cheap loans, and lead to a position in which public loans are used
to pay off private lenders. It may be argued that private credit is in a
different category, and that if the underdeveloped country is benefited
by the private export credit, then it must be in a better position to
service its public debt. This is a weak argument. First of all, some
countries at least have taken expensive private credit for uneconomic
projects, ministers or others having been over-persuaded by carpet-
bagging salesmen,[1] so that the country is harmed not benefited.

[1] See Little, *Aid to Africa*, p. 22.

Secondly, even if the projects yield more than the cost of this 'contractor finance', the contribution to the recipients' indebtedness is an 'external diseconomy' of the project which is not allowed for in any normal balancing of returns against interest cost.[1]

The question therefore arises as to what donor governments can do about the abuse of export-credits, an abuse which arises partly from competitive pressure to sell, and partly from recipients' gullibility in accepting costly terms for things they should not or do not really want (it is, of course, analogous to the hire-purchase problem). Clearly it is a problem which demands donor-country co-operation, and again the obvious body in which to try to get agreement is the DAC.[2]

But what should developed countries try to agree on? Clearly, export credits cannot be outlawed, nor could arrangements be made to discriminate against underdeveloped countries, even if developed countries thought this was for their own good. There seem to be two ways of limiting their use. First, donor governments can refuse to guarantee such credits unless they are satisfied, first that the recipient can, on general grounds of economic promise and present indebtedness, afford such credit; and, secondly, that the particular project or equipment for which the credit is given is likely to benefit the recipient. No doubt, governments pay some attention to the first of these conditions; but it is doubtful whether their decisions can be systematic or well-informed, both because full information of indebtedness is lacking,[3] and because the governments of donor countries often know little about the economies of the countries to which they lend. Secondly, donor governments can let it be understood that acceptance of much 'contractor finance' is likely to be a barrier to the extension of cheap public loans. Lastly, of course, if it is clear that an underdeveloped country is accepting contractor finance for projects which are clearly worthwhile, then it follows that they could have absorbed more public capital. Accepting expen-

[1] Equity finance is, in this context, no problem. First, the contribution to the economy cannot be less than the dividends remitted. It is normally far higher, both because of taxation and because companies generally plough back a considerable part of their profits. Secondly, it is not a liability which can give rise to default.
[2] It should be noted that the UNCTAD invited the IBRD to make a study of supplier's credits, submit it to the UN, and make recommendations.
[3] The IBRD has information on the public debt, and recipient-government guaranteed private debt, of the underdeveloped countries to which it gives loans. Even this is not a full picture, if only because there may be, and often is, private non-guaranteed debt. But one is not aware that developed governments themselves require information about indebtedness when extending loans.

sive contractor finance can either stem from irresponsibility on the part of the acceptor, or it can be a sign that the country concerned needed more aid.

At present much too little is known about this problem. We have figures only for increases in private export credits guaranteed by OECD governments. This may be only a small part of the total. But if one judges only by these figures, comparatively few countries increased their debt in this form very much in the period 1960–2. These few included Ghana, Mexico, Argentina, Brazil, and Peru. Some of these would seem to have been strong candidates for more aid.[1]

Certainly, an attack on the problem must form part of any general move to better co-ordination of aid terms. There is some good hope of co-operation by recipients in reaching a solution, for, among the UNCTAD resolutions, one can find the statement that 'developing countries, in their turn, should endeavour to limit recourse to short- and medium-term credits; in this effort industrialized countries and international institutions should co-operate'.[2]

In conclusion, one must emphasize that unification of the terms of public aid, and the elimination so far as possible of competitive private commercial credit, would not only help the underdeveloped countries, but would also improve the image of Western aid. Expensive loans, which are called aid, are bad for aid relations; and the image of Western capitalism is hardly improved by successful efforts to sell ill-conceived projects on expensive credit terms.[3]

3. BURDEN-SHARING, AND THE DEFINITION OF AID

The DAC partly owes its existence to the notion that the USA was bearing an unfair share of the 'burden' of assisting developing countries. It was hoped that the DAC would operate to increase the contributions of some of the European countries. There was some small success in the enterprise: but the main result was that the USA learned that it was not as generous as it thought it was. To quote an American judgment: '... even allowing for the inclusion of colonial and post-colonial expenses not strictly of an aid nature, the European-Japanese foreign assistance effort still looks impressive, and the USA has had some difficulty maintaining that it was carrying too heavy a share of the common burden.'[4]

[1] See Chapter X, p. 233.
[2] Final Act, A. IV. I, Section I, subsection j, Geneva, 1964.
[3] See also Chapter III, and Little, *Aid to Africa*, pp. 31–2.
[4] Salant *et al.*, op. cit.

But what is this burden to be shared, and how can it be measured? At present, there is a tendency to take the total flow of public loans and grants expressed as a proportion of GNP, and use this as a measure of a donor's performance. This is lumping together incommensurables with a vengeance.

The problem of arriving at the true cost of aid has already been discussed in Chapter II, where some tentative estimates were given. It is obvious enough that it is this 'true cost' that should form the basis of any burden-sharing exercise, rather than the figure for the total of loans, grants, commodity aid, etc. But it would be very hard to get agreement on a basis for assessing the true cost, especially taking into consideration surplus commodity aid, and making allowance for aid which although given for development was really a purchase of defence facilities. The dividing line between military and other aid would have to be found (unless defence and aid expenditures were to be lumped together in determining the burden—surely a horrific suggestion from the point of view of public relations with the underdeveloped world).

Even if all this were settled, there is not the slightest reason why the true cost should be the same proportion of GNP for countries which range in wealth from the USA and Canada, to Japan and Italy. So some progressive taxation formula would have to be found. The problem is further complicated by the fact that a determination of the amount of aid, would not also determine capital flows. It is reasonable that the poorer developed countries should provide more unsubsidized capital flows, and less by way of grants and cheap loans (although where they do give loans to 'long haul' countries, they should match the soft terms of the wealthier donors—they should just do less of this).

All in all, possibly enough has been said to suggest that a burden-sharing formula is more likely to cause trouble than do any good, at least until such time, if ever, as it has teeth—that is until there is some sanction against those who do not pay up their international tax, as it would then be. Meantime, the DAC confrontation procedure, whereby an understanding of what constitutes a fair contribution to public capital flows can be gradually built up, and pressure put on the obvious laggards, is probably more sensible.

4. THE WORLD DISTRIBUTION OF AID

The world distribution of aid is, mainly, a donors' problem. Yet, so far as we know, it is never discussed, even in the DAC which is the donors' club. It would be reasonable not to discuss it, either if there is no prima facie reason to suppose that it does not somehow sort itself out, as well as any exercise of reason might do; or if there is no hope of bringing such reason effectively to bear.

The distributions of both capital flows and aid proper can be conceived of as matrices with, say, the names of the donors at the top of the columns, and those of recipients to the left of the rows. The column totals give the distribution between donors. This was discussed under 'burden sharing', and we shall say no more. The row totals give the distribution among recipients. We have in Chapter X found cause to believe that this distribution can be faulted in the light of what we have presumed to be the self-interest of the Western world. We now wish to discuss how it may be improved. But changing a total implies changing the amounts in the cells of the matrix. Moreover, even if the totals were about right, it could still be the case that the amounts in the cells were not. Thus, both individual recipients and donors, more likely the former, may, apart from the total, regard the distribution of what they receive or give as unsatisfactory.

First, take recipients' totals. We discussed the facts in Chapter II. Now we must ask what determines the amount of public capital a country, or a continent, gets.

In 1962, USA bilateral grants and loans were about 56 per cent of the total of non-Communist aid. The USA gives aid almost everywhere, excepting other countries' dependent territories. A proximate answer would seem to be that the world distribution is determined by the USA, the next largest donor (France) accounting for only 15 per cent of the total. There is a lot of truth in this, but it is not quite the whole truth. First, apart from the fact that the administration may sometimes be restricted by Congressional rules, the USA can top up others' aid anywhere in such a way as to get the distribution more in accordance with its own liking. But it cannot reduce others' aid. Thus if French territories are over-aided the USA is powerless, or if the USA wants to reduce aid somewhere, possibly for political reasons, and other countries disagree, it may fail. Secondly, the USA feels bound to give aid to some countries which are heavily aided by the USSR, to prevent them being dependent only on the USSR (e.g. Afghanistan), and as a result may, so to speak, connive at their being over-aided. Thirdly, the USA sometimes ties its hands in the interest of trying to get others to give more. Thus, in the Indian consortium, it has on occasion matched other donors' contributions, and so left the aid level to be determined by them. The USA may also go slow in an area where it believes that other donors' political interests are involved, in order to limit the extent to which they might try to shift the 'burden' on to American shoulders. This may be part of the reason for the USA proclaiming its limited interest in Africa.[1] Thus donors may play at bluffing each other. But, Communist aid apart, it is doubtful whether this has been very significant.

If we take the big four, the USA, France, the UK, and Germany, together they account for 82 per cent of non-Communist flows. If one also includes the IBRD and its affiliates, 88 per cent is accounted for. We need look no further. Apart from Communist aid, agreement on policy between these four countries and the IBRD would be enough. But, in fact, there is little apparent agreement among the four as to the distribution or even the purposes of aid. The USA pursues a policy whose intent is very much in line with what, in Chapter III, we have described as the collective Western interest in aid. One may, of course, want to quarrel with USA judgment in particular cases, or with the effectiveness of their methods, but that is another matter. The French are very much bound to their dependencies and to ex-French countries, and do not appear to want others to contribute. They certainly do not see their aid as primarily serving the interests of the West. The British are likewise bound to the Commonwealth, more by historical accident than grand design, although there is, of course, a Commonwealth interest. The Germans, like the Americans, give aid very widely, and hence mostly in small amounts, but its distribution and purpose is more commercially oriented than one would like to see.[2] Finally, the IBRD (though not the IDA) has its hands tied to some extent by its appeal to private funds, so that it must preserve criteria of 'bankability'.

The apparent irrationalities in the world distribution of capital flows, which we discussed in Chapter X, are partly, but certainly not entirely, due to the above incoherence of policy. If France had been less concerned with French Africa, she might have given rather less to Africa and more to India (or Latin America). If Germany had been less concerned with commercialism, she might have concentrated her aid more on India. The IBRD would have given more to India, if India could have been described as a bankable proposition. But the chief causes of the low level of aid to India—the main anomaly, as we have suggested—has probably been a mixture of sheer unreason (her great size) and the absence of immediate apparent risk of political upheaval.

[1] cf. Clay Committee Report.
[2] These motives have been discussed at much greater length in Chapter I.

Turning to the distribution as between countries within the regions (India, we count as a region), the USA is so dominant in Latin América, the Far East, Southern Asia apart from India, and Europe, that any inconsistencies stem from USA judgment rather than incoherence. The same, of course, is true for the French in French-speaking Africa (apart from Morocco and Tunisia where both France and the USA are important). Thus it is really only in India and English-speaking Africa south of the Sahara, that inappropriate relative aid-levels may occur as a result of there being many donors. Some understanding between the UK, USA, and Germany, is essential to rational allocation here. No doubt such understanding exists, at least between the USA and the UK.

The remaining question is whether it is a good thing that such donor specialization on their ex-empires as exists for France, the UK, and Belgium, should continue.[1] On political grounds, it is surely a bad thing, if it prevents the recipients from receiving enough capital from enough sources not to feel too dependent. On economic grounds, minimization of the number of donors surely makes for greater efficiency. But one hopes that this multi-donor problem, which was discussed in Chapter VIII, can be reasonably well solved in a way which permits an element of donor co-operation sufficient for economic efficiency, without erecting the bogy of a monolithic Western donor. Whether or not this proves to be the case, the political consideration is probably most important.

Now British concentration on the Commonwealth does no harm, for British aid and capital flows are not large enough to make the recipients dependent on her, except in the remaining colonies, and perhaps the Caribbean. Moreover, the UK favours the entry of other donors. It is really only France that is the stumbling block to diversification, for the USA is dominant in many areas not so much by intention but because of the lack of other capital. There is some hope that France will increase her commitments outside the French Franc Area,[2] and one hopes that the UK and Germany will also increase theirs. But it is unfortunately true that at present the ex-colonial powers tend to be more interested in trade-promoting 'aid', than in development aid, when they turn to other areas.

We feel that, despite the fact that more diversified aid is probably less efficient, efforts should be made to promote it. Diversification of aid for Latin America and the Far East is possible only if other

---

[1] Of course no question of aid diversification can arise in the case of the Portuguese possessions until these become independent.
[2] cf. *The Jeanneney Report.*

donors increase their provision of capital, or if the USA increases her provision of aid to Africa against an understanding with the other three main donors that they will do more in Latin America and the Far East. But the USA is so large absolutely that her dominance could only be generally overcome if she delegated aid to, say, the UK and Germany by providing them with cheap long-term capital against an agreement that they would 'on-lend' it. We doubt if this would be acceptable to any of the parties! She could also, of course, delegate more aid to a multilateral institution. But this would almost certainly be unacceptable, unless it was controlled by the donors, with subscription-weighted voting, in which case the institution would be dominated by the USA, and diversification would again be nullified.

CHAPTER XIII

THE CO-ORDINATION OF
AID ADMINISTRATION

1. AT RECIPIENT COUNTRY LEVEL

The problems created for recipients, and indeed for development, by the multiplicity of donors were discussed in Chapter VIII. We there dismissed full multilateralism as impossible, and suggested that the most promising approach lay in co-operation between donors in the field of aid administration, if possible with recipient participation. The idea would be to set up an organization in the recipient country, multilateral but almost certainly donor-controlled, to carry out the job of plan and project evaluation, surveillance, etc., that all donors should be doing. Donors would delegate to this agency all the technical, advisory, and supervisory, functions that are at present carried out by AID Missions, or the UK's Middle East Development Division, and would follow the advice of the agency as to project selection, and the terms and conditions of aid, unless they had very strong and specific reasons for ignoring it. Donors would remain responsible for determining the amount of aid, and for drawing up specific aid agreements. They would also be free to make certain ideological stipulations—which should be kept to a minimum—for example that their aid may not be used to support public ownership of projects which they believe should be left to the private sector. There would be no question of bilateral aid losing its identity.

The agency's functions would be the same as the functions of a bilateral aid agency in a country where the donor's programme is fairly large, and the donor is genuinely concerned with development. It would study the economy and evaluate the government's economic plan and policies, co-ordinating its work where possible with the relevant UN regional organization. It would evaluate projects, help the recipient to fit available tied currencies and technical assistance into its plan, mediate between donor and recipient, investigate possible uses of aid, and sectors which have been neglected or are especially difficult to aid (e.g. peasant agriculture), and supervise the

THE CO-ORDINATION OF AID ADMINISTRATION

use of aid to whatever extent donors were willing to delegate their authority (it would probably leave auditing to the donor, and keep a more general check on the progress of projects, tendering procedures, etc.). It could also encourage and facilitate the co-operation of donors in particular projects. There are precedents for such co-operation, for example the joint FAO/UNICEF dairy training in central Kenya, the Nairobi water supply scheme financed by AID and CDC, and the East African development corporations which have attracted money from several sources. It is more difficult to quote examples of non-existent co-operation which would have been beneficial, but there is little doubt that they exist.

Institutions which already exist should be built upon as far as possible. It would be impossible to devise a single blueprint to suit the diverse needs and circumstances of all the countries in need of multilateral machinery for co-ordinating aid. Recipients vary widely in their ability and desire to negotiate and co-ordinate aid for themselves, and in the number of donors who provide them with aid. They also vary in their sensitivity to anything that may smell of a donor's club. Donors themselves also vary in the amount and kinds of co-ordination they are willing to accept. None of the Eastern countries has so far entered formally into even such co-ordinating institutions as exist, and Austria, Sweden, and Switzerland, have not so far joined the DAC because they associate it with NATO. Thus if Soviet, Chinese, Swedish, etc., co-operation is desired in a particular recipient country, certain types of organization and certain auspices have to be avoided. Whether the price of their co-operation is worth paying must depend on circumstances. While the price of Chinese co-operation is probably infinite, some Russian co-operation might be a real possibility in a few cases. It seems that in Afghanistan, Russians have attended regular meetings for the exchange of information between donors. Russian co-operation should not therefore be ruled out without consideration, for it would not merely help in improving the use of world aid, but would also be a step in the direction of peaceful co-existence.

The relationship between donors and the agency could vary between almost complete delegation of responsibility for project selection and surveillance, to consultation before the donors each drew up their own separate aid policies. The extent of delegation need not even be the same for all donors to a particular recipient country: one would expect a major donor (the USA in Latin America, France in West Africa) to be less willing to delegate responsibility than less important donors. But if the agency did a good job, confidence in it would grow, and one might hope that those donors who have exhibited more interest in export promotion than in the development of the recipient would be persuaded to change their emphasis as a result of the agency's work.

Donors would have much to gain from substantial delegation, if it could be achieved. They could be confident that conditions necessary for development were being attached to aid, without being exposed individually to the political embarrassment of interfering in the recipient's economy, They would also enjoy considerable administrative economy (assuming that donors shared the agency's expenses on a reasonable basis). Recipients would gain from the dilution of donors' non-development ambitions, and from the large amount of what would be, in effect, technical assistance provided by the agency. This would take the form of help in negotiating with donors, in solving the jig-saw puzzle of tied currency and aid in kind—including technical services and education—and in evaluation of economic policy, planning, and project design.

Let us next look at the extent of the apparent current need for coordinated advisory services on the lines suggested above, and the likely future need. The extent of the 'multi-donor problem' was discussed in general terms in Chapter VIII. Prima facie, available statistical evidence suggests that very few countries receive large amounts of aid from a wide variety of sources. Even India and Pakistan, for whom IBRD consortia help to arrange levels of aid from a number of sources, received 79 and 87 per cent of their OECD bilateral aid from the USA in 1962, and the corresponding percentage for Turkey was 89 per cent. These figures must, however, be used with caution, for several reasons. First, they exclude aid from all non-OECD sources, of which the most important are multilateral agencies and Communist countries; and the latter tend to concentrate their aid in relatively few countries, where they are significant donors. Secondly, they include for these three countries and for a number of others, such as Egypt, large quantities of USA commodity aid, and also re-finance credits, neither of which require the same type and degree of administration as other forms of public finance. Thirdly, they take no separate account of technical assistance, which to be effective needs careful administration and integration with financial assistance; and since many donors, such as Israel and some of the UN agencies, concentrate on technical assistance, figures expressed in money terms tend to understate the need for co-ordination.

The urgency of the need for co-ordination on the lines we favour cannot in any case be judged entirely on statistical evidence provided by donor countries. For instance, the main Indian source of statistics on aid,[1] which provides figures for aid commitments from all donors, gives a rather different impression from that presented by OECD,[2] and suggests that aid to India is in serious need of co-ordination. But, since other countries do not publish such clear statements of their sources of aid, we must revert to OECD figures which suggest that, on the basis of aid receipts for 1962, Nigeria, Yugoslavia, Israel, Morocco, Tunisia, Liberia, Chile, Iran, Tanganyika, Syria, and probably also Pakistan, Brazil, and Kenya, received aid on a large enough scale from a large enough number of donors to be faced with a considerable task of co-ordination. There are almost certainly other countries with considerable co-ordination problems, but this list covers most of the really important recipients, and a number of less important ones. However, one can eliminate Israel and Yugoslavia from the list, because their Governments are probably fully capable of co-ordinating aid for themselves, and probably also Brazil, and Chile, on the grounds that most of their aid from countries other than the USA consists of re-finance credits.

Pakistan and Turkey are countries which, like India, probably need more help in co-ordinating aid than would appear from OECD statistics, because the apparent predominance of the USA is due to large amounts of commodity aid. We are inclined to think that co-ordination of aid by means of some new multilateral machinery is most needed in India, Pakistan, Nigeria, and Turkey, perhaps followed by East Africa; our opinion is based on the existing pattern of aid, the impact that help with co-ordination might have on the appropriateness and utilization of aid, and the size and importance of the country or the area.

In these five areas, machinery for administering and co-ordinating aid should deal with the whole of assistance, both technical and financial, to the extent that the various donors would allow it to do so. This would imply a separate administrative unit in each country, except possibly in East Africa where a regional unit might be appropriate.

How much of a base already exists, on which a wider form of multilateral aid advisory service could be built? There are at present three main forms of co-operation between bilateral and multilateral donors (leaving aside all forms of multilateralism, including those restricted geographically or politically like the EDF or IDB). First there

[1] External Assistance, published annually by Ministry of Finance, Department of Economic Affairs, New Delhi.
[2] See Chapter VIII, p. 199.

are the consortia and consultative groups, run by the IBRD, OECD, and DAC. Consortia bring aid donors together, usually once a year, to pledge themselves to levels of aid. Subsequent negotiations for spending the amounts pledged remain strictly bilateral, and commitments to projects are not made at consortium meetings. Where consortia exist, greater multilateralism might be achieved by setting up the kind of multilateral advisory service described above, run by the IBRD or OECD, whichever convenes the consortium.

Such an institution could go some considerable way towards getting projects into a form in which they might then be more quickly accepted by some consortium member, and which would also shorten the subsequent negotiations. It could also try to persuade donors to standardize their procedures and requirements. Many of the delays in project aid arise out of the fact that serious work on project agreements occurs only after the pledging at the consortium meeting. The V. K. R. V. Rao report on aid utilization in India[1] has suggested that funds be committed, as well as pledged, at consortium meetings. This seems to imply that the donors shall have satisfied themselves about projects before aid is pledged, which could mean a lot of wasted work. But if such work as would be common-ground to any donor's requirements could be done by a multilateral agency trusted by the donors, a bank of projects being established with the agency's stamp of approval, then there would be little risk of the work being wasted, and the process of utilization could thus be speeded up. The work of such an agency could go much further of course, if aid were untied, and if donors could bring themselves to pledge for more than one year ahead.

Consultative groups, distinguished from consortia by the fact that no aid is pledged, have thus far achieved very little by way of coordination. They have served a tentative function of mutual information on problems and policies, but little more than this. An informed multilateral agency (which need not always be run by the IBRD, OECD, or DAC) would help to make these consultations more effective, and might help to convince donors that they should pledge aid levels, and turn themselves into consortia. Too much cannot be achieved unless the chips are down.

A second type of multilateral agency, or rather group of institutions, has been set up under the Alliance for Progress. The Alliance itself is a treaty, signed by all Latin American republics except Cuba, and by the USA, committing the Latin American signatories to aim at

[1] *Report of the Committee on Utilization of External Assistance*, Ministry of Finance, New Delhi, 1964.

a 5 per cent rate of economic growth, and to carry out certain social and administrative reforms thought to be necessary to that end, and committing the USA to help with financial and technical aid. The Alliance is in some respects similar to the Marshall Plan, although the time-horizon is much longer—ten years, initially, and far more than that will be needed if the 5 per cent growth rate is to be sustained —and the aid to be provided by the USA is on less generous terms than Marshall Aid. The interesting aspect of the Alliance for our present purposes is the multilateral machinery that has been set up. Existing organs of the Organization of American States (OAS), especially the Inter-American Economic and Social Council (IA-ECOSOC) and the IDB, are closely involved in the Alliance. Special committees have also been established. The first, the Panel of Nine and its sub-committees, evaluates the development plans drawn up by Latin American governments, and reports on them, to the government concerned, to the IDB, to AID, and to any other agencies that might provide aid for the plan. The second, established as recently as 1964, is the CIAP. This studies aid requirements and makes recommendations on the distribution of aid. There is, naturally, so far very little evidence as to CIAP's effectiveness. But if AID, as the principal bilateral agency, is willing to follow its recommendations even fairly closely, it will be an important pioneer, since its membership is almost entirely Latin-American and it is therefore virtually a recipients' committee.[1] On the other hand, it is not clear that any Alliance for Progress institution performs the functions of our proposed country-level co-ordinating agencies. Indeed, there are IBRD consultative groups in Latin America, e.g. for Colombia, in addition to Alliance for Progress machinery.

Thirdly, one should mention that aid administrators in the field do meet informally to try to keep track of what each is doing, ensure that technical assistance requests are filled only once, and discuss other issues that may arise. In a few countries, Jordan and Thailand for instance, committees of donor and recipient representatives have been set up to discuss aid utilization. The idea is a good one, and could form a first step towards some more comprehensive institution with staff for evaluating development programmes and aid requests. But, in the absence of an economic secretariat to carry out evaluation of aid proposals, and help to brief the recipient government's delegates, these committees have had limited success because they have thrown too much strain on the recipient government.

[1] CIAP is in some ways reminiscent of the OEEC, which had a say in allocating Marshall Aid.

Having picked out a small group of countries or areas which we believe should be the first to receive attention, it is worth considering which of the above kinds of organization might be developed towards the greater degree of multilateralism proposed, and under whose auspices. In India, Pakistan, and Turkey, it seems obvious that the consortium organization should be retained, and that the sponsors of the consortium should manage the new multilateral agency proposed. The most promising method in Nigeria and East Africa, for which the IBRD and DAC respectively have organized consultative groups, is rather more difficult to see. DAC, and probably also the OECD itself, are handicapped as sponsors because recipients associate them with NATO. The IBRD appears to be regarded with less suspicion, because its membership is less restricted, and because it does not exclude Communist members as such. IBRD-sponsored agencies would certainly be preferred to DAC-sponsored ones in non-aligned countries.

One would like to recommend that the Economic Commission for Africa (ECA), and the other UN Area Commissions, take responsibility for setting up aid administrations. There are, unfortunately, some serious objections to this. First, recipients' control of these organizations, however indirect, would probably make donors rather unwilling to delegate to them any responsibility for decisions relevant to financial aid. Secondly, the quota restrictions on the nationality of members would be a handicap. Thirdly, too many local people of talent might be attracted away from their own countries, where they are needed, defeating one of the major purposes of the exercise, which is to supplement the shortage of competent local administrators, economists, and other technical experts, by bringing outsiders in to aid administration.

The Alliance for Progress is an attractive model in some ways, but it is more of a continental than a country organization, and it is very doubtful whether it could be applied to any other continent. The countries of Asia are too divided. In Africa, there is the barrier of the special relation of the African and Malagasy States to France and the EEC. Also, sufficient competent, and qualified, Africans could at present hardly be found to man the range of institutions analogous to the Panel of Nine, CIAP, the IDB, etc. Nevertheless, mention of the IDB naturally suggests the possibility of using the African Development Bank (ADB)—so far a fairly small, purely African, institution, established in November 1964 in Abidjan with a distinguished Sudanese governor—as a vehicle for aid. If the ADB can set an example by its choice of projects and integrity of development purpose, then Western governments should certainly seek to use it as an intermediary for soft loans to the African continent, in a manner analogous to the Social Progress Trust Fund of the IDB.

Apart from the countries where there seems to be a case for a new multilateral agency, because there are several major financial aid programmes, there is also a large number of countries where small amounts of assistance, especially technical assistance, are received from a number of sources, even though most financial assistance comes from a single source. In many of these countries there may be a case for establishing some machinery to co-ordinate these little aid programmes with one another, and as far as possible to make them complementary with that of the major donors. Co-ordination at this level might take the form of an office which would administer all the smaller aid programmes (to the extent acceptable to the minor donors —as discussed earlier in this chapter), and co-ordinate these with the major donor's programme as closely as the major donor and the recipient would find acceptable. The office of the UN Regional Representative, which exists in most countries, and already is supposed to co-ordinate UNEPTA/UNSF activities with those of the UN Specialized Agencies, is the obvious candidate for this activity. Similarly, something would be gained by joint administration of several small technical assistance programmes even in countries where the major donors were unwilling to co-operate in efforts to administer aid in a co-ordinated way. There is a precedent in the form of joint Scandinavian projects in a few countries. But, even if no new institutions can be established, meetings of aid administrators or diplomatic representatives, together with recipients, probably under the chairmanship of the UN Regional Representative, to sort out problems of overlap and to inform each other of mutual intentions, are clearly desirable.

One final problem, which, although apparently one of administrative convenience, could have far-reaching effects on long-run political and economic development, is whether aid advisory agencies should be set up on a country or on a regional basis. For large countries—India, Pakistan, Nigeria, Brazil—country agencies would certainly be appropriate. For many smaller countries, especially in Africa and Latin America, a regional agency would be much more desirable on economic grounds. An obvious set of candidates for such a regional agency would be Kenya, Tanzania, and Uganda: or even, in addition, some or all of the surrounding countries, Malawi, Ruanda, Burundi, Somalia, Ethiopia, and the Sudan. From an economic point of view the optimum area would depend very much on the need for inter-country planning and for regional schemes. Unfortunately, political factors probably make any donors' regional aid agency inadvisable. For instance, it would be impossible for an aid agency to maintain cordial relations with Ethiopia, Kenya, and Somalia: or with Ghana, Togo, Dahomey, and Nigeria: or with Jordan and Israel. Even where the countries of the area are not in any obvious conflict, there would be grave difficulties. Although a regional agency would not decide the levels of aid to be received by each country in the region (aid would still be bilateral), it must needs have some influence on them if it were doing its job. This alone would probably make the position of such a donors' agency unviable. On the other hand, in some areas, the need for regional co-operation is so great that we must consider in what other ways donors might be able to promote such co-operation.

2. REGIONAL CO-OPERATION

For many developing countries, particularly in Central and South America, and Africa, the scope for economic development is very seriously limited by their small size, and the seriousness of the limitation is likely to increase as opportunities for fairly small-scale import substitution in existing national markets are exhausted. The combination of small size with the desire for large-scale industrialization cannot fail, in the absence of effective pressure from outside, to lead to waste, inefficiency, and a stifling of development opportunities. There has already been a great waste of capital involved in an unnecessary national multiplication of economic infrastructure—the number of ports being built in West Africa is a good example.

To what extent can donors (assuming that they act together) persuade recipients to co-operate and plan across national boundaries? It is difficult to answer this question, since so little persuasion of this kind has been tried. On the positive side, there is the success of Marshall Aid in promoting the OEEC and in fostering the EEC, though how far these organizations would have succeeded in any case, because Europeans themselves wanted them, is hard to say. In East Africa, the Common Services Organization (EACSO) is still in existence, although its future is somewhat precarious, and no political federation has been formed. This is in spite of the fact that only the major donor (Britain), and one minor donor (the IBRD), have assisted EACSO in any way; other donors seem to be unaware of its existence. More vigorous action on behalf of donors might possibly have given the extra push needed for federation in East Africa, although, on the other hand, it is possible that pressure from donors would have been resented and used as an argument against federation, and against even a common market. The experience of the Central African Federation showed that outside pressure is useless when political differences are too great.

If federation is seldom likely to be the answer, what possibilities remain? We have already suggested that a regional donors' aid agency is hardly likely to be politically feasible. It is a sensitive enough business to interfere, through aid, in a single country's economy. The active promotion of inter-regional planning by donors is likely to be even more difficult. The best hope appears to be that recipient-controlled organizations should make regional sector plans, and design inter-regional schemes, especially for transport and large-scale industry. The UN Regional Commissions are well aware of the need, especially ECA and ECLA, where the problem is most acute. The ECA is reported to be forming sub-regional commissions in Africa. The UNSF is also particularly interested in promoting regionalism, and the IBRD has had the most notable success in solving an international resource problem through the Indus Waters scheme.

But neither UN Regional Commissions, nor any other possible candidate for the role, such as the IDB or ADB, could produce effective supra-national plans, in the face of obdurate nationalism, without some financial sanction to enforce acceptance of them. If they were themselves aid-giving organizations on a large scale, they would very probably be too open to the political pressures of nationalism to be effective. But the combination of donor countries' financial power, and planning by recipient-controlled organizations, offers some hope of a solution. The political difficulty involved for donors in regional interference would be much less if such interference were in conformity with, say, the Regional UN Commission's advice and planning. The UN Commission itself would not have the awkward problem of imposing its own solutions. Moreover, East Africa, for example, might not be averse to regional planning in West Africa, and vice versa; and so the planning agency might have some support within its own demesne.

It would still be necessary for the donors to act together. If, for instance, the ECA produced a good plan for industrialization in West Africa, or for transport, it would be essential for each donor to refuse to finance projects in particular countries which did not conform. Donors' desires to please particular recipients, for political or commercial reasons, have already resulted in infrastructure projects which, they were aware, made no sense from a regional point of view. This is where a donor's regional consultative group would have a real function. Thus if the ECA could produce a plan for certain economic sectors in West Africa, a West African consultative group could operate a 'confrontation procedure', by which donors mutually disciplined each other only to support projects which conformed with ECA's plans. The DAC, which already operates the confrontation procedure for different purposes, would be the obvious body to organize such groups where needed: they could also then serve the additional function of promoting common and suitable terms for members' aid.

A difficulty for such a solution to the regional problem is that Regional Commissions are barely equipped at present to fulfil the role assigned to them. Donor countries would have to give them further support in providing the consultants and planners needed for particular operations, especially as other UN agencies, on which they might call, are short of expertise in some of the sectors which most need regional planning. But there would seem to be no good reason why technical assistance should not be provided to the United Nations!

CHAPTER XIV

SUMMARY CONCLUSIONS, AND THE ROLE OF THE DEVELOPMENT ASSISTANCE COMMITTEE

First, the amounts which, and/or the form in which, the rich countries have been willing to give or lend to the poor countries have been affected by their concern with balance of payments problems. This has primarily been true of the USA and UK. It is no accident that these countries' currencies are used as reserves by other countries. That this concern should exist is unfortunate, and damaging for the poor countries. It results in reduced amounts of aid, in aid-tying which reduces the value of aid, and also at times in damaging trade restrictions. Of course, from time to time, some rich country or other will always have a temporary balance of payments problem. But that, simultaneously, four or more of the donor countries should have severe problems is a clear indication of a basic deficiency in the international monetary mechanism. An essential feature of any improvement is the creation of an international reserve money. Part, at least, of the required creation of money can be neatly linked with world aid by financing the IDA, and other UN Funds, by such credit creation through the IMF. But whether or not some variant of this scheme—which is, broadly speaking, the Stamp Plan[1]—be adopted, it remains true that any improvement of the world's monetary mechanism, which will reduce the magnitude of rich countries' payments problems, is of the highest priority for any improvement in the quantity and quality of world aid, and hence for an improvement in the economic and political relationships between the rich and the poor countries.

Secondly, recognizing that complete elimination of aid-tying must wait upon an improvement in international payments, the question arises as to whether some code of behaviour, such that surplus countries are prevented from tying, is possible. The difficulties are

[1] See Chapter XI, p. 244.

great. The operation of the French Franc Area is a barrier, and so also are the commercial motives of other surplus donors. Furthermore, tying is difficult to define, and hence any agreement would be difficult to implement. These problems would remain even if a sufficient improvement in the world's payment mechanism allowed one to advocate a complete embargo on procurement tying. One can only hope that increasing recognition of the extent to which the value of aid is reduced by procurement-tying, and of the reduction in goodwill which it occasions, will permit the DAC to make some progress in the fight to reduce aid-tying. The most important line of attack on the problem is to increase the donor countries' willingness to finance local costs, and also procurement from underdeveloped third countries.

Thirdly, as in the case of aid-tying, the DAC is the main forum in which donors should try to reach agreement on suitable terms for aid in general, and also for particular countries, except where more specialized bodies such as CIAP or the various consortia exist. Lack of co-ordination in the past, and excessive optimism as to poor countries' capacity to repay debt and grow fast, has led and is leading to very embarrassing and difficult situations.[1] There is now much greater recognition of the problem than a year or two ago, and the DAC has made some progress. What is primarily needed, as in the case of aid-tying, is a greater recognition on the part of the hard donors of the collective interest of the West in a smooth and amicable transfer of resources for development, the political impact of which should not be damaged by frequent renegotiations of debt with all the potentiality for ill-will which they engender. The USA sets much the best example, and one hopes that other rich donors will become more willing to copy her approach. The problem is considerably complicated by private short- and medium-term export credits, the excessive acceptance of which has reduced several countries to positions of extreme difficulty. (Ghana is one of the most recent examples.)

Fourthly, the DAC came into existence partly to solve the problem of 'burden-sharing'. It may have had some slight success in increasing the flow of capital from a few European countries. But we believe that attempts to find an agreed community of interest and purpose in Western aid giving, and to establish common principles, is probably a more important focus for DAC meetings than putting pressure on apparently laggard donors to increase their lending, regardless of terms. In this connection, however, it might be useful if DAC could

[1] See also Chapter IX.

agree to a definition of 'aid', which would exclude loans either of short maturity, or bearing commercial or near-commercial rates of interest. This would both focus attention on what is an essential feature of aid proper—that the terms should be subsidized—and also help to differentiate loans given for primarily commercial reasons from those given primarily in the interest of long-run development.[1]

Fifthly, we considered how far the divergences of policy on the part of the major donors, and the lack of any unified mechanism for deciding on a rational allocation of world aid, contributed to such maldistribution of development aid as appears to exist.[2] The causes of maldistribution lie more in national policies, such as the French concentration on aid to the Franc Area, and in misjudgment on the part of the other major donors of some countries' economic potentiality or political importance, than in any lack of co-ordinating mechanism. It would probably be harmful for the DAC to discuss the distribution of world aid, for an apparent unification of donors' decisions on the amounts of aid for particular recipients would tend to remove one of the advantages of bilateral aid in the latter's eyes. In any case, far fewer countries than are members of DAC effectively determine the distribution of aid. In connection with the world distribution of aid, we considered also the extent to which aid could and should be more diversified, in order to satisfy the desire of most recipients to avoid dependence on a single donor. While the possibility of increased diversification is limited by the large relative size of USA aid, Europe might increase its contribution to Latin America and the Far East, if the USA increased its share in Africa, and possibly also in India.

Sixthly, we discussed how the problems of aid-administration in the field, where there are many donors, might be solved.[3] We suggested that in some countries, where several large donors operate, a new multilateral aid agency might take over much of the work of economic appraisal and supervision that is done either by donor aid missions, or, sometimes superficially, by a ministry or other organization in the donor country, or is not done at all. India, Pakistan, Turkey, Nigeria, and East Africa (depending on federation), were suggested as countries or areas, where such an office or offices might be beneficial. The first three of these already have donors' consortia

---

[1] The need to make this distinction more clear-cut was argued in Chapter III, pp. 114–15.
[2] The distribution itself was discussed in Chapter X.
[3] The 'multi-donor problem' itself was discussed in Chapter VIII.

operating. But consortia do not do the kind of work envisaged. Indeed, Nigeria is a strong candidate for the formation of a consortium, and East Africa might be if the political problem of a single consortium for these countries could be solved. Such agencies might be run by the IBRD or OECD, but most recipients are likely to look more favourably on the IBRD as a sponsor. Where the problem is more that there are many small donors, especially of technical assistance, we hoped that these might put themselves more under the co-ordinating wing of the UN Resident Representative, whose office could be strengthened to co-ordinate small-donor programmes and keep their offers of assistance complementary with those of the major donor or donors.

Lastly, the problem of promoting regional development was considered. If the African map remains unchanged, its long-run importance in this highly fragmented continent is difficult to exaggerate. We felt that the most promising solution at present appears to lie in some supra-national planning by a recipient-controlled organization—most probably the ECA—in specific key sectors. To be successful, and to get national plans to conform, the donor powers would not only have to support and encourage the efforts of the ECA (and possibly also the UNSF, IBRD, and ADB) in this respect, but also would have to tailor their aid to suit. This in turn would demand closer collaboration by donors than has yet been in evidence, a collaboration which could be fostered by two or three regional consultative groups for Africa, set up by the DAC in consultation with the ECA. But there is little point in such groups, until the ECA, or other UN agency, has in fact been able to produce, with whatever encouragement and assistance by donors as may be necessary, a viable regional plan in at least one important sector of economic activity.

PART FOUR

CONCLUSIONS

CHAPTER XV

CONCLUSIONS

The flow of official resources from rich to poor countries, loosely referred to as 'aid', reached approximately its present level of $6 billion per annum in 1961, after five years' rapid increase from a much lower level. Aid is considerably greater than the flow of private funds, and is also large in comparison with any deliberate transfer of resources that is likely to result from changes in rich countries' trade policies.

It is not easy to measure the capacity of poor countries to use aid to increase the rate of growth of output. Nevertheless, we believe that, over the next few years, around $1–1½ billion more public aid could be applied with considerable effect, mostly in India. But, for many recipients, improvements in the conditions and forms of aid might do more to raise the rate of economic growth than an increase in the volume of aid. More liberal trading policies on the part of rich countries would also, of course, assist growth: but, for most recipients, such policies would not do a lot to reduce the need for aid.

We believe that the political impact of aid, and consequently its ultimate benefit to the West, could be improved if Western donors would concentrate more on economic development, and worry less about the effects on their own economies and trade, and less about their own particular political aims. Each donor inevitably has its own special preference for certain recipients, and also particular objectives such as new markets or political influence. Nevertheless, the general aim of promoting stable and independent government in recipient countries, based on mass support and rising standards of living, is one to which all Western donors—and possibly also the USSR—should be able to agree to give priority. Disagreements and rivalries between donors would become easier to resolve if this common objective, and the need for economic growth as a means of achieving it, were recognized more explicitly, and aimed at more single-mindedly.

The tendency to allow other considerations to interfere with the main objective is increased by the inability or unwillingness of many industrialized countries either to adjust their cost levels by internal measures, or their exchange rates, or find any other action to rectify their balances of payments within the grace periods permitted by the levels of their reserves. As a result, either the level of aid suffers, or aid is strictly tied, the donor's balance of payments becoming almost as important an influence on the amount of aid, and the manner of aid-giving, as is the primary purpose of aid-giving. Aid and trade-promotion become confused. In the case of many recipient countries it has been stressed that aid-tying not only reduces the effectiveness of aid for economic development, but also damages the political impact of aid by giving recipients cause to doubt the benevolence of the donors' motives.

An increase, or several increases, in world liquidity would surely help to ease this problem of aid-tying. Aid could be directly linked with such increases, in an almost painless manner for Western governments, by putting some of the increased credit at the initial disposal of poor countries—this being the essential feature of the so-called Stamp Plan.[1] However, an increase in world liquidity would not remove the need for countries to adjust their balances of payments. It merely gives more breathing space. Changes in exchange rates should not be ruled out as an occasional measure of adjustment. But, especially for the USA and the UK, they are at present virtually excluded by the nature of the world's payments system. Any movement towards an international reserve currency, and away from the present gold-exchange system, would permit an improvement in the terms and conditions of aid, and a consequent improvement in the political relations of rich and poor countries.

However, in the meantime, some degree of aid-tying is probably unavoidable. But donors should bear in mind that a weakening of aid-tying, designed to prevent it having a distorting effect on the recipient's economy, may do as much for growth as an increase in the amount of aid. Aid is most effectively tied by giving it only for the import cost of particular projects. But, where aid is a significant part of total investment, this procedure inevitably has adverse repercussions on the recipient, by twisting its import pattern in favour of capital goods. This results in an underutilization of domestic resources—either of labour, because enough consumption goods cannot be imported to satisfy the demand which results; or of local industrial capacity, because it becomes starved of imports of materials

[1] See Chapter XI, p. 244.

and components. Underutilization of local resources is widely observable in developing countries: and aid-tying, if carried to excess, contributes to this deformation.

The promotion of economic development in particular recipient countries requires a nice combination of economic knowledge and flair, and diplomacy. Many donors pay too little attention to the uses to which their aid is put. Much waste undoubtedly occurs, and money is often spent on things which have a low priority. Some donor countries and agencies are beginning to pay closer attention to the economics of aid usage. We approve of this, despite the greater liability to accusations of neo-colonialism. We believe that many recipients will tolerate a considerable amount of supervision, provided it is clear that the objective is the most economic use of resources from the recipient's point of view. But such supervision of aid requires expert knowledge of development, and the particular difficulties and problems of each recipient. Many donors lack the expertise, and the local administration required.

This brings one to the difficult problem of co-ordination between donors in the field. In some countries, the number of donor agencies is large, and the capacity of the recipient itself to co-ordinate them limited. It goes almost without saying that, on economic grounds, close co-ordination by donors' agencies themselves would be advantageous. The forms which this might take must clearly depend in each case upon the willingness of donors to give the highest priority to economic development, and upon the welcome and respect which recipients are willing to extend to co-ordinating institutions or mechanisms. Ideally, teams of professional advisers might be established in each recipient country or sub-region, under joint donor, or donor/recipient, auspices. Donor governments would then have access to well-informed advice on which to base their aid programmes, while the expense and waste of scarce resources, for both donors and recipients, which must occur if each donor independently makes serious efforts to assess aid needs and opportunities in detail, in each potential recipient country, would be avoided. But political considerations may make less formal consultation sometimes the more desirable mode of making progress in this matter.

Lastly there are the financial terms of aid. Considerable progress has been made, and is being made, in this respect. But, in the case of almost all donors, repayment terms are still far too short to be appropriate for development aid. Donors as a whole cannot seriously expect to be receiving resources back from the present recipients in this century. With few if any exceptions, if a single donor gets paid back it will be from the aid of others. Interest payments also serve no function in aid to governments. Logically, all such aid should be grant-aid. Although we do not, in fact, advocate this, we do suggest that all development aid should be in the form of very long-term loans at merely nominal rates of interest. High rates and short repayment terms tend to distort the pattern of world aid, first because people confuse gross and net aid; and, secondly, because there is a bias against lending to a heavily indebted country, even where more rational criteria suggest that the extension of more aid to that country should be a high priority. Lastly, short-term loans create awkward problems of 'rolling over' debt, which can result in ill-will.

GLOSSARY

ADB	African Development Bank
AID	Agency for International Development
CALS	Commonwealth Assistance Loans
CDC	Commonwealth (formerly Colonial) Development Corporation
CD and W	Colonial Development and Welfare
CENTO	Central Treaty Organization
CIAP	Inter-American Committee for the Alliance of Progress
CO	Colonial Office
CRO	Commonwealth Relations Office
DAC	Development Assistance Committee
DTC	Department of Technical Co-operation
EACSO	East African Common Services Organization
ECA	Economic Commission for Africa
ECGD	Export Credits Guarantee Department
ECLA	Economic Commission for Latin America
ECOSOC	Economic and Social Council
EDF	European Development Fund
EEC	European Economic Community
EFTA	European Free Trade Area
EIB	European Investment Bank
FAO	Food and Agricultural Organization
FO	Foreign Office
GATT	General Agreement on Tariffs and Trade
GDP	Gross Domestic Product
GNP	Gross National Product
IA-ECOSOC	Inter-American Economic and Social Council
IBRD	International Bank for Reconstruction and Development
IDA	International Development Agency
IDB	Inter-American Development Bank
IFC	International Finance Corporation
IMF	International Monetary Fund
MEDD	Middle East Development Division
NATO	North Atlantic Treaty Organization
OAS	Organization of American States
ODI	Overseas Development Institute
ODM	Overseas Development Ministry
OECD	Organization for Economic Co-operation and Development
OSAS	Overseas Service Aid Scheme
OXFAM	Oxford Committee for Famine Relief
PL480	USA Public Law No. 480
SEATO	South East Asia Treaty Organization
SUNFED	Special United Nations Fund for Economic Development
UNCTAD	United Nations Conference on Trade and Development
UNEPTA	United Nations Expanded Programme for Technical Assistance.
UNESCO	United Nations Economic, Social and Cultural Organization
UNICEF	United Nations Children's Fund
UNTAB	United Nations Technical Assistance Board
UNSF	United Nations Special Fund
WHO	World Health Organization

WORKS CITED

The original list of "Works Cited" contained in the English edition of this book has been enlarged for the American edition by the generous efforts of Professor Wilson E. Schmidt. This more complete list was based in considerable part on a bibliography of foreign aid prepared by Dr. Goran Ohlin, and his contribution is gratefully acknowledged. Dr. Ohlin's bibliography has been published in his book, *Foreign Aid Policies Reconsidered,* Development Center of the Organization for Economic Cooperation and Development, Paris, 1966.

Adler, John H. *Absorptive Capacity: The Concept and Its Determinants.* Brookings Institution. June 1965.
Agency for International Development. *Policy Guidance for Foreign Assistance.* Washington. 1963.
Agency for International Development. *A Study on Loan Terms, Debt Burden, and Development.* Washington. April 1965.
Agency for International Development. Program Coordination Staff. *Principles of Foreign Economic Assistance.* Washington. 1963.
Alavi and Khusro. "Pakistan: The Burden of U.S. Aid," *New University Thought.* Autumn 1962. Reprinted from *Pakistan Today.*
Allen, George. "Food for Peace," *Lloyds Bank Register.* July 1963.
Alpert, Paul. *Economic Development.* The Free Press of Glencoe. 1963.
Alter, G. M. "The Servicing of Foreign Capital Inflows by Underdeveloped Countries," in H. S. Ellis, ed., *Economic Development in Latin America.* St. Martin's Press. 1961.
Aly, Bower, and Edward Rogge, eds. *Foreign Aid.* The National University Extension Association, Columbia, Missouri. September 1957.
Arey, Hawthorne. "History of the Operations and Policies of the Export-Import Bank of Washington," in *Study of Export-Import Bank and World Bank. Part I, Hearings.* Senate Banking and Currency Committee, 83d Congress, 2d Session. 1954.
Asher, Robert E. *How to Succeed in Foreign Aid Without Really Trying.* Brookings Institution. 1964.

Asher, Robert E. *Multilateral versus Bilateral Aid: An Old Controversy Revisited.* Brookings Institution. 1962.
Avramovic, D., *et al. Economic Growth and External Debt.* Johns Hopkins Press. 1964.

Bailey, F. *Caste and the Economic Frontier.* Manchester University Press. 1957.
Balassa, Bela. *Trade Prospects for Developing Countries.* Yale University Press. 1964. '
Baldwin, David A. "International Aid for Underdeveloped Countries: A Comment." *The Review of Economics and Statistics.* May 1962.
Bandera, V. N. "Tied Loans and International Payments Problems." *Oxford Economic Papers,* Vol. XVII. July 1965.
Barna, T. *Redistribution of Incomes through Public Finance, 1937.* Oxford University Press. 1945.
Basch, Antonin. *Financing Economic Development.* Macmillan. 1964.
Bauer, Peter. *United States Aid and Indian Economic Development.* American Enterprise Association. November 1959.
Bhagwati, J. "On the Under-invoicing of Imports," *Bulletin of the Oxford University Institute of Statistics.* November 1964.
Boskey, Shirley. *Problems and Practices of Development Banks.* Johns Hopkins Press. 1959.
Brittain, J. A. "Some Neglected Features of Britain's Income Levelling," *A. E. R. Papers and Proceedings.* May 1960.
Broekmeijer, M. W. J. W. *The Developing Countries and NATO: Strategic Importance of the Developing Countries for NATO.* A. W. Sythoff, Leyden, The Netherlands. 1963.

Cairncross, A. K. "Did Foreign Investment Pay?" in *Home and Foreign Investment 1870-1913.* Cambridge University Press. 1943.
Carrter, A. M. *Redistribution of Incomes in Post-War Britain.* Yale University Press. 1955.
Cartier, Raymond. In *Paris Match.* Spring issues 1961.
Ceylon. Ministry of Finance. *External Economic Assistance, A Review from 1950-64.* Colombo.
Chenery, Hollis B., and Alan M. Strout. "Foreign Economic Assistance and Economic Development." Agency for International Development. Office of Program Coordination. June 1965.
Cooper, Richard. *A Note on Foreign Assistance and Capital Requirements for Development.* The Rand Corporation. February 1965.
Coppock, J. D. *International Economic Instability.* McGraw-Hill. 1962.

Diamond, William. *Development Banks.* Johns Hopkins Press. 1957.
Dumont, Rene. *L'Afrique Noire est mal partie.* Editions du Seuil. 1962.

Enke, Stephen. *Economics for Development.* Prentice-Hall. 1963.

Fatouros, A. A., and R. N. Kelson. *Canada's Overseas Aid.* The Canadian Institute of International Affairs. 1964.

Feis, Herbert. *Europe the World's Banker.* Yale University Press. 1930.

Feis, Herbert. *Foreign Aid and Foreign Policy.* St. Martin's Press. 1964.

Finch, David. "Investment Service of Underdeveloped Countries." *International Monetary Fund Staff Papers.* September 1951.

Gaitskell, A. *Gezira, A Story of Development in the Sudan.* Faber and Faber. 1959.

Geertz, Clifford. *Agricultural Involution: The Problem of Ecological Change in Indonesia.* University of California Press for the Association of Asian Studies. 1963.

Great Britain. Her Majestey's Stationery Office. *Aid to Developing Countries.* Cmnd. 2147. 1963.

Great Britain. Her Majesty's Stationery Office. *Plowden Committee Report.* Cmnd. 2276. 1964.

Great Britain. Her Majesty's Stationery Office. *Select Committee on Estimates, Fourth Report, Colonial Office.* 1959-60.

Great Britain. Her Majesty's Stationery Office. *Treaty Series No. 73 (1961)—Loan Agreement with Brazil.* Cmnd. 1463.

Great Britain. Her Majesty's Stationery Office. *Treaty Series No. 65 (1963)—Loan Agreement with the Argentine.* Cmnd. 2164.

Great Britain. Her Majesty's Stationery Office. *United Kingdom's Role in Commonwealth Development.* Cmnd. 237. July 1957.

Gulick, Clarence S., and Jean M. Nelson. "Promoting Effective Development Policies: A.I.D. Experience in the Developing Countries." Agency for International Development. Office of Program Coordination. September 1965.

Hagen, E. E. *The Theory of Social Change.* The Dorsey Press. 1962.

Hanson, A. H. *The Process of Planning: A Study of India's Five-Year Plans, 1950-63.* Oxford University Press. 1965.

Harrod, R. F. "Desirable International Movements of Capital in Relation to Growth of Borrowers and Lenders and Growth of Markets," in Roy Harrod and Douglas Hague, eds., *International Trade Theory in a Developing World.* St. Martin's Press. 1963.

Higgins, Benjamin. *Economic Development.* W. W. Norton. 1959.

Higgins, Benjamin. *United Nations and U.S. Foreign Economic Policy.* Richard D. Irwin, Inc. 1962.

Hirschman, Albert O. *Journeys Towards Progress.* Twentieth Century Fund. 1963.

Hirschman, Albert O. *The Strategy of Economic Development.* Yale University Press. 1958.

284   INTERNATIONAL AID

Hoffman, Paul G. *One Hundred Countries, One and One Quarter Billion People*. Albert D. and Mary Lasker Foundation. Washington. 1960.

India. Ministry of Finance. *Economic Survey*. New Delhi. 1964-65.
India. Ministry of Finance. *Report of the Committee on Utilization of External Finance (V. K. R. V. Rao Report)*. New Delhi. 1964.
India. Ministry of Steel and Heavy Industries. *Report of Steel Control (K. N. Raj Report)*. New Delhi. October 1963.
India. Planning Commission. *Memorandum on the Fourth Five-Year Plan*. New Delhi. October 1964.
International Bank for Reconstruction and Development. *Economic Growth and External Debt*. 1964.
International Bank for Reconstruction and Development. *Eighteenth Annual Report*. 1962-63.
International Bank for Reconstruction and Development. *Policies and Operations of the World Bank, IFC, and IDA*. 1963.
International Bank for Reconstruction and Development. *Some Techniques of Development Lending*. September 1960.

Jacoby, Neil H. "An Evaluation of U.S. Economic Aid to Free China, 1951-1965." Agency for International Development. Bureau of the Far East. January 1966.
Jordan, Amos A. *Foreign Aid and the Defense of Southeast Asia*. Praeger. 1962.

Krassowski, Andrezej. "Aid and the British Balance of Payments." *Moorgate and Wall Street Review*. 1965.
Krause, Walter. *Economic Development*. Wadsworth, San Francisco. 1961.
Kreps, Clifton H., and Juanita M. Kreps. *Aid, Trade, and Tariffs*. H. W. Wilson Co. 1953.

Lewis, John P. *Quiet Crisis in India*. Brookings Institution. 1962.
Liska, G. *The New Statecraft*. University of Chicago Press. 1960.
Little, I. M. D. *Aid to Africa*. Pergamon Press. 1964.
Little, I. M. D. "The Strategy of Indian Development," *National Institute Economic Review*. May 1960.

MacBean, Alisdair I. "Causes of Excessive Fluctuations in Export Proceeds of Underdeveloped Countries," *Bulletin of the Oxford University Institute of Statistics*. November 1964.
McClellan, Grant S., ed. *U.S. Foreign Aid*. H. W. Wilson Co. 1957.
MacDougall, G. D. A. "India's Balance of Payments," *Bulletin of the Oxford University Institute of Statistics*. May 1961.

McKinnon, R. I. "Foreign Exchange Constraints in Economic Development and Efficient Aid Allocation," *Economic Journal*. June 1964.

Mason, E. S. "Foreign Money We Can't Spend." *Atlantic Monthly*. 1960.

Meier, Gerald. *International Trade and Development*. Harper and Row. 1963.

Meier, Gerald. *Leading Issues in Development Economics*. Oxford University Press. 1964.

Mikesell, Raymond F. "Commodity Agreements and Aid to Developing Countries." *Law and Contemporary Problems*. Spring 1963.

Mikesell, Raymond F. *Public External Financing of Development Banks in Developing Countries*. University of Oregon. Bureau of Business and Economics Research. 1966.

Mikesell, Raymond F. *Public International Lending for Development*. Random House. 1966.

Mikesell, Raymond F. *United States Economic Policy and International Relations*. McGraw-Hill. 1952.

Millikan, Max F. "New and Old Criteria for Aid." *Proceedings of the Academy of Political Science*. January 1962.

Millikan, Max F., and Walt W. Rostow. *A Proposal: Key to an Effective Foreign Policy*. Harper and Brothers. 1957.

Moore, Frederick T. "The World Bank and Its Missions." *The Review of Economics and Statistics*. February 1960.

Nehru, Braj Kumar. "Foreign Aid from the Viewpoint of the Recipient Countries." *Proceedings of the Academy of Political Science*. January 1962.

Nevin, Edward. *Capital Funds in Underdeveloped Countries: The Role of Financial Institutions*. St. Martin's Press. 1961.

Ohlin, Goran. *Foreign Aid Policies Reconsidered*. Development Centre of the Organization for Economic Cooperation and Development. Paris. 1966.

Organization for Economic Cooperation and Development. *The Flow of Financial Resources to Countries in Course of Economic Development, 1956-59*. Organization for European Economic Cooperation. 1961.

Organization for Economic Cooperation and Development. *The Flow of Financial Resources to Less-Developed Countries, 1956-59*. 1964.

Overseas Development Institute. *British Aid 2: Government Finance*. London. 1963.

Overseas Development Institute. *British Aid 4: Technical Assistance*. London. 1964.

Overseas Development Institute. *Jeanneney Report;* an abridged translation of *La Politique de Coopération avec les pays en voie de developpement.* London. 1964.

Pakistan. Planning Commission. *Preliminary Evaluation of Progress during the Second Five-Year Plan.* Karachi. March 1965.

Pearson, Scott R., and Wilson E. Schmidt. "Alms for AAMS: A Larger Flow?" *The Journal of Common Market Studies.* Autumn 1964.

Pincus, John A. "The Cost of Foreign Aid." *The Review of Economics and Statistics.* November 1963.

Pincus, John A. *Economic Aid and International Cost Sharing.* Johns Hopkins Press. 1965.

Ranis, Gustav, ed. *The United States and the Developing Countries.* W. W. Norton Co. 1964.

Reddaway, W. B. *The Development of the Indian Economy.* London. 1962.

Report to the President on Foreign Economic Policies (Grey Report). U.S. Government Printing Office. November 1950.

Rimalov, U. *Economic Co-operation between the USSR and Underdeveloped Countries.* Foreign Languages Publishing House. Moscow. n.d.

Rosenstein-Rodan, P. N. "International Aid for Underdeveloped Countries." *Review of Economics and Statistics.* May 1961.

Ross, Anthony Clunies, with R. I. Downing *et al. One Per Cent; The Case for Greater Australia Foreign Aid.* Melbourne University Press. 1963.

Rostow, W. W. *The Stages of Economic Growth.* Cambridge University Press. 1960.

Rostow, W. W. "The Take-Off into Self-Sustained Growth." *Economic Journal.* March 1956.

Ruthenberg, H. *Agricultural Development in Tanganyika.* Springer-Verlag. 1964.

Salant, W. S. *et al. The United States Balance of Payments.* Brookings Institution. 1963.

Schelling, Thomas. *International Economics.* Allyn and Bacon. 1958.

Schmidt, Wilson E. "The Case Against Commodity Agreements." *Law and Contemporary Problems.* Spring 1963.

Schmidt, Wilson E. "Default of Public International Debts." *The National Banking Review.* March 1965.

Schmidt, Wilson E. "The Economics of Charity: Loans vs. Grants." *Journal of Political Economy.* August 1964.

Schmidt, Wilson E., and I. O. Scott. "Capital Exports and Capital Export Capacity." *Finanzarchiv.* 1965.

Schultz, T. W. "Value of Farms' Surpluses to Underdeveloped Countries." *Journal of Farm Economics.* Proceedings Number. December 1960.

Seers, D. "A Theory of Inflation and Growth in Underdeveloped Economies Based on the Experience of Latin America." *Oxford Economic Papers.* June 1962.

Shonfield, A. *Economic Growth and Inflation.* Council for Economic Education. Bombay. 1961.

Siegert, Robert, ed. *Entwicklungshilfe—Einmal Anders.* Verlag August Lutzeyer, Baden-Baden. Bonn. 1963.

Singh, Manmohan. *India's Export Trends and the Prospects for Self-Sustained Growth.* Oxford University Press. 1964.

Stamp, Maxwell. "The Stamp Plan—1962 Version." *Moorgate and Wall Street Review.* Autumn 1962.

Streeten, Paul. "Hilfe, Handel und Entwicklung." *Schmollers Jahrbuch für Gesetzgebung, Verwaltung und Volkswirtschaft.*

Strout, Alan M. "Factors Affecting the Allocation of Foreign Economic Aid." Agency for International Development. 1964.

Thorp, Willard. *Trade, Aid, or What?* Johns Hopkins Press. 1954.

United Nations. *External Development Financing in the Economic Development of Latin America.* E/CN. 12/649. April 1963.

United Nations. *International Compensation for Fluctuations in Commodity Trade.* E/3447. 1961.

United Nations. Conference on Trade and Development. *Final Act.* Geneva. 1964.

United Nations. Conference on Trade and Development. *Financing for an Expansion of International Trade.* E/CONF. 46/9. Geneva. 1964.

United Nations. Conference on Trade and Development. Secretary-General (Raul Prebisch). *Towards a New Trade Policy for Development.* New York. 1964.

United Nations. General Agreement on Tariffs and Trade. *International Trade, 1961.* Geneva. 1962.

United Nations. International Monetary Fund. *Compensatory Finance of Export Fluctuations.* February 1963.

United States. *Composite Report of the President's Committee to Study the Military Assistance Program.* Washington. 1959.

United States. *Report of the President's Committee to Strengthen the Security of the Free World (Clay Committee Report).* Washington. March 1963.

University of Arizona. "Policy for United States Agricultural Export Surplus Disposal." *College of Agriculture Technical Bulletin 150.* August 1962.

Viner, Jacob. "Economic Policy on the New Frontier." *Foreign Affairs*. July 1961.

White, John. *German Aid*. Overseas Development Institute. 1965.
White, John. *Japanese Aid*. Overseas Development Institute. 1964.
Wiggins, James W., and Helmut Schoeck, eds. *Foreign Aid Re-examined*. Public Affairs Press. 1958.
Williams, Peter, and Adrian Moyes. *Not by Governments Alone— The Role of British Non-Government Organizations in the Developing Decade*. Overseas Development Institute. 1964.
Williamsen, Jeffrey G. "Projected Aid Requirements for Turkey: 1960-1975." Agency for International Development. Office of Program Coordinatio.:.

Wolf, Charles, Jr. *Foreign Aid: Theory and Practice in Southern Asia*. Princeton University Press. 1960.
Woods, George D. "Address to the Boards of Governors, Tokyo, September 7, 1964." International Bank for Reconstruction and Development.
Yale University. South East Asia Studies. *Indonesia: Perspective and Proposals for United States Economic Aid; A Report to the President of the United States*. New Haven. 1963.

INDEX

absorptive capacity (for capital), 93, 94, 104, 132-7, 235
  of Africa, 222-3, 236
  of India, 226, 228
  and need for aid, 139-40, 155, 214, 215
  technical assistance and, 178, 179
  trade and, 154
ADB (African Development Bank), 264, 272
Aden, 115
administration
  of aid, 201, 258-68; by France, 41; by Germany, 43-4; by UK, 33; by USSR, 29
  in India, 186, 229
  of recipients, 140; burden of procurement-tying on, 165, 189
Afghanistan
  aid to, 27, 28, 225, 254
  donors' meetings in, 259
Africa
  absorptive capacity of, 222-3, 236
  aid to, from China, 29; from Israel, 56
  flow of finance to, 219, 221
  lack of central banks in, 141, 145, 162
  lack of skills in, 136, 223
  needs of, 234, 235, 256
  new independent countries of, 17, 18
  outflow of capital from, 218, 219, 220
  planning in, 186-7
  population growth in, 123
  power and transport in, 133
  rate of growth in, 216n
  USA and, 255, 271
  see also Central, East, South and West Africa, and individual countries
African Development Bank, see ADB

Africanization, in former colonies, 36, 40
agencies, multilateral, for donors, proposals for, 258-66, 271, 277
Agency for International Development, see AID
agriculture (including forestry and fishing), 124, 152, 154
  aid to, 69, 71
  commodity aid and, 170
  demand for products of, 126
  in India, 170, 186
  need for more aid to, 135-6, 164, 190
  in Pakistan, 170, 225
  production of, often unknown, 183
  Western, excessive potential of, 169, 174
AID (Agency for International Development), 25, 26, 92, 174, 215n
  and CIAP, 263
  and Congress, 26, 240
  in French Africa, 115, 199
  loans from, 236, 249n, 259
  Missions of, 180, 258
  and planning, 229
  and recipient governments, 116
  technical assistance through, 180
'aid benefit', calculation of, 105, 132
aid counsellors, professional, need for, 112
Algeria
  aid to, 66, 68; from France, 38, 39, 60; from USSR, 28
  outflow of capital from, 218, 220
Alliance for Progress, 231, 264
  and policy of recipients, 25, 110, 111, 262-3
amortization of loans, 207-8, 210, 230n, 233n; amounts of, 58
Argentina
  aid to, 66, 232

exports of, 151
interest rates on loans by, 82
population growth in, 107
Jeanneney Report on French aid, 39
Jordan
 aid to, 66, 68, 213n, 223, 266
 joint donor and recipient committee in, 263
 USA and, 26, 213n

Kabul, paving of streets of, 88
Kenya
 aid to, 66, 261, 265, 266; for purchase of White Highlands from settlers, 68n, 222; tying of, 162; from UK, 60, 85, 222; from USSR, 30
 population of, 122n
Khrushchev, on aid, 28
Korea, South
 aid to, 26, 60, 66, 199, 213n, 224
 commodity aid to, 166

labour gangs, art of managing, 170
land, improvement of
 in India, 144
 systems of tenure and, 124, 136
Laos, aid to, 213n, 224
Latin America
 aid to, 219, 221, 231-3; from Europe, 271; from France, 40; from USA, 17, 24, 26, 198, 256, 259
 deterioration of terms of trade of, 148
 inflation in, 143n, 163
 outflow of capital from, 218, 219, 220, 231
 population growth in, 123
 underaided, 234
 see also individual countries
Lenin, 81
leverage effects of aid, 103, 110-13, 281
Liberia, aid to, 66, 68; German, 60; multidonor, 261
liquidity, international, increase needed in, 242-3, 245, 324
loans
 from AID, 236, 249, 259
 amounts of, 52-3, 57; by category

of donor, 48, 49, 58; by recipient, 60; per head of recipient, 66
cheap and expensive, 249-50
on commercial terms, should not count as aid, 21, 82, 114, 252, 271
from Communist countries, 61
for development, from USA, 25
element of aid in, 13, 82
from IDA for infrastructure, 19
to India, 227-8
to Latin America, 232
from multilateral agencies, 55, 58, 211
see also CALS, grace periods, interest, maturities
'local cost' problem, see 'home cost'
Luxembourg, aid from, 58n

Malagasy Republic, French aid to, 38, 40, 41, 60
malaria, control of, 45, 46, 109, 122
Malawi, aid to, 265
Malaya, 33
Malaysia, 56, 156, 224
Mali, 28, 38-9
Mali-Senegal federation, 39
Malta, 92
Malthusian cycle, 107, 110n, 129
Marshall Aid, 24, 26, 27, 232, 263
maturities of loans, 13, 59, 73
 from Communist countries, 61
MEDD (Middle East Development Division, UK), 180, 197, 258
Mexico, 125, 136, 210n, 233, 252
 aid to, 66, 231, 232
Middle East, 218, 221, 223-4
Middle East Development Division, see MEDD
military aid, 22, 24, 79n, 83-4, 253; see also defence support
mining, minerals, 125, 126, 127
monetary system of recipients, and balance of payments, 141
monopoly, and project-tying of aid, 165
Morocco
 aid to, 66; from France, 38, 39, 41, 60; multidonor, 256, 261
 US bases in, 26

planning for economic development
in recipient countries, 18, 111,
113, 181-8
advance commitments and, 44
aid and, 111, 113, 185, 188-91
donors' interest in, 110, 193
fluctuations of export earnings
and, 159
technical assistance for, 177-8, 197
USSR and, 29
see also India, Pakistan
Plowden Committee Report, 327
Poland, 121
commodity aid to, 166, 172*n*
political aspects of aid, 84-6, 90,
102, 115-17
in Communist countries, 28
in France, 39, 41-2
population
age distribution of, 122
aid per head of, 66, 221, 234; Far
East, 224; India, 227, 230; Latin
America, 231, 232, 233; Pakistan, 255
rate of growth of, 94, 95, 122-4,
181, 183; and aid, 103, 107-10;
in India, 230; and savings, 105,
106
size of, and aid, 67*n*, 94*n*, 234
Portugal, 87, 121
aid to colonies by, 30, 42, 214,
233, 256*n*; figures for, 64, 65,
75-7
power, aid for supply of, 133
poverty
and aid, 121, 122
and population growth, 94-5
and saving, 129, 146
and self-sustained growth, 208
Prebisch, Dr, 146, 148
pre-investment schemes, UNSF and,
19
pre-revolutionary régimes, aid to, 85
prestige projects, 86, 113, 138, 200,
223
prices
agreements on, as aid, 51
of commodities, fall of, 18
of farm products, support of, by
France, 38, 157; by USA, 168,
169

in recipient countries, 132
primary production
dependence of poor countries on,
125-8
rate of growth of, 147, 154-5
private enterprise in recipient countries, donors and, 26, 43, 133,
189, 194, 258
private investment
in colonies, 23, 30-1
in developing countries, amount
of, 52-3, 216, 219, 220
from France, in Czarist Russia,
22-3
in Greece, 233
in IBRD, IDR and EIB, 53-4
must be estimated in development
plans, 182
sometimes included in 'aid,' 13
from USA in Mexico, 233
procurement-tying of aid, 21, 61; by
Communist countries, 27, 61-2;
by France, 39, 61; by Germany,
44, 61; by Japan, 54; by UK, 18,
33, 61; by USA, 61
and balance of payments, 57, 246-
9, 269-70
combined with project-tying, 72
effects of, 163-6, 185, 199
loss of value due to, 51, 57
product, national
of donor countries, aid as percentage of, 42, 63, 64, 65, 117, 239,
253
estimates of, 183
exports as proportion of, 126
rate of growth of, 123-4
of recipient countries per head,
and amount of aid, 66, 122,
181, 214, 221, 224
trade and, 153
productivity
of aid, 103, 103-4, 314
of investment, 131-9, 181, 204,
214-15
project-tying of aid, 57, 111, 160-6,
185, 188-91
combined with procurement-tying,
72
by Communist countries, 29, 61
extent of, 69, 70

For Product Safety Concerns and Information please contact our
EU representative GPSR@taylorandfrancis.com Taylor & Francis
Verlag GmbH, Kaufingerstraße 24, 80331 München, Germany